HOW TO
HOME REPAIR

D0435637

HOW TO CHEAT™ AT HOME REPAIR

Time-Slashing, Money-Saving Fixes for Household Hassles and Breakdowns

JEFF BREDENBERG

STERLING

New York / London
www.sterlingpublishing.com

STERLING and the distinctive Sterling logo are registered trademarks
of Sterling Publishing Co., Inc.

Library of Congress Cataloging-in-Publication Data
Bredenberg, Jeff.
  How to cheat at home repair : the sneakiest, time-slashing fixes for
household wear, tear, hassles & breakdowns / Jeff Bredenberg.
     p. cm.
  Includes index.
  ISBN 978-1-4027-5629-0
  1. Dwellings—Maintenance and repair—Amateurs' manuals. I. Title.
  TH4817.3.B738 2008
  643'.7—dc22

                                        2008007160

10 9 8 7 6 5 4 3 2 1

Published by Sterling Publishing Co., Inc.
387 Park Avenue South, New York, NY 10016
© 2009 by Jeff Bredenberg
Distributed in Canada by Sterling Publishing
C/o Canadian Manda Group, 165 Dufferin Street,
Toronto, Ontario, Canada M6K 3H6
Distributed in the United Kingdom by GMC Distribution Services
Castle Place, 166 High Street, Lewes, East Sussex, England BN7 1XU
Distributed in Australia by Capricorn Link (Australia) Pty. Ltd.
P.O. Box 704, Windsor, NSW 2756, Australia

Book design by Richard Oriolo

Printed in China
All rights reserved

Sterling ISBN: 978-1-4027-5629-0

For information about custom editions, special sales, premium and
corporate purchases, please contact Sterling Special Sales
Department at 800-805-5489 or specialsales@sterlingpublishing.com.

ACKNOWLEDGMENTS

The author is grateful to the following sources for their generous contribution of time and ideas:

Dean Bennett, architect, contractor, builder, Castle Rock, Colorado. ◇ Jeff Bishop, technical advisor, Institute of Inspection, Cleaning and Restoration Certification, Dothan, Alabama. ◇ Paul Bizzarri, vice president of innovation, TimberTech, Wilmington, Ohio. Scott M. Brown, a.k.a. "Samurai Appliance Repairman," proprietor of Fixitnow.com, New London, New Hampshire. ◇ Richard Bullock, owner, Bullock's Furniture Restoration, Odenton, Maryland. ◇ Mark Bruley, vice president for accident and forensic investigation, ECRI Institute, Plymouth Meeting, Pennsylvania. ◇ James Dean of Lewiston, Maine. ◇ Dave Donovan, electrician, writer for DoItYourself.com, Atco, New Jersey. ◇ Joe Dussich, CEO, JAD Corporation of America, New York, New York. ◇ Sara Fisher, professional organizer, Atlanta, Georgia. ◇ Doug Gagliardi, office furniture repairer, The Chair-Man, Twin Falls, Idaho. Henry Hendrix, brand manager, Combat Insecticides, Scottsdale, Arizona. ◇ Victoria Higgs, inventor, Adelaide, Australia. ◇ Mike Kozlowski, director of product quality and support, Sears Home Services, Hoffman Estates, Illinois. ◇ "Handyman Scott" Kropnick, Blue Bell, Pennsylvania. ◇ David Lupberger, home improvement expert for ServiceMagic.com, Denver, Colorado. ◇ Reggie Marston, president, Residential Equity Management Home Inspections, Springfield, Virginia; "House Detective" on Home & Garden Television. ◇ Tom McCormick, president, McCormick Electrical Services, North Liberty, Indiana. ◇ Chuck McLaughlin, plumber, Glenside, Pennsylvania. ◇ Steve Nearman, furniture restorer, The Master's Touch, Fredericksburg, Virginia. ◇ Paul Pearce, vice president, Institute of

Inspection, Cleaning and Restoration Certification, London, England. ◇ Tim Puro, owner, Monroe Furniture Restoration, Bloomington, Indiana. ◇ Cheri Russell, wicker restorer, Wicker Fixer, Ozark, Missouri. ◇ Tom Scherphorn, Wyndmoor, Pennsylvania. ◇ David Shapiro, electrical contractor, Colmar Manor, Maryland. ◇ Craig Vetters, furniture repairer, the Chair Dr., Evansville, Indiana. ◇ Scott Vincent, Oreland, Pennsylvania. ◇ Raymond VinZant, Roto Rooter's Ask-the-Plumber, St. Paul, Minnesota. ◇ Ed Waller, co-founder, Certa-Pro Painters.

The author also is grateful for the contributions of editor Jo Fagan, the rest of the staff at Sterling Publishing, and agent Linda Konner.

CONTENTS

The Repair Book for the Rest of Us

IF YOU HAVE BUILT YOUR OWN TEN-BEDROOM MANSION WITH YOUR BARE HANDS, AND IF YOU WEAR A TOOL BELT TO BED INSTEAD OF PAJAMAS, THEN YOU MIGHT NOT CARE MUCH ABOUT WHAT I HAVE TO SAY IN RESPECT TO KEEPING A HOME IN GOOD REPAIR. THAT'S OK. THIS REPAIR BOOK IS FOR THE REST OF US: PEOPLE WHO WANT PRESENTABLE HOMES IN GOOD REPAIR—WITHOUT WORKING TOO HARD FOR IT.

Yes, the title is *How to Cheat™ at Home Repair*, and you might well ask how you could possibly cheat at fixing things. Am I talking about skirting building codes, using chintzy materials, and slapdash techniques? Not at all. Building regulations protect us all, and none of us likes the look of careless work in our homes. Cheating at home repair means using ingenious shortcuts that will save you time, energy, and money—while getting the repair done properly. It means selecting the most durable furnishings and materials for your home so you have to make repairs less often. It means walking away from the myths, misconceptions, and counterproductive traditions that sap hours out of your home life. It means stocking your toolbox with simple-but-versatile tools so you're ready for any mishaps and breakdowns that homeownership throws at you. And it means knowing your limits—when to call in a professional rather than doing a sloppy repair yourself.

This book is jam-packed with sneaky tips and techniques that any homeowner or apartment-dweller can perform with the most common tools and materials. Many of these tips come from professional repair people themselves. I put this question to each of them: "When you arrive at a customer's home, which are the jobs that cause you to shake your head and say to yourself, 'They could have taken care of this themselves'?" With their replies in hand, I put together instructions for the simplest, anybody-can-do-it home repairs. Even more tips come from inspectors, architects, professional organizers, inventors, and regular folks with clever ideas. Now, the how-to-cheat movement is not confined to one continent, and discussing home repair gets tricky when you consider the differences in building techniques, measuring systems, tools, and product availability. Nevertheless, we've done our best to provide tips that can be understood and carried out by the broadest possible audience. That's why you will find mention of both imperial and metric measurements, generic product names alongside specific brand names, and occasional instructions for finding supplies on the Internet.

And speaking of regular folks, now that you're in the "how to cheat" fold, I invite you to join the growing throng of ingenious homeowners who submit their own sneaky ideas about home management for use in future books. Just drop me a note in care of Sterling Publishing, or submit tips electronically by visiting one of my websites, HowToCheatBooks.com or JeffBredenberg.com.

Please use common sense when you make repairs, follow the appropriate safety precautions, and don't proceed with any repair you don't fully understand. Hire your trusted professionals to deal with jobs that entail dangerous elements, such as live electricity and heights. As cheaters at home repair, we're looking for sanity in our home lives—not the added stress, expense, and time loss that come with injuries.

And resist the pressure to be a super do-it-yourselfer. Sure, it's easy to admire the people who have gone through the specialized training and licensing required to do professional-level building, plumbing, electrical work, and such. You may gawk dreamily as a television personality remodels a kitchen in twenty-five minutes. And some corner of your heart may envy Toolbelt Tom who lives down the block, the DIY freak who buys every power tool in the local home center. But, in reality, you don't want to be them—you chose a different career path, and life is hectic enough without trying to pack a second one into your schedule. You have your own priorities, ones that preserve your sanity: A presentable home, efficient ways to get repairs done, time for your family, and a hassle-free lifestyle. Ah, that's the cheatin' life!

The Cheating Frame of Mind

HOW TO CHEAT AT HOME REPAIR IS ALL ABOUT ACHIEVING A PEACEFUL COEXISTENCE WITH YOUR POSSESSIONS. YOU WANT A HOME ENVIRONMENT YOU CAN BE PROUD OF—WHERE EVERYTHING LOOKS GOOD AND FUNCTIONS WELL. BUT MODERN LIFE IS ALREADY INSANELY STRESSFUL, AND YOU'D RATHER NOT WORK TOO HARD TO REACH A GOAL LIKE THAT. NO PROBLEM. WHEN YOU APPROACH HOME REPAIR ISSUES WITH THE RIGHT FRAME OF MIND, YOU CAN REDUCE STRESS, SAVE TIME, AND SAVE MONEY, TOO—ALL WHILE GETTING YOUR HOME REPAIR ISSUES PROPERLY ADDRESSED. LET'S TAKE A LOOK AT SOME CORE CHEAT-AT-HOME-REPAIR PRINCIPLES THAT WILL HELP.

When Something "Breaks," Resist the GULP Response

It's peculiar how we can leap to conclusions. When something you own doesn't perform as you expected, you may find yourself immediately assuming the worst—that a complex, expensive repair is in your immediate future. This is what psychologists call the GULP response, which stands for Giving Up Logic Prematurely. (OK, they *might* have called it that if they had a little less dignity.) Instead of GULPing, condition yourself to troubleshoot the situation. When you troubleshoot, you start by thinking about the symptoms of the object that's not working. Then you methodically check all the simplest, most direct possible reasons for those symptoms. And only when you have eliminated the simplest reasons for the breakdown do you move on to more complicated causes.

To illustrate, let's walk through an exaggerated example: You turn on a lamp's switch but you get no light. Do you immediately declare that the lamp's switch is broken or that the lamp's wiring has shorted out? No, that would be GULPing. If the lamp has been in perfect working order up to now, those reasons are not very likely. But you do know that lamp cords often get pulled out of their outlets, so you would check that first. If that's not the problem, you would check whether the outlet is supplying electricity (perhaps a circuit breaker tripped), so you plug a different appliance into the outlet to test it. If the outlet is not the culprit, there's yet another common cause—a blown light bulb—so you would check that. By this point in your troubleshooting, 99.9 percent of the time you will have solved the problem—in minimal time at no expense (except for a new bulb). Had you GULPed, you would be halfway to the home center to hand over big bucks for a new lamp.

Sure, in real life maybe you would have figured out the lamp's problem immediately, but professional repair people will tell you that a shockingly high percentage of house calls are for problems that are about that simple—a circuit breaker that wasn't on, a cord that wasn't plugged in, a filter that had gotten overloaded, or a reset button that was overlooked, for instance. GULPing is expensive, time-gobbling, stress-inducing, and embarrassing. A simple trouble-shooting habit will save you time and again.

Build a "Support Staff"

Here's another situation where a panic response will lead to misery and unnecessary expense: the times when you need to call in a professional to perform repairs around the house. At a minimum, you want to have on hand the names and contact information for a handyperson, a plumber, and an electrician—professionals whose backgrounds you've already checked. If you just flip open the telephone book and pick the first name that sounds professional—or the first company with an impressive display ad—you're in deep trouble. Your odds of getting good work at a reasonable price that way are very low. When you do your research and find repair professionals that you're comfortable with, it's wise to treat them like family, pay them fairly, and pay them promptly. For more on hiring professional help, see chapter 13.

Know Your Limits—
and Don't Be Ashamed of Them

As long as you're going to have a reliable "support staff," you might as well make sensible use of them. As in an office environment, you need to know how to delegate—let the professionals available to you do what they do best, while you handle the work that you do best. Much of *How to Cheat at Home Repair* is devoted to simple fixes that any of us regular Janes and Joes can make with common tools and no special training. Pass the tough tasks to the pros without hesitation or a guilty thought. Sure, you might have a shred of admiration for the neighbor who has a basement packed wall-to-wall with sophisticated tools and can add a new floor to his house single-handedly. But that's not you. You have your own priorities and will still manage to keep your home in great repair—in less time, for less cost, and with less chance of getting shoddy results. Remember these two acronyms:

◇ If a repair is a Super-Easy Lightweight Fix (SELF), you get the job.

◇ If the work is Hard, Important, Rarely done, and Elaborate (HIRE), pass it along to a professional.

Be Methodical about Your Home and Possessions

I probably don't have to persuade you that your car needs regular inspections, oil changes, tire rotation, and such. The same is true of many parts of your home as well. I'm not trying to turn you into a clerk with a clipboard forever tucked under your arm, but neglecting your home invites breakdowns and wear and tear—which is actually the more expensive and angst-ridden path in life. Here are some approaches that will help:

◇ Keep your owner's manuals in a predictable place. You might want to store the owner's manual for your DVD player on the shelf of your entertainment center. If you're not going to stash a manual near the item it covers, keep it in the same place with all your other manuals—perhaps in a file or box in your office. That way, you'll never be at a loss when you need to do simple troubleshooting.

◇ And speaking of manuals . . . if you're the "I never read owner's manuals" kind of consumer, get over it. Most manuals are quick reads, and all sorts of crucial information is lurking in there.

◇ Enter regular maintenance duties into your family calendar or computerized calendar. Don't try to keep all your home's recurring maintenance issues in your head—months and years can slip by before you're surprised by a breakdown. This includes yearly servicing of your furnace, changing of smoke detector batteries, and the like.

◇ Pick a spot in your home to be Tool Central—a depot where you will store all the most basic home repair tools, arranged in a way that makes any item easy to find.

◇ Practice your MBO. No, you office geeks, I'm not talking about Management By Objective. This stands for Maintenance by Observation. In several different parts of this book you will find mention of signs of trouble to watch out for. Just keep your eyes open— you couldn't ask for an easier task!

◇ Follow the Materials on a Program (MOP) philosophy. This means learning about an advantageous, low-maintenance material or tool— but not feeling like you need to buy it just yet. For instance, perhaps you're infatuated with the plastic-and-wood decking that hit the market in recent years. But your current deck has a good three years of life in it. So study up on the new material, price it, talk to neighbors who use it, and set aside some cash in a future budget. Just don't build the new deck until the old one is kaput.

Don't Rush an Unfamiliar Repair Job

When you're making a new kind of repair—even a simple one— relax and don't commit yourself to a tight schedule for getting it done. Look at the task as a learning experience. Also, don't be astonished or frustrated if you end up taking more than one trip to the hardware store or the home improvement store in the course of the project.

Embrace Innovative Products

Sure, you're assaulted by hundreds of advertising messages a day about new "miracle" products. But now and then a truly innovative product—perhaps a building material, perhaps a tool, or perhaps a pest control device—will emerge that will truly save you time, effort, and money. Some good ones are mentioned in this book, and you will discover others on your own. As with any hype aimed at consumers, engage your B.S. detector and then make your own decision.

Getting the Right Tools in the Right Place

JUST OWNING TOOLS IS NOT ENOUGH. IF YOU WANT TO BE READY FOR THE MOST COMMON HOME REPAIRS, IF YOU WANT TO SAVE YOURSELF ENORMOUS AMOUNTS OF TIME, ENERGY, AND AGGRAVATION, THEN YOU NEED TO ADOPT SOME SIMPLE PRINCIPLES ABOUT YOUR RELATIONSHIP WITH TOOLS. WHICH ONES YOU BRING INTO YOUR LIFE, FOR INSTANCE, WHERE YOU PUT THEM IN THE HOME, AND HOW YOU ORGANIZE THEM. NONE OF THIS IS DIFFICULT— IN FACT, *NOT* TAKING THESE MEASURES IS THE DIFFICULT WAY TO GO. WE'LL ALSO TAKE A LOOK AT SOME SNEAKY WAYS TO USE YOUR TOOLS, PLUS ANOTHER SURPRISE OR TWO.

Power Up Your Tools
with Wise Selection and Storage

A lot of the advice in *How to Cheat at Home Repair* involves the very moment when you put a tool to use. However, there are many factors in the background that influence how efficient, powerful, useful, and hassle-free that tool is. Here are some simple strategies for selecting and storing tools that will have an enormous impact on your cheat-at-home-repair efforts.

Versatility. When you were a kid, a kind uncle might have given you a screwdriver set with one small plastic handle and several different kinds of driver tips that snapped into it. If that was your introduction to multiuse tools, then you might have soured on them when the plastic cracked and the cheap tips shredded after only a few uses. Well, multiuse tools aren't kid stuff any more. The cleverest home-repair people I know rave about them because they're so convenient. Basically, it's the Swiss Army knife concept on a slightly larger scale. Rather than having to carry several tools around to make a repair, you have several high-quality tools combined into one compact object. Multiuse tools can make good economic sense too, because their cost is often less than the combined cost of the individual tools they represent. They also add less weight to your toolbox.

Now, not all multiuse tools are alike, of course. Buying one depends on what kind of work you typically do. Some are geared more for electrical work, carpentry, or even recreational pursuits, such as camping and fishing. A good one for around-the-house use might include multiple screwdrivers, knife blades, a saw blade or two, an awl, and pliers with a wire-cutting edge. Some versatile tools focus on a single function, but adjust to all the sizes and varieties of that function. For instance, Chuck McLaughlin, a plumber in Glenside, Pennsylvania, loves his Lenox multitip screwdriver that offers Phillips, flat, square, and nut drivers. Similarly, an adjustable socket wrench has an opening that will expand and shrink to fit any size nut—much better than lugging around a half-dozen wrenches. So put a little thought into what kind of repair work you do most and what kind of multiuse tools can help you shrink the size and weight of the tool kit you take along. Then you get to do one of my favorite things: go browsing in hardware stores and home improvements stores for the ingenious multiuse tools that will make your cheat-at-home-repair life even easier.

Portability. If you had a workbench in your basement with all your tools at hand and that was the only place where you ever did repair work, then portability of your tools would not be an issue at all. But life doesn't work like that. Your attic, shed, roof, siding, and clothes washer will all cry out for attention occasionally, which means that you need to be able to move just the right tools to a location far from your tool storage area—with a minimum of hassle. This is where clever use of tool-carrying devices comes in.

Sara Fisher, a professional organizer in Atlanta, recommends buying a small, lightweight toolbox and stocking it with the tools you use most often around the house. You'll be able to grab it from your tool storage area whenever you need it without hunting around for your screwdrivers, hammer, and pliers. Oreland, Pennsylvania, resident Scott Vincent has multiple toolboxes, and they're stocked according to purpose; for instance, drilling equipment goes in one box, and tools for working on home siding go in another. Raymond VinZant, Roto Rooter's Ask-the-Plumber expert, likes to keep a small bucket supplied with the four or five tools he most often needs for plumbing jobs around the house. And yet another alternative: Post a small-but-rugged-handled tool bag in your tool storage area, but leave it empty. Each time you need to fix something, toss in only the items you need, and return those tools to their proper places when you're done.

Resist the temptation to cram all your tools into one box—you'll never feel like lugging *that* around. Also, don't attempt to store all your hardware—nails, screws, bolts, and picture hangers—in your toolbox. A small selection would be helpful, but the entire supply is needless weight.

A Bag in Every Toolbox

Scott Vincent keeps multiple toolboxes handy, their contents depending on the repair jobs he has to do most frequently around the house. But every one of his toolboxes has an item in common: a clear plastic bag full of miscellaneous, commonly used hardware (a variety of screws, nails, picture hangers, and such). This way, no matter what kind of job he's doing, he can save himself an annoying trip back to his workbench if he needs a common hardware item.

Availability. Being able to get to your tools readily when you need them is crucial to successful cheating-at-home-repair. The easier your tools are to find, and the closer they are at hand, the more likely it is that you'll snap them up and make simple repairs the moment you're aware of the need. So if you don't already have a single location where you cluster all your tools, choose a spot now. Garages are often ideal, as are basements. In a pinch, a walk-in pantry, laundry room, or mudroom might suffice, too.

Make sure that your Tool Central has some wall space open. To make your tools super-available, you need to be able to display the tools that don't reside permanently in toolboxes. The classic ways of doing this are by installing either pegboard or shelving. Pegboard comes with an enormous range of movable hooks that can accommodate tools of any size and shape. For storing tools on shelves, Fisher prefers the "ventilated" wire style of shelf. You can add hard plastic, easy-to-clean shelf liners to wire shelving to prevent teensy objects from falling through and getting lost. An alternative (or in addition to wall storage): Fisher also loves storing tools in a cabinet with multiple shallow drawers that have dividers in them (Elfa is one brand).

Durability. We all keep an eye out for bargains. But the most experienced repair people I know are unanimous about this: The tools that work better and are more durable cost more money than the tools that don't perform as well and fall apart quickly. Now, if you only intend to use a particular tool once or twice for a rare job and its longevity doesn't matter to you, then a cheaper tool may suffice. Otherwise, invest in quality. A screwdriver that will last you twenty years is a sounder investment than twenty screwdrivers—each of which falls apart after a year.

Understand that many tool manufacturers offer their products to different kinds of consumers. They may create a line of less expensive tools to appeal to everyday homeowners, and they may create a separate line of the same tools to appeal to fix-it professionals. There's a reason that the pros will only buy the latter. You often will get hints of this phenomenon from tool packaging in the stores—look for such terms as *professional grade*.

Are You Properly Equipped to Start Cheating?

If you've been running your own household for more than a few years, chances are you've been accumulating tools in self-defense—just to keep your house or apartment from collapsing in on you. And it's also likely that you have many or all of the following basic tools already. But just to be sure, let's run down a list of the must-haves for any household toolbox. These tools are versatile, easy to use, and relatively inexpensive. If you're missing any of these, put them on your shopping list the next time you visit a hardware store or home improvement center.

Screwdriver. You'll need various sizes and with various tips—flat, Phillips, and square tips, plus hex nut drivers.

Crescent wrench. For grasping various sizes of nuts and bolts, crescent wrenches have a jaw that can widen or narrow by turning a screw on the side of the wrench's head.

Channel-lock pliers. These pliers have an adjustable jaw size and are used for a wide variety of grasping purposes.

Pipe wrench. This is an adjustable wrench with a toothy jaw meant for

GETTING THE RIGHT TOOLS IN THE RIGHT PLACE

15

grabbing the rounded part of a pipe or some other fitting (not nuts). Unless you expect to do a lot of heavy-duty plumbing, one of the smaller sizes—say, ten inches (25.5cm) or so—will do nicely.

Hammer. At the very least have one classic, sixteen-ounce hammer with a two-pronged claw on the head for pulling nails out of wood. Look for a forged steel head. The handle might be steel as well, or it might be wood or fiberglass.

Utility knife. Also called a box cutter, this gizmo features a sharp, retractable blade that protrudes from one end of the handle. Yes, it will cut open cardboard boxes, but it's also handy for slicing other tough materials, such as carpet. The blades are replaceable and often stored inside the handle.

Chisel. A chisel has a sharp, flat end that's used for sculpting gaps or recesses into wood.

Power drill. While they come in larger sizes, the classic $3/8$-inch (1-cm) electric drill (that's a measurement of the maximum drill bit size) is probably all you need for general-purpose home repair. Whether to go with the corded variety or cordless is a matter of personal preference—and whether you intend to do a lot of drilling away from a convenient electrical outlet. Buy drill bits in a variety of sizes, plus a few screwdriver bits for times when you want to drive multiple screws quickly.

Hand saw. At a minimum you will want a crosscut saw, the conventional carpentry tool for cutting across the grain of wood. However, you will find two other saws very handy as well: a hacksaw for cutting metal and a pruning saw for cutting tree branches and other yard work.

Staple gun. A spring-powered device that allows you to squeeze the handle and drive hefty staples into wood and other firm-but-penetrable surfaces.

Caulking gun. A lot of the materials you use for filling holes, sealing around the bathtub, and filling cracks in the driveway come in standardized tubes with a nozzle on one end. A caulking gun has an open cylinder that you set such tubes into, and then you snip the end of the nozzle to make an opening. When you squeeze the handle of the caulking gun, a rod presses into the back of the tube and forces the patching material out the nozzle.

Tape measure. A long, thin metal tape with inches and/or centimeters marked on it that coils up, spring-loaded, inside a small metal or plastic casing. For home use, get one that's at least twelve feet (4m). It's a must-have for any kind of carpentry, of course, but also take it with you any time you're buying bulky items that will have to fit into your home—furniture, shelving, or appliances, for instance.

Eight Sneaky, Highly Versatile Repair Tools

Enough about conventional tools. Full-fledged cheaters-at-home-repair love to use common household objects to solve everyday problems, too. Here are some of my favorites, chosen for their versatility, durability, and reasonable cost. In fact, I suggest that you collect each of these eight items into several kits (stuff them into a mini-toolbox, a zip-closing bag, or some other small container). Store these kits in multiple locations—your main tool storage area, in the shed, in the garage, in your car trunk, and perhaps even in the kitchen. You will find yourself inventing zillions of ingenious uses for these tools as you run into daily hassles and dilemmas.

1. **Spray lubricant.** Spray it anywhere you need two parts to slide against each other more easily. Will prevent metal corrosion, too, and is a great solvent in many cleaning situations. Available in a wide variety of retail stores. WD-40 is one common brand.

2. **Compressed air.** A second entry from the aerosol-can department. Use this "instant wind" for dusting delicate or intricate items, cleaning electronics and other equipment that's sensitive to cleaning chemicals and moisture, and blowing dust out of spots you can't

GETTING THE RIGHT TOOLS IN THE RIGHT PLACE

17

A Ready Lubricant, Right Before Your Eyes

You probably don't carry an oilcan around with you day in and day out. So do you know what to do when you need just a little light lubricant—say, to loosen up a pair of balky scissors? The solution is as plain as the nose on your face. That's right: Rub your finger against the side of your nose—it's a ready source of lubricant!

If your tummy is turning flip-flops just now, let me point out that the cleverest cheaters-at-home-repair consider all the tools at their disposal when they confront a problem. You can't afford to ignore the potential of nose oil any more than you can afford to throw your favorite screwdriver into the trash. Legend has it that old-time clockmakers used nose oil to lubricate fine lock mechanisms. If clockmaking isn't your career path, then you will want to know about these other uses for the world's handiest lubricant. (By the way, the best place to harvest nose oil is at either side of your nostrils, in the crease where your nose meets the rest of your face.)

◇ Use nose oil to remove the foamy head from a glass of soft drink or beer. Yes, rub your finger against the side of your nose, dip it into the foam, and swirl. You see, the oil disturbs the water in the bubbles and causes the bubbles to rupture. *Highly recommended:* Only try this on your own drink.

◇ Rub nose oil into a scratch on your sunglasses to make it less visible. After you rub it in, wipe off the excess around the scratch so you don't have a big smudge.

reach in any other way. Hold the can straight up so the propellant sprays out. Buy cans of compressed air at office-supply stores, computer and electronics stores, and camera stores.

3. **Fishing line and needle.** Buy a spool of four- or five-pound test (1.8–2.5kg) monofilament fishing line. Fishing line is handy for

◇ Use nose oil to rub away the sticky residue left by a label on glass or plastic.

◇ Use nose oil as lip balm. Probably the kind of application you would want to employ discreetly.

◇ Use nose oil to add a quick gloss to your fingernails.

◇ If you haven't yet converted to digital photography, use a touch of nose oil to mask scratches in a negative when you're printing photographs in the darkroom.

◇ Use nose oil to make hazy glass transparent. For instance, if your low-voltage kitchen counter lights have hazy bulbs and you want to see if their filaments are burned out, rub on a little nose oil and you'll be able to see right through the glass.

◇ Rub nose oil onto the bowl of your tobacco pipe to keep it shiny.

◇ Use nose oil to lubricate your fingertips while playing a stringed instrument, such as a guitar or a banjo.

Note: A grateful salute—right off the side of my nose—goes out to Mark Bruley, a vice president at ECRI Institute in Plymouth Meeting, Pennsylvania, and also an accomplished nose oil scholar.

scores of impromptu repair jobs, including stitching up ripped jackets, pants, backpacks, and upholstery. Also use it to hang things or make an impromptu clothesline. Because it's clear, any stitching you do will be inconspicuous. To go with your fishing line, select a needle that's hefty enough to penetrate sturdy materials and has an eye that will accommodate the thickness of your fishing line. Store the needle in its original packaging to keep it from getting lost and to protect your fingers from pokes.

4. **Bailing wire.** This thin, strong galvanized wire is great for hanging pictures, outdoor decorations, and more. Wrap it around objects that need to be bound together, twist the ends together, and snip off the excess with wire cutters or pliers.

5. **Zip ties.** These are sturdy nylon straps with a slotted opening on one end and a ridged band that slides through the slot and locks. They're commonly used for forcing some order in spots where you have multiple wires or cables. They're also very handy for an impromptu fix when you need to bind two or more objects together. Secure a weak plant stalk to a garden stake, hold several washers together "key ring" style, or bind two objects together when their bolt comes loose and is lost. You can buy zip ties at home improvement stores in a variety of lengths. Cluster the unused ones in a zip-closing bag.

6. **Bungee cords.** These are strong-but-elastic cords with hooks on each end. They come in a wide range of lengths and colors and are available in hardware stores and home improvement centers. Use them anywhere you need to temporarily hold one thing to another—say, binding a bed roll to a backpack, holding your car's trunk lid down when it won't close over an oversized object, or securing your garbage can lid to prevent the wind—or varmints—from removing it. There's an annoying thing about bungee cords: When you store several of them together, those little hooks love to reach out and grab one another and any object they happen to be near. The solution to this: Store unused bungee cords in a large zip-closing bag, which will curb their grabby tendency.

7. **Duct tape.** Strong, waterproof, and more versatile than a Swiss Army knife. The Scouts I know include in their backpacks a small pencil wrapped in several feet (1m or so) of duct tape. That makes it lighter and more compact than an entire roll—and you have something to write with as well!

8. **A bag of plastic supermarket bags.** Squash together three plastic supermarket bags, stuff them into the bottom of a fourth bag, roll the entire thing into a tight wad, wrap a rubber band around it, and drop it into your toolkit. The ultimate way to recycle supermarket bags is to get a second use out of them. Naturally, they'll be handy when you need to carry several things at once. But they're also great for keeping your hands out of grimy or disgusting messes. Slide one over you hand while you're changing the lawnmower's oil, for instance, or while you're picking up that dead mouse that your cat left on the sidewalk. Throw out the bag, of course, when it gets messy, and replenish your stock when it runs low.

Sneaky Tool-Specific Tips

Here's a collection of clever ways to save time and effort while you're using specific tools:

For one-handed screw driving, tear off some tape. It's very easy to drop a screw when you're trying to drive it, especially if you don't have your second hand free to hold the screw, or if you have to reach for the spot where the screw needs to go in. Here's "Handyman Scott" Kropnick's tricky solution: Tape the screw to the tip of the screwdriver. Here's how you do it: Tear off about two inches (5cm) of tape (electrician's tape or masking tape work well) and poke the tip of your screwdriver through the center of the tape so that the tip emerges on the sticky side. Then set the slot of your screw against the tip of the driver, and fold the tape up so it grasps the head of the screw. Now you can drive the screw one-handed without fear of dropping it.

Reduce the damage—and effort—of pulling nails. Many people do too much damage—and work way too hard—when they're pulling nails out of wood with a claw hammer. The novice's approach goes like this: You slide the head of a nail between the two prongs of the hammer's claw, then you push the handle of the hammer down so the leverage pulls the nail out of the wood. If the nail gives you any resistance at all, the head of the hammer leaves a mark—and sometimes a sizable dent—on the wood. Instead, here's Kropnick's take-it-easy approach: Before you push the hammer's handle down, slide a thin piece of wood under the hammer's head to protect the wood below. Then, instead of pushing straight down, loosen the nail by pushing side to side, and lower the handle gradually. "This is especially good for bigger nails," Kropnick says.

Keep a "notepad" on your measuring tape. When you're taking measurements for a job around the house, you probably know better than to try to keep the figures in your head. When you go to buy materials at the home store, the length of the shelves you need will have vanished from your mind quicker than last night's dream. The obvious solution is to write all measurements down immediately. But that requires carrying yet another object around with you—a notepad. To simplify matters, and to make sure you're never without a scratch pad, do this: Buy a roll of 2-inch-wide (5-cm-wide) masking tape. Tear off five 2-inch (5cm) lengths of this tape and affix these squares, one on top of another, to the case of your tape measure (the outer side, not over the belt clip). Now when you take measurements, you will have a "notepad" right there in your hand. Jot the figures on the top piece of masking tape. Peel it off and stick it to your materials list when you go shopping. Replenish the tape squares as needed.

Seal your plumbing connections. You may not consider yourself a master plumber, but now and then you might make a plumbing connection that you want to be leak-free—say, when you install a new showerhead. So you will want to know about a material that plumbers use anytime they're connecting one pipe to another: joint sealer. This stuff comes in two forms. Teflon tape is a material you wrap around the threads of a pipe. "Pipe dope" is a liquid that you brush onto the threads. These products, available at home improvement stores and hardware stores, prevent leaks by sealing any voids left in the joint, says Chuck McLaughlin, a plumber in Glenside, Pennsylvania.

Put a rust-buster in your toolbox. Collect those little packets of silica gel that come with so many consumer products (sneakers, electronics, medicines, and camera accessories, for instance). The packets are designed to absorb moisture, so they make an excellent rust preventer to toss into your toolbox. When you get a new one, toss out an old one, since they become saturated after a while and will no longer draw the damaging humidity out of your toolbox's interior. If you would rather buy your silica gel, ask for it at a hardware store, a home improvement store, a camera store, or a craft store.

On ladders, let your power tool dangle. Working with power tools on a ladder has its ups and downs. Specifically: You go up the ladder with your power drill to drive some screws. When you need to set the drill down for a moment, you have to go down to the ground again to set it in a safe place. Up and down, up and down. Well, save yourself the steps with this simple trick, says Scott Vincent. When you're at the top of the ladder, tie the cord of the drill around a side support of the ladder, leaving yourself enough slack that you can reach the spots where you need to work. When you're not using the drill, just let it hang along the side of the ladder. It will be right at your fingertips the next time you need it.

Label broad categories on your tool display. Wherever you display your tools on pegboard or shelving, using labels will help ensure that your tools always find their way back to the proper place. Now, quit rolling your eyes—I'm not suggesting that you create a label to go with every screwdriver and pair of pliers. Depending on what kind of work you do around the house, you probably will get away with three to five labels, because we're going to use broad categories for our labels rather than narrow ones—CARPENTRY, PLUMBING, and ELECTRICAL, for instance. When you have your tools clustered and labeled this way in your storage area, anyone in your household who borrows a tool is much more likely to return it to the proper place. Which means that you're much more likely to be able to find it the next time you need it.

"I'm label crazy—I love labels," says Sara Fisher. "Help the home-

Spills: A Sticky Solution

A container slipped through your fingers, and now your floor is covered with hundreds of minuscule objects. Whatever they are—pins, brads, beads, nails—you're envisioning an hour of meticulous work to gather them all up again. But the situation is not really that bad. All you need to do is wrap your hand in tape with the sticky side out—cellophane tape or masking tape will do nicely. Then pat your hand against the errant objects and brush them off into their original box. You'll be done in just minutes.

If the spilled objects are metal, there's another easy alternative: Just drag a magnet over the floor and pick the objects up a score at a time.

less items in your home. I have a home, and you have a home—we know where we go. So we've gotta be sure our tools know where they go."

A slick way to make screw driving easy. When you have to drive a lot of screws into wood, the friction from the screwdriver can leave your hand raw or even blistered. Making screws easier to drive is simple. Keep an old candle in your toolbox just for this purpose. When you have to drive a screw, rub the candle against its threads first, lubricating the metal. This makes the screw much easier to turn and saves the hands a lot of pain. If you don't have a candle handy, soap will work well, too (but with greater potential to get messy). Or spritz the pilot hole for your screw with spray lubricant.

YOU'VE LEARNED ALL about the home repair cheatin' frame of mind, about selecting and storing your tools, and now you're rarin' to go. Let's move on to some simple and downright sneaky fixes you can make in and around the house.

Furniture: Top-Shelf Shortcuts and Fixes

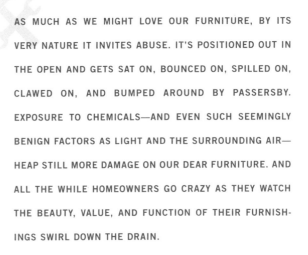

AS MUCH AS WE MIGHT LOVE OUR FURNITURE, BY ITS VERY NATURE IT INVITES ABUSE. IT'S POSITIONED OUT IN THE OPEN AND GETS SAT ON, BOUNCED ON, SPILLED ON, CLAWED ON, AND BUMPED AROUND BY PASSERSBY. EXPOSURE TO CHEMICALS—AND EVEN SUCH SEEMINGLY BENIGN FACTORS AS LIGHT AND THE SURROUNDING AIR— HEAP STILL MORE DAMAGE ON OUR DEAR FURNITURE. AND ALL THE WHILE HOMEOWNERS GO CRAZY AS THEY WATCH THE BEAUTY, VALUE, AND FUNCTION OF THEIR FURNISH-INGS SWIRL DOWN THE DRAIN.

Well, sit back, put your feet up (not on the coffee table, please), and let's review some repair and maintenance shortcuts that will restore your sanity in no time.

Wood Furniture: When Life Goes against the Grain

A lot of our most beautiful and expensive furniture is made of wood. We think of it as hefty and solid, but wood furniture is actually rather sensitive stuff. So as a first step in getting long life out of our furniture, we're going to do something touchy-feely: Sit down on or beside every chair, table, dresser, shelf, and cabinet in the house and feel what they're feeling. Yup, look carefully all around you and think about the close environment of each piece: Is it in direct sunlight? Is it close to a heating or air-conditioning vent? If either is the case, move that piece into a safer spot immediately. The ultraviolet rays in sunlight cause "tremendous fading" in your furniture's finish, says furniture restorer Steve Nearman of The Master's Touch in Fredericksburg, Virginia. Streams of cold and hot air change the humidity around your furniture, too, and that's bad for it. Sure, there are some practical concerns involved, and you'll just have to be inventive. For instance, if your dining-room table and chairs are exposed to bright sunlight, you can't very well move them to another room. However, you may be able to keep the shades drawn in the room during the day. Also, try this trick: Simply turn the table and rotate the chairs every few weeks, so at least the colors will change evenly.

Refinish? Scratch that idea. The best fix for deep gouges and scratches in wood furniture is simple and fun: Pull out a ninety-six-count box of crayons and start coloring, recommends Tim Puro, owner of Monroe Furniture Restoration in Bloomington, Indiana. Professional repairers use special wax fillers to do these fixes, but a big box of crayons from the kids' aisle of a discount store will work just fine. Such collections contain many of the same colors as the pros use, he says. Select the color that most closely matches the wood, and hold the crayon so your finger is near the tip and the crayon is nearly horizontal with the wood. Rub the colored stick back and forth across the crevice in the wood, so the edges scrape wax off the crayon. Keep going until you have *over*filled the gouge, Puro emphasizes.

Now take a credit card from your wallet (or take one of those fake credit cards that the companies send you in the mail every day) and scrape it over the top of the repaired spot to remove any wax bulging out of the gouge. This will leave you with a perfectly smooth, color-matched spot where the defect was just moments before.

If using crayons makes you feel a little childish, a device called a stain pen will disguise the shallower scratches in your wood furniture. Pick one up in a matching color at your hardware store or home improvement store, and use that to darken the scratch.

Stash some "gold" in the pantry. Here's the other way to insure your furniture and other woodwork against scratches and gouges: Put a can of scratch remover on your shopping list the next time you visit a home improvement store, and tuck it away in an accessible cabinet, says "Handyman Scott" Kropnick. (His favorite brand is Scott's Liquid Gold.) Scratch remover is a polish you apply to nicked wood with a soft rag. The polish adds a slightly darker tone to the wood, filling in the bright mark of a scratch with disguising color.

Rub away water rings. Ouch! An oafish guest set down an iced tea glass on your tabletop, and it left a water ring. Or perhaps you did it. All that matters is knowing how to get that blemish out. For starters, look at the color. If it's white, it's fixable. The moisture has penetrated the finish and forced apart its molecules, creating little bubbles of moisture or air, says Richard Bullock, owner of Bullock's Furniture Restoration in Odenton, Maryland. If the ring is dark, the water penetrated the wood and you either have a lengthy project on your hands or your favorite furniture repair professional does.

All you need to do is warm the white ring to melt those bubbles out of the finish. Squirt on a dab of nongel toothpaste, and aggressively buff it onto the ring with a rag. The toothpaste isn't magic—it's just transferring the heat from the rag to the tabletop, Bullock says. When the white in the wood is gone, you're finished.

If you don't have toothpaste, or don't enjoy buffing, you can use a hair dryer to heat the ring. Be careful with this approach, however—hair dryers can easily get hot enough to damage the finish. Spread your fingers and hold your hand so the dryer blows between your thumb and forefinger onto the blemish. If the air gets too hot for your hand, then you know it's too hot for the furniture as well, Bullock says.

Or coast right past those water rings. We love our party guests dearly, of course, but the problem is that those who have drinks in their hands, by definition, have been drinking. And often they don't bother searching for coasters when they want to set down those drinks. A guest who doesn't find one quickly is likely to put his glass right on your tabletop, where it could leave an unsightly ring. The solution, says furniture restorer Tim Puro, is to liberally distribute coasters around your home before guests arrive, and point them out as you're serving drinks. That's much easier than restoring your furniture's finish the next day.

Get steamed up over furniture dings. Oops—you dropped a casserole dish on the kitchen table. Oops—your child slammed a toy dump truck onto the coffee table in a moment of overexuberance. Now that perfectly smooth surface is marred by a dent. If the dent didn't break the surface of the wood, all you have to do is steam it out, says Craig Vetters of the Chair Dr. in Evansville, Indiana.

If you have a steamer—the kind you see advertised on television for steaming clothes or cleaning tile surfaces—that will work fine. Position the device so that the steam will spray straight into the dent, and fire up the appliance. The moist heat will cause the wood to swell and "raise the dent right back out of the wood," he says.

If you don't have a steamer, your clothes iron can serve as a sub-

Protection: Wax Works, But Pass on Polish

We don't know what four out of five dentists would recommend about polishing your furniture, but here's what the advisors we talked to had to say about furniture polish across the board: Don't use it!

"I'm opposed to furniture polish," says Richard Bullock, owner of Bullock's Furniture Restoration in Odenton, Maryland. The polish doesn't protect the wood. If your furniture is sealed with lacquer, shellac, or another coating, *that's* the layer of protection it needs from the outside world. Nor does it need any oil in the furniture polish for nourishment. The furniture's wood takes on moisture depending on the humidity in your home, adds Puro. It doesn't need polish for that purpose. Neither should you believe any nonsense about polish replacing the wood's natural oils. It doesn't have any natural oil to replace!

What furniture polish may do is leave an oily film on your furniture. This sticky sheen collects dust more quickly than nothing at all. You then use *more* polish while dusting, and the cycle repeats. Not surprisingly, the owners of the furniture-polish companies can afford very, very nice furniture in their own homes.

In addition, furniture polishes may contain silicone, which bonds chemically with the finish on the wood. If you take the furniture to professionals for refinishing in the future, they'll have to "fight like hell" to refurbish the piece, Bullock says. For that kind of job, he sighs, "I should charge more—but I don't." Don't count on *your* professional to be that nice.

Instead of polish, a much better alternative for protecting your furniture is wax. It's harder than oil, and it does provide a protective barrier, Bullock says. Pick up a can of the paste wax variety. Unlike polishes, a single can of wax could last you for the rest of your life. Apply a thin layer every five to six years to dressers, buffets, and china cabinets. For surfaces that see more wear, such as tabletops and the arms and backs of chairs, use it annually.

And when you want to dust or clean your furniture, our advisors also agree on a method that's cost-free and hassle-free as well: Take a hand towel, lightly dampen it with water, and apply it to the furniture, wiping in circular motions until the dust is removed.

stitute. Place a damp towel over the dent, set your iron so it steams, and run the iron over the towel-covered dent until it pops out.

Keep old dressers properly lubed. In old dressers, the runners that hold the drawers as they slide in and out are made of wood. The wood-on-wood friction of the moving drawers gradually causes the runners to wear down, Steve Nearman says. Then the drawers start closing at a crooked angle, which can chip the finish on the faces of the drawers. An easy way to prevent this insidious problem is to take a clear or white candle and rub it down the length of the runners. Also give a waxy rubdown to the parts of the drawers that fit into the runners. Doing this every few months will add years of life to your dresser.

New cabinets? Grab this opportunity. Have you ever lost or damaged one of the knobs or pulls on your cabinets? It's almost impossible to find an exact matching replacement. So your only alternative is to buy new knobs for every cabinet in the room—that's a lot of money and a lot of work. So plan ahead whenever you buy or build new cabinets. Always buy a few extra knobs when you get new cabinets. If they're wood knobs that require staining, stain the extras at the same time you stain the ones you'll be using, so they'll be sure to match when you need them in the future. Then store the extras away as backups.

Keep furniture cool. You picked up your refinished end table on a blistering summer day. You need to stop at the mall for a new window air-conditioner, and the convenience store for a bag of ice, and maybe the grocery store for some ice cream. While you're shopping, the new finish on that end table is blistering and cracking in the hot car.

Instead, treat your furniture like pets, kids, and other passengers that could be harmed by high heat—don't leave them in the car during warm months for any length of time, warns furniture restorer Richard Bullock.

Scrub away a smudge. If your vacuum cleaner leaves a mark on the bottom of your bookcase, you splattered paint on the dining-room

Bungled Chair Repairs Don't Sit Well with the Pros

If there's one thing a furniture repairer dreads hearing, it's the customer who says, "I tried to fix this wobbly chair, and nothing worked!" In general, if you try to fix a wobbly chair, you're just going to further damage it, which will cost you more money when you have to take it to a professional for repair.

"Most of the time, if you left it alone I could fix it for half the price," says Steve Nearman of The Master's Touch in Fredericksburg, Virginia. Most people start drilling holes and inserting screws into a loose chair joint, not realizing that by drilling out that little bit of wood they're making the joint weaker, not stronger. In addition, nails and screws work their way out of chairs before long, due to people moving and shifting around on the furniture. And that results in yet another hole in the joint.

Another common problem: Over time, people squirt several different kinds of glue into a loose joint, creating an ineffective, globby mess. Or they unwittingly use a kind of glue that expands when it dries (the popular Gorilla Glue, for instance), which can break a joint in the chair if not managed correctly. (*Hint:* Read the label!)

"We get stuff in here that looks like four or five guys have tried to fix it, then you have a big glob of goo you have to remove," Nearman says. If a joint in your chair is a little loose, he says, take this one shot at fixing it: Apply a small amount of instant glue, such as Super Glue. If that doesn't work, bite your lip and resist the temptation to try another kind of glue. Oddly enough, old glue and new glue will not bond well. So the wisest next move is to leave the chair alone and call your local furniture repair shop.

table while painting, or you found some other smudge on your furniture, do what you'd do for a dirty skillet: Break out the steel wool.

Using extra-fine steel wool—called 0000-gauge steel wool—with paste wax can remove smudges and clean off "years of accumulated dirt and grime," Bullock says. Use your steel wool as an applicator and brush on the wax. Move back-and-forth along the grain. Don't make circular motions that go across the grain. Let the wax stand for fifteen minutes, and then buff it out with an old T-shirt. The smudge will be gone, and the shine will be back!

It's a bed, not a towel rack. Fresh and chipper after your shower, you stroll into the bedroom, toss your damp towel over the footboard of your bed, and start pulling clothes out of the closet. Hold it, says furniture restorer Steve Nearman. A warm and moist towel draped over your wooden headboard or footboard will leave water marks on the furniture, making it look shabby long before its time. Give your bed a break and hang your towel where it will dry without causing damage. The towel rack in the bathroom is a good bet, or buy a stand-alone towel rack at a bath store and position it in a corner of your bedroom.

Make veneer get a grip. That veneer layer on your tabletop looks nice when it's flat on the table—but not so nice when it's loose and flopping up and down. Just take out a knife, stab it, and the problem is gone.

Well, it's a little more complicated than that, but not much. Take a thin, flexible artist's palette knife and coat it with white glue or hide glue (a glue long used in woodworking), Puro recommends. A dull kitchen knife might work just as well. Slip the knife waaay back as far as you can under the veneer, slide it back and forth to distribute the glue, and then pull it out.

If sliding the glue in with a knife isn't workable, here's an alternative approach. Take a drinking straw and bend one end over to seal it temporarily. Then carefully drip your glue into the open end of the straw until you have accumulated enough to hold the veneer down. Now flatten the straw enough to slide the open end under the popped-up veneer. Unbend the protruding end, and blow into the straw to push the glue out.

And one more option for inserting the glue: Pick up a glue syringe (a reusable device available where woodworking products are sold), draw some glue into it, and squeeze it into the gap.

Whichever method you choose, once you have the glue in place lay a piece of wax paper over the area and stack some books on top of it until the glue dries. The wax paper will keep any stray glue away from the books.

Just say no to amateur stripping. Sure, there's something romantic about finding an old end table at a yard sale, stripping and refinishing it, and then displaying the gleaming new treasure in your home. But in the cheat-at-home-repair world, furniture stripping will never qualify as a Super-Easy Lightweight Fix (SELF). You have to pay for pricey chemicals that are harsh enough to peel the finish off wood. And while you do the work, you have to breathe in the noxious fumes and risk getting toxins on your clothing and skin. (If you have any doubts about how caustic stripping chemicals are, just read the scary warnings on their containers.) So this is where the HIRE principle kicks in. Let's all recite it together: When a job is

A Super Fix for Sticky Fingers

It's the conundrum that arises every time you fasten items with instant glue, such as Super Glue: You need to apply pressure to the two objects you're gluing together until the pieces set—and in the meantime, your fingers inevitably get caught in the sticky ooze.

Furniture restorer Tim Puro has a sneaky solution: All you have to do is whip out a stretch of high-density polyethylene. No, you don't have to be a chemical engineer to find this stuff. Go to your recycling bin, pull out a plastic milk or water jug, and look for the initials HDPE stamped somewhere. This kind of plastic is resistant to instant glue. So use a utility knife or kitchen shears to snip out a flexible shield for protecting your fingers while you press on the items you're gluing together. Alternatively, if you're using a book (or some other heavy object) to press down on the items you are gluing together, use a stretch of milk or water jug plastic to protect your book.

Hard, Important, Rarely done, and Elaborate, hire a professional to do it. If you like, we can extend the acronym to HIRED by adding *Dangerous*. Professional furniture strippers already have the chemicals, the safety gear, and the know-how to do it right. And you get to devote the time you save to something much more fun—like going to another yard sale.

Preventing Even More Furniture Boo-Boos

Tread softly with those felt pads. Putting self-adhesive circles of felt under lamps, bowls, and other heavy items before setting them on your furniture can help protect the finish. But beware—that's not a foolproof solution. Sometimes the adhesive in such pads will seep through the felt and mar the furniture's finish, says furniture restorer Steve Nearman. It's hard to tell which felt pads will cause this problem, or which furniture is prone to this kind of damage. So to stay on the safe side, just use felt protectors without adhesive.

Change your vacuum's trajectory: Pop quiz: What's this sound? Whirr . . . *klunk*. Whirr . . . *kachunk*. Give up? It's the sound of your vacuum bashing into your coffee table, entertainment center, and china cab-

---

THE MOST LIKELY PROBLEM 👁

Silencing a Squeaky Bed

Every time you lie down, your bed announces it to the world with a loud squeak. There are two probable causes for this annoyance, depending on what your bed frame is made of. If the frame is wooden, look for a weakening joint and firm it up with an application of instant glue. If your bed frame is metal, it probably has a rivet shifting in its hole when you put pressure on the bed. Give any rivets you can find a tiny drop of oil, and tell them to shut up—it's sleep time.

inet, leaving colored marks from its rubber bumper. The occasional tap and bump with the vacuum cleaner may seem like a minor concern, but it will definitely leave your furniture looking tired and shabby well before its time. So establish this little course correction in your head: When vacuuming near furniture, always vacuum parallel to the piece rather than straight into it.

Choose your duster wisely. Feather dusters may be as light as, well, a feather, but they can scratch like sandpaper. The feathers are slightly abrasive, Puro says, and the dust they pick up is scratchy, too. If you were to use a feather duster on a highly polished piece of black lacquered furniture, after just six months it would be covered with light swirls from the dusting. Instead, he recommends using a disposable electrostatic duster (Swiffer, for instance).

Upholstery: Splotches, Drips, and Rips—Oh My!

And now for the softer side of furniture repair—the fabric coverings on our chairs, couches, pillows, and more. With this sneaky collection of tools and techniques, you will no longer live in dread of the spills, tears, and other travails suffered by our cushy furnishings.

Recycle those thread holes. Is your upholstered piece of furniture coming apart at the seams? Calm down—you needn't do the same. Just gather a curved needle, a spool of thread and, if your vision isn't sharp, your eyeglasses. Usually curved needles come in a pack of three or four at fabric stores, says Craig Vetters of the Chair Dr. in Evansville, Indiana. They're easier to use on upholstery than straight needles, he says.

Select the smallest needle and thread it. Now take a close look at the gap in your upholstery. Do you see the tiny rows of holes where the seam was originally sewn together? As long as they haven't been ripped through, use these holes to resew the gap. This method helps ensure that the gap will pull together tightly without puckering. Also, before you start sewing, pull the edges of the gap together and make sure the matching holes on each side are lined up as you sew. Start your stitching by putting your needle through the *underside* of the fabric, a trick that helps to hide the knot and some of the thread. Then sew straight across between the holes, following the path of the original thread; that way, you'll cut down on puckering as well.

Fish around for "thread" that won't break. When repairing rends in your upholstery, skip the cotton or polyester thread you'd use on your clothes—it breaks too easily. If you have nylon thread, use that instead, since it's stronger. No nylon thread? Go look in your tackle box. Craig Vetters buys monofilament fishing line in 1,500-yard (1,400-m) spools, not because he's such a fishing enthusiast, but because it makes a great thread for sewing upholstery. Relatively thin monofilament—four- or five-pound test—handles easily. Besides, because it's clear, you don't have to worry about matching thread color with fabric. Also, due to its transparency, "The nice thing about it is if you make a mistake, it blends in well," Vetters says.

Fix tears in an instant. When you're dealing with little holes, snags, or tears in your upholstery, in many cases *gluing* the edges together is a better bet than sewing. Instant glue (such as Super Glue or Krazy Glue) can fix little rips in leather, vinyl, or even cloth. To use it, first pull the edges of the tear together. The more easily you can pull them together, the more likely it is that the glue will hold the repair. If you have trouble making the edges meet—or if the rip is in a spot where someone's weight will put a lot of tension on the fix—it might not work as well. Apply the glue to the very edge of the material on just one side of the rip, not both sides. Then pull the edges together so they make contact. Hold for a few minutes until the glue dries.

Fix pilling with a close shave. When a rough spot develops on your cloth upholstery from wear, the little "pills" on the material feel a bit like five o'clock shadow. The solution is the same one that you'd use for your own stubble: a razor. Use a disposable razor, and lightly

"Top Secret" Upholstery Cleaner— Straight from the Bathroom

When Indiana furniture repairer Craig Vetters was in the business of cleaning up after fire and water damage, he kept his favorite upholstery-cleaning tool a top secret. "We used to wrap a piece of paper around the can so clients couldn't see what the label was, and we'd tell them it was a secret product developed especially for us."

But it wasn't, he confesses. You, too, can easily get this ultimate weapon against stains and spots. It's bathroom cleaner—more specifically, Scrubbing Bubbles.

"That's the most incredible cleaner you'll ever run across for upholstery," Vetters says. Simply spray a small amount onto the spot or stain on your fabric upholstery, then lightly brush it into the material with an old toothbrush or a fingernail brush. Let the cleaner sit for a few moments until the foam disappears. Once the bubbles have worked their magic, blot up the cleaner with a clean, damp cloth.

shave off the pilled area. (Unlike your face or your legs, your upholstery will be better off if you skip the shaving cream.) If fabric pilling is a big problem in your house, drop by a fabric store or browse the Internet for a small appliance called a fabric razor or jumper shears, says Paul Pearce, the London-based international vice president for the Institute of Inspection, Cleaning and Restoration Certification. Reminiscent of a man's electric razor, such devices quickly clip the pilling off your upholstery, plus they will give a fresh new look to wool, cotton, and knit clothing as well.

Remove greasy spots with naphtha. When a guest drops an oily hors d'oeuvre onto your living room upholstery, your heart sinks. After all, oily and greasy spots are famously tenacious. Around the house,

This Suedelike Upholstery Is No Softie

Sure, you have plenty of ideas about what kind of upholstery you prefer on your home's furniture—what color, look, and feel. But how's an everyday homeowner supposed to know which of the myriad materials available for covering furniture will actually make your life easier over the years—by resisting wear, tear, and stains while looking great at the same time? After all, at the beginning of this book we committed ourselves to the Materials On a Program (MOP) philosophy. This means knowing what kind of materials we will welcome into our homes the next time a purchase is necessary—in this case, what kind of upholstery will keep repair and maintenance to a minimum.

So I put the question to a guy who ought to know, Paul Pearce, the London-based vice president for the Institute of Inspection, Cleaning and Restoration Certification. His vote for the most hassle-free furniture upholstery on the planet: a high-tech material called Alcantara, which also is used in automobile interiors and other applications. It has a rich, suedelike feel and resists wear and staining. Cleaning dribbles off Alcantara is usually a simple matter of blotting with a white paper towel or white cloth. You can use upholstery cleaners on it, too, although it's a good idea to avoid scrubbing the material. Also avoid using heat-based cleaning techniques, such as steamers.

Alcantara is especially hassle-free upholstery if you have children in the house, Pearce says.

though, "Handyman Scott" Kropnick fears no grease. His favorite cure: the cleaning solvent naphtha, available at hardware stores and home stores. Just dribble a little bit of naphtha onto the spot, let it sit for six seconds, and then blot at the spot with a clean white towel. Don't scrub—that will just move the grease around and broaden the offending spot. This technique will remove greasy or oily spots from upholstery, carpet, and fine fabrics, too. Move cautiously, though, and test the naphtha first on an inconspicuous spot so you can tell if there's a chance the solvent will harm the material.

Wicker Wisdom

For many of us, wicker is the "comfort food" of the furniture world. Casual, homey, and elegant, wicker furniture has an emotional appeal whether we park it in the den, in the sunroom, or on the back porch. But the same qualities that make wicker furniture light, soft, and comfortable also make it easily damaged, says Cheri Russell of Wicker Fixer in Ozark, Missouri. You simply can't handle wicker the same way as wooden furniture—and for those times when you treat wicker too roughly, well, you need some sneaky ways to repair the results. But first let's take a look at ways to prolong the life of your wicker furniture:

◇ **Avoid stepping on it.** If you need to retrieve something from a high shelf, don't stand on your wicker chair—you're likely to damage the seat or put your foot right through it.

◇ **Stand up under your own power.** When you rise out of a wicker chair, lean forward and get up without putting your weight on the armrests— which will crush the wicker and cause gradual damage.

◇ **Stop tilting back.** Sure, it's comfortable and relaxing to push back with your feet so your chair is resting on its back legs. But this practice puts too much stress on a wicker chair's legs, weakening them. Russell had a customer who did that—and fell backward through a sliding-glass door. That turned out to be neither comfortable nor relaxing.

◇ **Rotate the seating.** If the same people regularly sit in the same wicker chairs around a table, the repeated strain from their weight and posture will warp and wear out the furniture. Rotate the chairs every few weeks so none of them is exposed to two-hundred-pound (91-kg) Pa, bouncy Susie, or fidgety Bobby all the time.

◇ **Keep the weather at bay.** Covers for outdoor furniture are expensive. If you have a nice piece of wicker furniture that's exposed to the elements, the official *How to Cheat at Home Repair* approach is to buy a fitted waterproof twin mattress cover at a discount store and slide that over your outdoor wicker.

◇ **Blow it off.** All those crevices in wicker furniture can hold a lot of dust. An easy way to get it out is to affix the attachment hose to your vacuum cleaner and set the airflow on reverse. Blow air on the furniture while you brush it with a soft-bristled brush—for instance, a toothbrush, a nail brush, or even a clean toilet brush, Russell says. Don't use a wire brush on your wicker—that would damage it. But if using a vacuum cleaner set on reverse isn't practical, you can easily use a hair dryer set on "cool" for your wind power.

◇ **Wash it carefully.** It's OK to gently wash wooden wicker pieces outside with soapy water, Russell advises. Fill a bucket with water from your garden hose, stir in two squirts of gentle dishwashing liquid, and use a soft-bristle brush to clean the furniture. Then rinse the wicker clean with the hose. Set the furniture in the shade to dry, not in direct sunlight. Too much sun can cause wicker to dry too fast, making the paint pop off.

◇ **Tape up unraveling strands.** Sometimes the legs of wicker furniture will unravel near the seat. Sure, you could haul that piece off to a professional for a by-the-book repair. But why hurry? A quick-and-simple fix will keep the damage from spreading. Position the errant strand of wicker into its proper place, then wrap that part of the leg in a snug layer of clear cellophane tape or clear packing tape. Chances are, you'll be pleased enough with this repair job that you'll "forget" about arranging for a more costly and elaborate fix. Otherwise, you couldn't call it cheating, could you?

◇ **Give wicker a trim.** If you notice that a strand in your wicker furniture has broken off and is sticking up, snip it off with a pair of diagonal cutters (a tool that looks like wire cutters), recommends Cheri Russell of Wicker Fixer.

Brush Up on Painting Wicker

When repainting wicker furniture, follow these steps to protect the piece's value and appearance, says wicker expert Cheri Russell.

Clean it first. Some people will just slap a new coat of paint over their wooden wicker when it gets dirty. This will produce a lumpy, sloppy look. Remove dust and crud before painting.

Protect the label. Many pieces of old wicker bear a paper label that tells you where it was made—a bit of authentication that's worth preserving on a venerable piece. Before you paint wicker furniture with such a label, mask the label with aluminum foil, and secure the foil with easily removable tape that won't do damage when you pull it up.

Prime it. Before painting, cover the furniture with a primer, such as Kilz. If you don't, the wicker will suck up the paint, and you'll have to apply thick coats that won't look as good. By priming first, you can use thin coats.

Use spray paint. Since you're looking for thin coats to create the best look, spray paint is definitely the way to go. Give your paintbrush a rest.

For some reason, kids love to fiddle with and pick at loose wicker, and this habit will only increase the damage to your furniture. Even worse, someone scooting out of the chair could catch the protruding strand of wicker on a pair of pants—or skin—and harm the chair and possibly herself. So giving your furniture a close "haircut" is the best way to prevent damage all around.

◇ **Reconnect broken strands.** What if a strand of wicker has snapped, but none of the pieces has broken away from the furniture yet? Let's put that strand back together with a little quick surgery, using masking tape and a pair of scissors. First, use your fingers to push the two broken ends of wicker back together. Snip a piece of masking tape about a half-inch (13mm) wide and long enough to wrap around the wicker strand twice. Wrap the tape around the joint snugly and press it flat. If you still have a bit of the paint that you last used on this piece of furniture, apply it to the tape to camouflage the repair. Otherwise go your child's collection of 10 zillion markers, select the one that most closely matches the wicker's color, and use that to touch up the masking tape.

◇ **Tighten up a saggy seat.** If you have a kitchen chair with a sagging caned seat (the material that looks like woven netting), don't despair. Here's the easy way to give your chair a "fanny tuck"— without a trip to the repair shop. Wet a rag or dish towel under hot water. Flip the chair over and lay the cloth on the underside of the seat for twenty minutes, says Cheri Russell. Remove the cloth and be sure not to sit in the chair again until it dries. The heat and moisture will cause the material to shrink and tighten. If the seat has not tightened up satisfactorily after the first try, repeat the process two or three more times.

When Office Furniture Calls in Sick

Most furniture repair tricks will work whether you use the furniture for watching television or writing sales reports in your home office. But in some specific instances, office furniture is a species unto itself, so here are some secrets that will save you a lot of grief.

Turn this for more comfort. Many an office worker sits down in a desk chair only to find himself tipping backward alarmingly. Or, conversely, he finds that the chair back is suddenly stiff as a board. Woefully, he contemplates a trip to the office supply store in search of comfy new support. Not so fast! Many people think the only adjustment gadget beneath the seat of an office chair is the lever that moves the chair up and down, says Doug Gagliardi of The Chair-Man, an office-furniture repair store headquartered in Twin Falls, Idaho. But with just a little bit of exploration under the seat, you will find a small device called the tension knob.

Turning the knob one way will tighten the tension as you lean against your chair's seat back, and turning it the other way will loosen the tension. Next time, don't be so quick to push the panic button!

To protect their arms, give office chairs a hand. A common problem that swivel office chairs develop is threadbare fabric on the fronts of the armrests, says Gagliardi.

The damage typically comes from sliding the chair up against your desk after you stand up—there's not enough clearance for the arms to fit cleanly under the desktop, and the repeated abrasion of the desk against the chair arms adds wear each time. So preventing wear and tear on the arms is simple: Don't just push your chair against the desk. At the same time that you slide in the chair, reach down for the lever that lowers the seat, so the arms clear the underside of the desk. That's negligible added effort, and it's not nearly the hassle involved in ordering new armrests and installing them.

Take one extra step when moving office furniture. If you ever need to move your office desk or file cabinet, first either empty the drawers and tape them shut, or remove the drawers completely, Gagliardi warns. Failing to heed this simple step can cause a desk drawer to fly out and break—or bang a hole in your doorframe or your shin. If a file cabinet drawer lunges out, it can damage the frame of the cabinet so that the drawers never work properly again.

Watch your seat. Usually when the casters (the wheels) on your office chair go bad, it's because the chair has slid off the protective mat underneath it too many times, and you've slid it back onto the plastic mat without getting up. Dragging the casters over the edge of the mat damages them. If you slide off the mat, get up, pick up the chair, and place it back on the mat. If you find yourself frequently drifting off the edge of the mat, it's time to buy a bigger mat—much less expensive that fixing or replacing your chair.

NOW YOU HAVE an entirely new relationship with the furniture in your house. You have a set of amazingly powerful furniture-fixing tools stashed away—which, in the cheat-at-home-repair tradition, happen to be easy-to-find household items. You also have a host of strategies that will lengthen the life of all your furniture and thus totally avoid zillions of future repairs—which, in the cheat-at-home-repair tradition, happens to mean you get more time in the hammock. Don't forget your sunscreen.

Home Electricity:
Powerful Moves

WHEN YOU GO TO SCHOOL TO BECOME A RESIDENTIAL ELECTRICIAN, THEY DON'T TELL YOU THAT YOU'RE GOING TO NEED A REALLY GOOD NECK BRACE. THAT'S BECAUSE ELECTRICIANS SPEND MOST OF THEIR TIME WALKING THROUGH THEIR CUSTOMERS' HOMES SHAKING THEIR HEADS. EVERYWHERE THEY GO, THEY SEE POORLY AND DANGEROUSLY DONE ELECTRICAL WORK ACCOMPLISHED BY WELL-MEANING DO-IT-YOURSELF ENTHUSIASTS. THIS IS PARTICULARLY WORRISOME BECAUSE OF THE FORCES INVOLVED. IF YOU MESS UP A PLUMBING PROJECT, MAYBE YOU'LL FLOOD THE BASEMENT OR RUIN A CARPET. IF YOU MESS UP AN ELECTRICAL PROJECT, YOU COULD DESTROY YOUR HOUSE AND FAMILY.

Not only is the electricity flowing into your home extremely powerful. Even under ideal conditions, household electricity is pretty deep science, too. You need to have a good grasp of complex circuitry, scores of different sizes of wiring, current strengths, safety procedures, and a zillion code specifications that are changed more often than your underwear. What's more, unless your home was built in the last year or two, it's probably an astonishing grab bag of poorly done wiring and antiquated equipment—all waiting to reach out and fry your sneakers.

Now, don't pout. Since you're reading this, I know that you have at least a touch of do-it-yourself spirit. Rest assured that in this chapter you will find plenty of sneaky tips, tricks, and shortcuts for managing your home's electricity that will save you time and hassle. Just tread very carefully, and let a professional electrician handle any situations involving direct exposure to live current.

The Big Picture: Your Service and Panel

Strap on your seat belt. In the realm of home electricity, you are about to rocket past three-quarters of other homeowners. That's because you are going to accomplish an easy—yet vital—project that is woefully neglected in most households. This little complement to your home wiring will make your home much safer. It will save you, and any electrician who works for you, tons of frustration and time. And it's the least technically involved electrical task you can perform in your home.

First, so you'll get a good understanding of how electricity gets into your house and is then distributed, let's take a little stroll. If your home's electrical system is a big mystery to you, in just three minutes you're going to learn some valuable facts. Chalk these items up toward your MBO (Maintenance by Observation, a tactic you committed to while reading chapter 1).

Walk into your backyard and look for wires leading from telephone poles to your house. The electrical feed to the building is that group of two or three lines either hanging together or wound around one another. (Underground feeds exist, too, but they're less common.) Overhead power lines attach to a bracket high on the side of your house. From that attachment spot, you'll see a thick service cable running down the wall, probably leading into your electric meter, possibly also into an electrical box, and then disappearing through the side of your house. (Just to confuse you, there may be other overhead wires leading to your house, skinnier lines bringing you such services as phone and cable television.)

Note the spot where the electrical cable enters your house. Now go inside, find that same power feed (often it's in the basement), and see where it goes. In short order, it should lead you to a metal box mounted on the wall, perhaps sixteen inches (40.5cm) wide and a few feet (1m or so) high. This is your home's electrical panel, Command Central for all the wiring and everything that depends on electricity. Just to keep you on your toes, your home may have similar, smaller boxes, too—called subpanels. They often have specialized functions—governing one of your home's large appliances, for instance, housing a special set of circuits, or housing the main electrical shutoff for the entire house. (*An aside:* Remember that box I mentioned near the meter outside? If you have one, there's probably another main shutoff in there. When firefighters arrive at your house, they can cut off the juice before they start squirting water all over the place.)

If you open the little door of your main electrical panel, you will find a display of devices that control the circuits in your house. If you see a panel covered in switches, those are circuit breakers. If you see a wall of little metal-and-glass circles screwed into the panel and (possibly) cylindrical cartridges held by metal clips, those are fuses. Now, I may save you hundreds of dollars with this little observation: You probably have it in the back of your mind that circuit breakers are new technology (therefore good) and that fuses are old technology (therefore bad). There might be good reasons to upgrade your electrical panel to circuit breakers, but if you have fuses and the panel is still in good condition, you might be able to manage swimmingly for years to come. In fact, bad wiring that lies beyond your fuse box would be more of a danger to your home than a fuse box that's in good condition.

Whether you have circuit breakers or fuses, here are some signs that your electrical panel might need fixing or replacing—definitely a job for an electrician:

◇ You see rust or other corrosion on the box and other signs that the panel is exposed to moisture.

◇ There seem to be parts missing from the electrical panel and you can see the heavy-duty wiring inside the box.

◇ The panel seems to be coming loose from its mounting.

Map Out Your Circuits

While you're visiting your home's electrical panel, pull back the little door that covers the front and look on the inside of the door. You should see a chart pasted there, a system of numbers and blanks that correspond to each circuit breaker or fuse on the panel in front of you.

If your chart is typical, there is a smattering of handwritten notations in those blanks—maybe the person who installed central air-conditioning in your home wrote A/C over a couple of circuits, and maybe you scribbled MICROWAVE on another label back when you overloaded one of the kitchen circuits. And then there are numerous circuits indicated on the chart that have no labeling at all. If you were an ancient mapmaker, you might inscribe these with "Here be monsters." But being a modern hominid who wants to inflict a little order on your home's systems, you're going to do much, much better.

Why bother? Because of the oath you took when you read chapter 1: You're going to focus like crazy—and with equal effort—on basic safety and on eliminating hassles from your life. If your stereo system starts smoldering and you can't easily reach its power cord behind that mammoth entertainment center, you want to shut off the electricity to your music system before you start picking through those wires and components. If you have a poorly labeled chart in your electrical panel, you won't know which circuit breaker to switch off or which fuse to remove. Sure, you could just guess— if you're the sort who enjoys playing Russian roulette. Or you could go to that intimidating circuit breaker or fuse marked MAIN and shut down power to the entire house—not a fun prospect when you consider all the systems that will stop working (lights, heating, air-conditioning, hardwired smoke detectors, computers, answering machine, appliances, and the like), not to mention all the digital clocks that will reset themselves to noon.

Think how simple your life would be in this scenario if the chart in your electrical panel included the word STEREO in the blank for the appropriate circuit. Similar scenarios will play out scores of times over the years that you own your home—anytime you, or people working for you, need to react to emergencies, make repairs, troubleshoot, or install devices. With a precisely charted electrical panel, you may actually live longer, expensive repair folks will clock less time working for you, you'll be able to spot circuits that are stacked up with too many power-hungry devices, and your entire house will just glow with an aura of contentment and peace. As an added benefit, when you chart your electrical panel, you're automatically reviewing every electrical item that it feeds—and this is the perfect time to prepare a checklist of future repairs and improvements you'd like to make. So here are simple tips for creating a ready-for-anything chart on your electrical panel—advice recommended by David Shapiro, an electrical contractor, consultant, inspector, educator, and writer who does business as Safety First in Colmar Manor, Maryland (outside Washington, D.C.). By the way, his book *Your Old Wiring* would be a great addition to any homeowner's personal library.

Make a precise survey of the entire house. Take a pen and a pad of paper, survey the house inside and out, and list every single feature that's a standing part of the building's electrical system. (Quit rolling your eyes—this is a one-time job, precision is important here, and it's a heck of a lot easier than crushing boulders with a sledgehammer.) Inside, list all outlets, light fixtures, ceiling fans, hardwired smoke detectors (as opposed to the battery-only kind), appliances (stove, dishwasher, refrigerator, washing machine, dryer), heating and cooling, alarms, exhaust fans, thermostat, doorbell, garage door opener, and more. Outside, include on your list security lights, shed light, post light, exterior outlets, and such. List a precise location for each item so that *anybody* could locate the exact item you're referring to. For instance: OUTLET—2ND FLR, MASTER BDRM, SOUTH WALL. Use terms that will stand the test of time, not the name of a bedroom's current occupant or the current color of a wall in the family room.

Make sure everything works. As you survey the electrical features of your house, test every item to make sure it works. Flick on every fan, every light, and every appliance, and test every outlet (use a lamp you know is working, or use one of the voltage testers described later in this chapter). If you encounter a dead outlet, check whether it's actually controlled by a wall switch and note this on your list. Thorough testing of each item will give you a checklist of small projects to take care of in the future—broken equipment, missing bulbs, and mysterious devices of yet-to-be-identified function. Also, if one of these items turns up "dead" sometime, it will help to know that it was working in recent history.

Locate the circuit feeding each item. Now comes the fun detective work. At your electrical panel, start with all circuits on and then turn just one of them off by switching off one circuit breaker or disengaging one fuse. Then go around the house and check out the electrical items on your survey list. When you find an item that was working a few minutes ago but is now defunct, mark the number of that circuit beside that item on your list. Yes, you often will see patterns in the devices that are serviced by a single circuit—say, one entire bedroom—but never make assumptions. Odd things may have been done during repair work or installations in your home. Check all devices individually. Even when you have double outlets, check each receptacle separately.

Save yourself some steps. You probably quickly realized that turning off a single circuit and then locating every dead electrical device in the house requires a lot of walking back and forth from your electrical panel to various rooms. A clever person like you will want to save some steps if possible, and here are ways to do that. Use a radio—turned up really loud—to test outlets. You won't have to walk up a flight of stairs to see whether a lamp is on or off. You'll be able to *hear* whether the outlet is working. Alternatively, use a long extension cord to position your testing lamp closer to you so you won't have to walk as far to find out whether it's on. Or get a friend to help with your testing. Let her do the walking around the house, communicating via cell phones or walkie-talkies while you're standing in front of the electrical panel.

Now chart every circuit. Once you have matched up a circuit with every electrical device in and around your home, it's time to record that information in a way that anyone will be able to use for years to come. You have a decision to make. First, take another look at the original chart that's pasted inside the door of your electrical panel. Do the blanks provide enough room for you to neatly write down all the information on your list? Was the writing that was already entered on the chart done well enough that you can live with it? If the answer to either question is no, then write up your chart on your home computer, print it out, and tape that inside the panel door. But there's yet another approach to consider. Have you found that some of the circuits in your home have such a crazy layout—spanning multiple rooms and locations, for instance—that a text-only listing is hard to follow? If that's the case, sketch out an informal floor plan of your house (on multiple pages, if necessary) and mark each electrical device on the map. Beside each labeled device, mark the number of its circuit. This way, anyone will be able to understand the circuit layout at a glance.

Don't Reset Without Investigating

Ah, circuit breakers! The key to a hassle-free home electrical system. Or so goes the grossly mistaken thought process of some homeowners. Here's the dangerous mistake that many people make: A homeowner discovers that the electrical devices in one area of the house aren't working. He goes to the electrical panel and, thanking his lucky stars that he doesn't have to search around for a replacement fuse, just flips the circuit breaker back to the ON position. He might even repeat this operation again and again over the next few hours and days.

The problem is that circuit breakers are a safety system, and in this scenario they're crying out a warning and are routinely ignored while a dangerous situation could be developing somewhere in the home. When a circuit breaker trips, always investigate the possible reasons before turning it back on. If you realized that you were using too many heavy appliances on the same circuit at the same time, that's probably easy to remedy. But if you're blowing circuit breakers for no apparent reason, a call to an electrician could save you from disaster.

Make the panel's numbers legible. Let me ask you: If you were going to print up any kind of text that was meant to be read in an emergency, would you use tiny typography, stamp it onto a metal sheet, paint that sheet in one solid color, and then post it in the dim light of your customer's basement? Probably not, but for some reason that's how you will find circuit numbers indicated on your electrical panel. You'll usually find the circuit breakers or fuses arranged in two columns side by side, each circuit marked with a faint number on the metal box cover—typically, even numbers are on the left side and odd numbers are on the right side. If you have to squint and search for the circuit numbers, do yourself a favor: Take a permanent marker and reenter each circuit number in the appropriate spot. In those situations where every second counts, you'll save yourself a lot of time and anguish trying to find the right circuit breaker or fuse.

The Care and Feeding of Your Electrical Panel

Now that you're on speaking terms with your electrical panel, here are some tricks that will make your life easier and safer:

Give it the back of your hand. Whenever you visit your home's electrical panel, check its temperature, says Tom McCormick, president of McCormick Electrical Services in North Liberty, Indiana. No, you don't need a thermometer. Just lightly touch the back of your hand to several spots on the front of the electrical panel, including the circuit breaker switches. It should feel room temperature. If you feel an unusually warm spot, tell your electrician. A wiring problem could be generating heat, and a pro should investigate. As much as you might be tempted, do not try to remove the cover of your electrical panel to look inside yourself. Among other horrors, you could easily tip a corner of the panel cover into the hot wires and cause an "arc flash"—a nasty electrical explosion of molten metal that could burn or blind you.

Make sure dead circuits stay dead. It sounds like a scene from a bad television sitcom: You decide to work on part of your electrical system and turn off the appropriate circuit breaker or disengage the fuse. You return to work and start handling "dead" wiring. However, another family member realizes there's a dead circuit in the house, goes to the electrical panel, and dutifully flicks the power back on. In the TV world, you would have a brand new perm. In the real world, you could be dead. So give yourself an extra level of protection anytime you kill power in your home and then expose yourself wiring or electrical devices:

◇ **Put tape over the breaker or fuse you have disengaged so another family member will think twice before tampering with it. Also, tape a sign to the electrical panel warning people away.**

Feeling the Heat

Not only is Tom McCormick a professional electrician, but many of his customers know that he has been on his local fire department for nearly twenty years. One day he informed a customer that his main electrical panel had a defect that made it a fire hazard and it needed to be replaced.

"How bad is this really?" asked the customer, apparently suspicious that McCormick might be angling for unnecessary business for himself.

"It doesn't matter to me," the firefighter replied. "The next time you call me I can either bring the red truck or the white truck."

The customer pondered this vision of fire trucks pulling up in front of his house and decided quickly, "Okay, let's fix it."

◇ Educate everyone in your house about the seriousness of electricity and explain to them your system for taping and posting signs.

◇ Use work habits that will help to reduce your risk of being injured. Only use tools with insulated handles. Don't wear metal jewelry. Cover your eyes with protective goggles. Work only with one hand, and keep other body parts away from objects that could serve as an electrical ground, completing an electrical circuit through your body. Avoid moisture. If there's any dampness underfoot, stand on dry wood.

Remove those barriers. Make sure that all the elements of your electrical system—the circuit breakers or fuses, any subpanels—are easy to get to. Don't stack storage boxes in front of them and make sure nothing gets in the way of opening a panel door. Also, assess whether your panel and subpanels have been mounted at the right height. Can an adult of normal size reach all the controls? If not, talk to an electrician about having such panels remounted within easy reach.

Down to the Wires

If you have an older home and you had the electrical service upgraded in the last several years—you might be ignoring an important factor about the condition of your home's electrical system. Yes, there's a beautiful new cable snaking into your house and ending in a handsome electrical panel. And that gleaming new panel has oodles of capacity for adding new circuits when you need it. But don't forget that those enhancements do nothing to improve the condition of the rest of the wiring in your home—the plastic-covered copper lines that distribute electricity to all the rooms and appliances in your house. If you have a house that's several decades old, there's a good chance that you have a lot of several-decades-old wiring still running through your walls. These wires may be in tip-top shape, or they may be degenerating into a serious hazard.

Now and then you probably get a glimpse of some of your wiring (say, in the basement where it's not hidden inside walls, or inside an electrical box when a fixture is getting replaced). Keep these pointers in mind so you'll be able to spot decrepit wiring and call in an electrician:

◇ Wires that have insulation that's cracked or falling off need to be replaced.

◇ Wires that appear to have been baked black or brown are kaput.

◇ If a wire's insulation appears to be intact but you want to test it, do this: Make absolutely certain that power to that wire is off. Then bend the wire in half. If this causes the insulation to crack, the wire will need replacing soon.

By the way, out of all the wires in your house, those feeding your kitchen light fixture are the most likely to be deteriorating, says electrical contractor-author David Shapiro. Such wiring is often exposed to more heat than wiring in other parts of the home, and kitchen lights are typically in use for longer periods. Unless these wires were replaced during a renovation, good wiring feeding a kitchen light fixture bodes well for the wiring in the rest of the house.

Heroic Circuits That Know When to Quit

A few centuries in the future, someone is going to write a history of lifesaving inventions. Bicycle helmets, automobile seat belts, airbags, and smoke detectors will all get prominent mention. And enshrined among them will be a comparatively new device, a style of electrical outlet called the Ground Fault Circuit Interrupter (GFCI—an acronym which, I suppose, is pronounced much like a sneeze). These are the serious-looking, rectangular-faced receptacles that you have seen popping up in bathrooms, kitchens, garages, crawl spaces, outdoor receptacles, and other locations in recent decades. They essentially are "smart" receptacles. When a GFCI senses that the electricity they provide is going somewhere it ought not (maybe you dropped your electric hair dryer into a sink full of water), it's designed to shut down immediately, protecting you from electrical shock.

Now, let's reflect for a moment on the HIRE principle, which you tattooed to your forearm while reading chapter 1. When a job is Hard, Important, Rarely done, and Elaborate, it's sensible to HIRE a professional to do it. So consider this: I'm not even recommending that cheaters-at-home-repair bother with replacing *standard* electrical receptacles in their homes. Wiring a GFCI receptacle is even trickier, so that definitely goes on your professional electrician's to-do list. That said, there are still plenty of things you want to know about GFCIs. Here are some powerful bits of knowledge that will make you the on-top-of-things homeowner you aspire to be.

Retire an aging GFCI. The early GFCI receptacles that appeared in homes were undoubtedly an innovation, but they had a drawback.

It's easy to incorrectly wire a GFCI so that you're not getting the protection you expect. On early models, you could push the TEST and RESET buttons without getting a clue to the problem. The newer generation of GFCIs come with a feature called something along the lines of RESET LOCKOUT. This more sophisticated version will not reset itself and restore power if it has been wired incorrectly. If you think you have old-style GFCIs, have your electrician replace them with the lockout type the next time he passes through.

Replace that two-prong outlet with a GFCI. Here's a sneaky way to use GFCI outlets to your advantage. Many older homes were wired without a separate ground wire. The living areas are populated with two-prong receptacles (providing only the hot and neutral contacts) that are not safe for the tools and appliances that have three-prong plugs on their cords. With some effort, an electrician might be able to create a proper ground and install a three-prong outlet for you. But electrical experts say it's also perfectly acceptable to have a three-prong GFCI outlet installed where no ground actually exists— a person using a tool or appliance plugged into such a receptacle will be protected from shock in the event of a short in the machine. (*Note:* The practices of snipping off the ground prong from a cord's plug or using an ungrounded adapter are dangerous—stop that.)

Spread the protection. GFCI is a wonderful technology that saves lives in lots of different situations. There's really no reason not to apply it generously to your home, experts say. When an electrician is pulling out one old receptacle for any reason, ask him about installing a new GFCI in its place—even outside of bathrooms and kitchens, where they're commonly used. In some cases, an electrician can wire a GFCI receptacle so that it also protects other fixtures that come after it in the circuit's sequence. GFCI protection can also be installed at your electrical panel to cover entire circuits.

In these cases, don't forget which fixtures are covered by remote GFCI protection. Otherwise, you might spend hours or days—or money on a service call—trying to figure out a mysterious "outage"

Top Priority: Kill the Power

If you suffer a short-term electrical shock from home wiring or an appliance, you probably don't need to be told to get your body away from the voltage. The pain sends an obvious message, and you're a fast learner. There's a physical phenomenon, however, that can complicate matters when humans and live electricity mix: Electricity can cause your muscles to freeze up. So, unfortunately, if a person grabs a live wire and the electricity completes a circuit through her body, she might not be physically capable of letting go and backing away. The result: extensive injury or death. All too often, the tragedy is compounded when someone tries to remove the victim from the source of electricity and the rescuer gets electrocuted as well—two deaths instead of one.

So what should you do if you see someone who's unable to extricate herself from electrical voltage?

- ◇ The lower-risk approach is to kill the power. If there's a switch governing the current, turn it off. If there's an electrical cord involved, pull it out of the receptacle—assuming you can do so safely; that is, there's no moisture present and the cord is in good shape. Killing power at the home's electrical panel is a good move, too.

- ◇ As mentioned above, heroics in this situation can get you killed, and trying to physically remove the victim from the source of voltage is not recommended. If you decide that you're going to accept that risk and try to move the victim away from the source of electricity, do not touch the victim or anything else that could be carrying live current. Push or pull at the victim using some kind of large, nonconductive item as a barrier. Make sure the item is dry and free from metal parts or filaments. Wood, heavy cloth and rubber are good candidates.

- ◇ A person who has suffered serious electrical shock is in need of immediate medical attention. Once the victim is free from the voltage, call your community's emergency services number.

when your GFCI just needs to be reset. "Handyman Scott" Kropnick of Blue Bell, Pennsylvania, gets the occasional call from a flustered customer talking about a "break in the electrical line"—which is often solved by scouting around for a remote GFCI outlet in the bath, kitchen, or garage that needs resetting.

Test GFCI outlets every month. The sad truth is that GFCI receptacles can fail. Electrician Tom McCormick says that half of the homes he visits professionally have GFCI outlets that don't work properly. So in your own defense, run them through their simple, built-in testing procedure once a month. You will see two buttons on the face of the receptacle, one marked TEST and the other marked RESET. Press the TEST button. If it's working properly, the RESET button will pop out and the electricity in the outlet will shut off. (If it doesn't do this, have an electrician replace the receptacle.) When you press the RESET button, power should be restored.

Before You Touch It, Test It

At certain points, a homeowner who decides to have anything to do with electricity ought to have some crucial questions come to mind. Such as: "Did the electricity in this outlet really go off when I flipped that circuit breaker?" Having a definitive answer to such a question will not only help you locate electrical problems in your home, but it will also help to extend your lifetime beyond the next few seconds. To get the answer, you need a gizmo called a voltage tester. There are several varieties of testers, some of them of dubious value and reliability, says Shapiro. He recommends a few styles. Each kind has two leads (electrical contacts), one that you touch to what ought to be the "hot" wire of a circuit and the other that you touch to the neutral wire or to the ground wire:

Solenoidal voltage tester. This tool, also known by the nickname "wiggy," has a needle indicator and typically lights and buzzing indicators as well. It is the long-time electrician's workhorse.

Neon tester. This looks like two wires hooked to a mini–light bulb. Because that's pretty much what it is.

Multimeter. This tool has a needle indicator inside a plastic window on a box. Make sure you follow the device's instructions for picking the right setting so you don't blow this gizmo's internal fuse. (After all, relying on a dead voltage tester can set you up for an unpleasant experience.)

If you explore this subject for a while, you're going to come across a handy-looking product called a receptacle tester. This is a plastic case with prongs on one end that fit into your electrical outlet and a few lights on the other end that are supposed to analyze whether the outlet is wired correctly. While electrical testers have many fans, electrical contractor David Shapiro says these devices are actually of limited value—they *may* be handy for merely indicating whether the outlet is "hot," but there's a lot of potential for misdiagnosing wiring problems. (*Know this:* Electricians call such gizmos "idiot lights.") One of the testers listed above would be the better choice.

Here are some crucial tips for using voltage testers:

Make sure your tester really works. Before you go leaping into a life-or-death situation, make sure the tester you rely on is functioning correctly. Try it out on a circuit you know is live. For instance, go into the living room where a lamp is working, turn the lamp off by its built-in switch (not the wall switch) and pull the lamp's plug out of the outlet. Apply your tester to that same outlet, and make sure your tester indicates a live circuit. Then you know your tester hasn't filed for early retirement.

Make sure a circuit is alive before you "kill" it. I know this sounds odd, but basically you want to be sure that something like defective wiring doesn't fool you into shocking yourself. Say you want to know for sure whether a particular circuit breaker controls a particular receptacle. First use your tester to detect the live current in the receptacle while its power is on. Now kill that circuit by turning off the appropriate circuit breaker or unscrewing the fuse. Then use your tester once again to make sure the electricity is really off. This way, you know that your "no current" reading isn't based on a faulty switch, a poor connection, or a broken wire—while there's actually electricity present.

Handle the leads carefully. The two wires attached to your tester have bare metal tips that conduct electricity and plastic-covered handles that protect you from that electricity. Keep your fingers away from the bare metal at all times. When you're testing, act at all times *as if* you're going to find live current.

Haul the Right Stuff Home

In chapter 13, "Getting Help," you'll find my argument for letting electricians and other professionals buy their own supplies when they install devices in your house. For example, if an electrician buys a receptacle and installs it in your living room, he will replace it if something goes wrong. If *you* supplied a defective part, it's your problem, and you will pay for parts and labor to have it replaced. There may be occasions when you want to be able to discern high-quality parts from lower-quality parts, so here are some things to know about product labeling, says Shapiro:

◇ The terms *hospital grade* and *heavy duty* are usually a good sign of higher-quality materials, better construction, and durability.

◇ *Deluxe* is meaningless balderdash.

◇ A term like *professional grade* is usually an indication of higher quality. It's likely that the manufacturer has a couple of separate product lines, one intended for do-it-yourselfers and a line of higher-quality devices that are intended for tradespeople.

More Tricks of the Trade

Detect—and replace—old smoke detectors. I probably don't have to sell you on the idea of having smoke detectors in your house. You may even have developed the admirable habit of changing the batteries every six months or at least every year. (Make it a ritual on the same day each year—perhaps your birthday, New Year's Day or the switch to Daylight Savings Time.) But here's a sobering thought: If you have a smoke detector in your home that's more than ten years old, it's been running constantly for more than 87,000 hours. You wouldn't expect any other appliance to last that long, so why should expect it of a smoke detector? In fact, electrician McCormick says that out of every ten homes he is called to professionally, seven will have at least one defunct smoke detector. So if you have a smoke detector that's at least ten years old, replace it with a new one, he says. Newer smoke detectors have their date molded into the outside casing, so you can read it from a stepladder. Older smoke detectors may have a date marked on the back side, meaning you have to remove the device from the ceiling to find the date. If there's no date anywhere on the body, it's definitely too old to keep, McCormick says.

Don't let all phones go dark. Cordless telephones are a great convenience that allow you to walk around the home while you talk without being tethered to the wall. If your family has converted to cordless phones, make sure you have a backup plan for making emergency calls if your power should go out, says McCormick. In that case, you will either need a hardwired phone still operating or a cell phone with a fully charged battery.

Look for the label. Whenever you buy electrical fixtures, tools, or other supplies, check that they carry the stamp of approval from an agency that inspects such products in your country. In the United States, that would be an organization like Underwriters Laboratories

(UL), for instance, and in the European Union it would be CE Marking. And speaking of foreign locales, don't forget that if you buy electrical products abroad and ship them home, you could be inviting compatibility problems, says Reggie Marston, home inspector in Springfield, Virginia, and "house detective" on Home & Garden Television.

Con-Fused? Tips for Dealing with Blown Circuits

As mentioned above, when a circuit breaker or fuse in your home blows, priority number one is not getting the electricity back on—it's figuring out what caused the circuit to shut down in the first place. That said, when it does come time to restore power, working with your electrical panel is not as simple as flipping a switch or screwing in a fresh fuse. Here are things you should definitely know.

Keep your breakers healthy. I know this sounds bizarre, but a circuit breaker that has been out of use for a long time can start to lose its calibration—that is, it's less likely to trip at precisely the right time and could fail altogether. The answer is to give your circuit breakers an invigorating workout once a year. No kidding. Pick a time when you're alone in the house. Switch off all devices, such as the televisions and the computers. Then stand at the electrical panel and, one by one, flick your circuit breakers off and then on again.

Another way to protect the integrity of your circuit breakers: Don't short out your circuits on purpose. Some people do this in order to figure out which breaker governs which circuit. The drawback is that this technique shortens the life of the switch. Stop that.

Hey, that's no light switch. When you look at a circuit breaker, well, it looks an awful lot like a wall switch. So you would be forgiven if you thought a circuit breaker worked exactly like a wall switch, too. Many of them don't, however, and this little observation may save you a long afternoon of puzzled head scratching some day: When a circuit breaker blows and shuts off electricity to the circuit it governs, it probably won't switch all the way to the OFF position. Confusingly, it will pop away from the ON position only a little bit and come to rest either midway between ON and OFF or even just a minuscule distance away from ON. Yes, when you first glance at your electrical panel, you might not be able to spot which breaker is actually off. To boggle you even further: You don't reset such a breaker merely by pushing it back to the ON position. You have to push the lever all the way over to OFF first, and then back to ON before it will hold in that position and restore the electricity.

Learn to spot a spent fuse. One of the main frustrations that homeowners report about dealing with fuses is trying to figure out whether a fuse has blown. The most common fuses are the round "plug" style that screw into a socket on your electrical panel. They have a window on the front that allows you to see a teensy strip of metal or a little spring inside. When the fuse's circuit gets overloaded, the metal melts, the circuit is broken, and you find yourself staring at the panel trying to figure out why your hair dryer quit working. Through the window, you will see a gap in the metal strip, soot inside the glass, or a collapsed spring that broke the circuit. As with a blown circuit breaker, this means it's time to investigate what went awry on that circuit. When you replace the fuse, it's vital that you use a new one with the right amperage (fifteen amps is most common, although you might find circuits rated at twenty or thirty amps for specialized situations involving heavier equipment).

Cartridge fuses are a more exotic item, somewhat inscrutable because they don't give you any handy visual cues that they have blown. These are heavy cardboard cylinders with metal contacts on each end. Cartridge fuses are used on heavy-duty circuits or as backup protection. They are typically set into a pair of spring-loaded metal clamps that run current through the fuse. They may just be mounted that way on the electrical panel behind a concealment door, or they may be encased in a little box that you pull out of the panel. When you pull the box out of the electrical panel, the circuit is broken and the cartridge fuses inside that casing are safe to

HOW TO CHEAT AT HOME REPAIR

What Blew My Fuse?

Plug fuses (the screw-in type) give you a good hint as to what went awry when they blow. If the little metal strip inside the cover window has melted, that's a sign of an overloaded circuit—say, too many kitchen appliances running at once. If the interior of the window has been blackened, that's usually a sign of a short circuit—say, a "hot" wire touching a neutral wire or a ground, creating extra current.

handle. If you have cartridge fuses behind a concealment door, opening that door may break their circuit—but don't bet your life on that. Use a voltage tester to make sure before handling them. (And once you have a cartridge fuse out of its brackets, you can use your voltage tester again to figure out whether it has blown.) Take your blown cartridge fuse with you to the hardware store or home store to make sure you get the right shape and amp rating when you buy a replacement.

Switch to tamperproof fuses. One of the most treacherous aspects of having a fuse box is that some homeowners talk themselves into the dangerous practice of "overfusing." It goes like this: A fifteen-amp fuse blows. The homeowner either has no backup fifteen-amp fuses, or he's afraid that if he does install another fifteen-amp fuse it will just blow again. So instead he screws into the socket a twenty- or thirty-amp fuse. Sure, such a few will blow less readily—but it bypasses a crucial safety system and leaves the house vulnerable to fire.

Part of this problem lies in the design of old-style fuses, the kind with a threaded base that's the size of a conventional light bulb's. These are called Edison-base fuses, and woefully they're all interchangeable no matter what their amp rating is. A newer style of fuse, called Fustat or type S, prevents overfusing because the bases

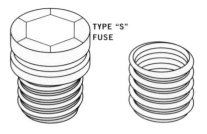

TYPE "S" FUSE

Fustat fuses (also called type S), like the one at left, are not interchangeable. The base adapter (right) can screw into an old-style Edison socket.

are not interchangeable. Only fifteen-amp fuses can screw into a fifteen-amp Fustat socket, for instance. The fuses and bases also are color-coded so you can tell at a glance which kind of fuse belongs in which socket.

If your fuse box uses the old wide-base Edison fuses, you can easily convert to Fustat and prevent dangerous "improvising" in the future. First, make sure what amp rating is required on each circuit. For example, in North America, the most common household circuits will be fifteen amps. If you're not sure about any circuits, don't go any higher than fifteen unless an electrician tells you otherwise. Then buy a set of Fustats for your panel, plus a base adapter made to fit each fuse. Installation is simple: Screw the Fustat into the base adapter, then screw the combined assembly into the old Edison-size socket on your electrical panel. The next time you unscrew a Fustat fuse, its base adapter will stay behind in the socket and it will only accept new Fustat fuses in the correct amp rating.

Keep the right spares in stock. Many people equate having a fuse box with inconvenience when compared to circuit breakers. But the truth is, replacing a fuse is a breeze if you use a few simple organizational tricks in managing the electrical panel:

◇ **Do a thorough labeling job for your electrical panel, as described above. When a circuit goes dark, you will have no trouble finding the suspect fuse.**

- ◇ **Keep an ample supply of fresh fuses on hand for each circuit.**
- ◇ **Throw away blown fuses immediately so they don't get mixed in with the new fuses.**

Respect those extra fuses. From the Just to Confuse You Department: Be aware that sometimes you will find fuses in a separate subpanel that governs one of your home's major appliances—even in homes that have circuit breakers on the main panel. This may be because the appliance manufacturer specified that fuse protection is necessary—a requirement that should not be ignored at installation time. When you're shopping for a new electric stove, an air-conditioning system, a water heater, or some other major appliance, check the installation instructions for circuit protection requirements and make sure they're followed. New wiring may be required, too. If the prospect of dealing with this makes you blow a *mental* fuse, then make installation a simpler matter by finding an appliance with specs that jive with your current electrical setup. Running an appliance that's mismatched with your electrical system could harm the machine and could be dangerous.

Screwing in Light Bulbs: It's No Joke!

I asked contractor David Shapiro for a list of the top mistakes that homeowners typically make concerning electricity—the kind of goofs that they ought to go back and undo right away. Unfortunately, there are a lot of choices. But after some rumination, he chose to shine the spotlight (sorry) on the issue of poor light bulb selection. Now, I know what you're thinking: Proper light bulb selection sounds like a school-marmish, Goody Two Shoes consideration. But think about it: When you supply a lamp with a bulb that's at a higher wattage that the lamp specifies, you're forcing the lamp and the wiring to accommodate more electricity than they were designed to carry, and the added electricity generates heat. That heat can cook nearby materials, making them highly flammable. Also, you have essentially converted that light into an impromptu toaster hanging around your living areas—often unsupervised. So which would you rather deal with in your life: A little care in light bulb selection, or the aftermath of a dangerous house fire?

Check out every bulb. Right about now, in the back of your mind, you're asking yourself how many times you might have surrendered to temptation and used a seventy-five-watt bulb in a lamp marked for sixty watts or less. There's one way to be sure: Survey your home from attic to basement and replace bulbs as required. In any spot where you can screw in a light bulb, you should be able to find a label or markings telling you what kind of bulb to use. If you're low on bulbs in a particular wattage you need, unplug and turn off those lamps until you can go shopping. No kidding—this is that important. And when you shop for bulbs, check the packaging of the bulbs you buy. Some bulbs carry a warning about the kind of lamp they can be used in. For instance, a specialty bulb might require a ceramic fixture, meaning it would get too hot for plastic and other less durable materials.

Have a plan for those soaring lights. Sometimes grand ideas can get the best of us if we don't take some routine maintenance issues into account. David Lupberger, the Denver-based home improvement expert for ServiceMagic.com, points out that many homeowners are bowled over by a showy two-story-high foyer—until the light bulbs start blowing in that chandelier that's dangling twenty feet (6m) out of reach. Yes, you can buy a pole that has a bulb-grabbing mechanism on the end, but those are generally designed for bulbs that are hanging down—not for chandelier bulbs that point upward. Another solution—an enormous ladder—might be OK if you have training as a circus acrobat. However, the official *How to Cheat at Home Repair* approach to this dilemma is having the chandelier suspended from a pulley that allows you to lower it to within arm's reach.

Outdoor security lights can present a similar quandary, Lupberger notes. If you're thinking of having spotlights mounted on the exterior of your house, first make sure you have a reasonable and safe way of reaching those fixtures when the bulbs blow out. Too many security lights have to "go dark" permanently because the homeowner can't reach the two-story-high fixture.

Check both circuits *and* bulbs. When you appear to have a power outage in part of your house, make sure your analytical skills haven't shut down as well, says electrician Tom McCormick. Before calling an electrician, look for the simple solutions first:

◇ For instance, say you discover that two or three lights in your living room aren't working. You rush to your electrical panel, find that your circuit breakers have not tripped, and start to panic. Calm down, says McCormick—it's possible that a power surge blew out more than one bulb in your living room and they merely need to be replaced.

◇ Or perhaps a lamp doesn't work, and you find that the circuit breaker governing that part of the house has tripped. You reset the breaker, but when you return to the lamp it's *still* not working! Well, try installing a new bulb in the lamp. Sometimes when a light bulb blows, that in itself trips a circuit breaker.

Kill the juice before switching bulbs. You might not think you need to read how to change a light bulb, but here's a bit of advice that just might save you from splashing blood all over the living room carpet. When you're replacing a light bulb in a fixture, first shut off the power to that socket. First of all, there's some chance your fingers will come into contact with metal that's carrying electricity, and the shock won't be pleasant. Furthermore, there's an odd phenomenon involving electricity rushing into bulbs, says electrician Tom McCormick: Occasionally the surge of power into a new bulb can cause it to burst. If that's going to happen, wouldn't you prefer to be across the room rather than having the bulb in the palm of your hand?

Broken Bulbs: A Crash Course

Breaking a light bulb while it's set in a socket presents quite a quandary—multiple dangers, including electricity and broken glass. In any case, priority number one is removing the electrical threat. Turn off the switch governing the light. If the bulb is in a freestanding lamp, pull its plug out of the receptacle, too. If the fixture is hardwired to your home's electrical system, go to the electrical panel and turn off the power to that circuit by flipping the circuit breaker off or unscrewing the fuse. Also, use a dustpan and whisk broom to sweep up any shards of glass.

Now put on a couple of protective devices: a pair of protective goggles and a pair of work gloves that are heavy enough to stand up to broken glass. You'll probably be able to remove the base of the broken bulb from the light socket using one of these techniques:

1. With your gloved fingers, try gingerly holding the bulb—low down, near the socket—and turning counterclockwise.

2. Take a potato, orange, or apple and set it gently into the top of the broken bulb and turn counterclockwise. (Dispose of the food when you're done.)

3. Use needle-nose pliers to grasp the upper rim of the bulb's metal base and turn counterclockwise.

4. If those measures fail, again use needle-nose pliers to grab the upper rim of the bulb's base. Bend the side of the base inward to reduce metal-to-metal contact inside the socket, and then try turning the base again. *An alternative:* Put the tip of your needle-nose pliers inside the base of the bulb and spread the handles of the pliers. The two sides of the pliers' tip will open and grab the inside of the bulb base. Now twist the pliers to remove the base.

Once you have extracted the bulb, inspect the inside of the fixture's socket. If the bulb was difficult to twist out, that could be due to corrosion in the socket and the fixture might need to be replaced.

Double-check your "global" security. A lot of ceiling or hanging light fixtures have a translucent glass globe that covers the light bulbs. Here are a few notes that may prevent a glass-smashing mini-disaster in your house. The suspended globe is typically locked into a metal rim through the use of a few screws that tighten against the globe from the side. The globe is held in place not by sideways pressure, but because the shaft of the screw fits under a protruding lip around the top of the globe. When you have to replace light bulbs and you are setting the globe back in its place, make sure none of the screws is holding the globe up only through side pressure and friction—an unstable situation, says Shapiro. Also, when you're tightening those screws, remember that the glass has no give and could break if the screws apply too much pressure. Check that the mounting feels secure before you wander off to your next project.

Help your fluorescents flourish. If you have a fluorescent light fixture in the home, change the bulbs regularly, says McCormick. The older a fluorescent bulb gets, the more energy it requires to light up. This puts extra stress on the fixture's ballast (the device inside that fires up the bulb) and wears it out more quickly. Replacing bulbs is a heck of a lot cheaper than having an electrician replace a ballast. If a fluorescent bulb is in use for eight hours a day, change it every twelve to eighteen months. If there's more than one bulb in the fixture, change all of them at the same time. Otherwise, an old bulb will create a drag on its newer mate and shorten its life.

The Ins and Outs of Compact Fluorescents

Now that you've added light bulb management to your roster of *How to Cheat at Home Repair* duties, you're going to want to know about compact fluorescent bulbs. For the uninitiated, these are an innovative substitute for the traditional incandescent bulbs that have been around since Thomas Edison started having bright ideas. Compact fluorescents are those weird-looking bulbs you see now in supermarkets, hardware stores, and home stores. They have a traditional threaded base and a little coiled tube of glass mounted on it. They cost more than traditional bulbs, but they last so long (several years) and require so little electricity that they easily pay for themselves. So you have to change them less often, you save money, and you can pat yourself on the back for doing a good turn for the environment.

However, I need to hang a great big asterisk on this discussion. There are a few points you should be aware of when it comes to compact fluorescent bulbs:

◇ **They contain a small amount of mercury, which is toxic. So if you are in the habit of smashing bulbs on the floor and lolling in the debris, compact fluorescents are not for you. Also, as compact fluorescents get more and more popular, communities will get increasingly serious about setting up special disposal systems for them rather than letting you just cart these bulbs off to landfills. So keep an eye out for recycling updates.**

◇ **You still want to be sure that the compact fluorescent bulb you have chosen is appropriate for the fixture you want to use it in, so check the wattage.**

◇ **Compact fluorescents don't perform well in all scenarios. They're better in situations where they stay on for long periods. Repeatedly flicking them on for a few minutes and then off again will shorten their life. They also don't perform terribly well in the cold.**

◇ **As popular as compact fluorescents are becoming, keep an eye out for other emerging technologies that might be even more environmentally friendly—LED (light-emitting diode) lighting is a possibility.**

Bottom line: Saving the planet is good. Compact fluorescent bulbs are a nice step, but keep an eye on their limitations, the ever-shifting technology related to them, and emerging alternatives that may be even wiser to use. Stay tuned, stay illuminated.

Plumbing Repairs: Putting Water in its Place

CHAPTER 5

AN ASTONISHING AMOUNT OF HOME REPAIR AND MAINTE-
NANCE HAS TO DO WITH MAKING WATER BEHAVE ITSELF—
THAT IS, MAKING IT GO WHERE YOU WANT IT TO GO AND
NOWHERE ELSE. REPELLING RAIN IS A MATTER OF GOOD
ROOFING, GUTTERS, AND DRAINAGE. BUT PLUMBING IS AN
ENTIRELY DIFFERENT MATTER. WE'RE ACTUALLY INVITING
WATER *INTO* OUR HOMES—UNDER HIGH PRESSURE, NO
LESS—LETTING IT KNOCK AROUND INSIDE TO ACCOMPLISH
VARIOUS TASKS. THEN WE KEEP OUR FINGERS CROSSED,
HOPING THAT THE RESULTING WASTEWATER WILL FIND ITS
WAY OUT OF THE HOME AGAIN WITHOUT DOING ANY
DAMAGE.

There might be some home repairs that you can ignore for months on end—a scuffed floor or a creaky hinge, for instance—but plumbing jobs rarely fall into that category. Leaks are a big-time waste of water and energy (in the case of heated water). They quickly damage building materials and furnishings. They encourage mold and other pests. And they never get better—just worse.

So if you have the kind of brain filters that allow you to ignore ongoing problems inside the home, at the very least wake up and pay attention to the signs of plumbing problems. After all, "Denial is not a river in Egypt," says David Lupberger, the Denver-based home improvement expert for ServiceMagic.com. To that I add: Denial *could* become a river in your basement.

Plunging into Drain Problems

The official *How to Cheat at Home Repair* weapon of choice against any kind of clogged drain is that simple device called a plunger, or "plumber's helper." You know—that tool with an eighteen-inch (45-cm) handle and a big suction cup mounted on one end. It's easy to use, it's very effective, and it doesn't involve dangerous chemicals. But first, there's a simple matter to determine—whether it's your toilet that's clogged or some other kind of drain—because there are two styles of plungers, and they work best on the drains they're designed for. If you don't have both styles, this calls for a trip to the hardware store. Every home should have at least one of each:

Toilet plunger. The business end of this plunger has a ball-shaped suction device with a narrow opening at the bottom that's designed to fit snugly into the drain hole at the bottom of your toilet bowl.

Cup-style plunger. This is the classic style of plunger with a cup-shaped suction device on the end and a wide opening at the bottom. Use it on all drains except for your toilet.

Once you have matched up the right plunger to the right kind of clogged-up drain, the procedure is pretty much the same. But don't

No Plumber's Helper? Make the Plunge!

Much to your horror, the toilet is stopped up and you don't have a "plumber's helper." Stop fretting—you probably have in your home all the materials you need to remedy the situation: a 1.5-liter plastic bottle, a knife, a wooden broomstick, and duct tape. Use the knife to cut the bottom off the bottle. Slide the broomstick into the small opening at the top of the bottle (perfect fit!). Now wrap duct tape several times around the top of the bottle and the broomstick to secure the two objects firmly together. In one minute, you have made a toilet plunger that's good for one-time use. Dip the wide, open end of the bottle into the toilet to let if fill partway with water, then fit that open end over the toilet's drain hole. Push down on the broomstick with one firm stroke. The plastic bottle will collapse, accordion-style, and the compression will shove water and any clogging material through the drainpipe. (Unlike a real plunger, this impromptu model won't create enough suction for pulling the clog up.)

start flailing away just yet—there are some who'd-a-thunk-it short-cuts to success.

Make the water work for you. Your plunger is a device designed to exert force against material that's clogging your pipe somewhere out of your reach. Keep this in mind: When your plunger works against a pocket of air, the air will compress somewhat and reduce the force that you're exerting against the clog. But water does not compress. If there's water in the drain and in the bell of your plunger, you'll be tugging against that clog more powerfully. So before you plunge, make sure the drain is full of water, and immerse the plunger in water if possible, too. Turn the bell of the plunger to the side underwater so it gets filled at least partway. This will be easy to do in the toilet, because water is typically already there. In a sink, run the faucet until you have a couple of inches (several cm) of water in the bottom.

Grinding Glass: A Not-So-Sharp Idea

There's a persistent—but destructive—myth going around that occasionally grinding up glass in your garbage disposal is a great idea. The mistaken theory is that the glass will sharpen the blades of your disposal and make it function better. In reality, says Raymond VinZant of Roto-Rooter, the glass will break down into fine, sandlike grains that will degrade the machinery. So save those unwanted jars for the recycle bin.

Get a good seal. Your plunging will be more powerful if you're careful not to let the pressure escape. So when you're about to start plunging, set the rim of the open end securely against the hard surface of the toilet, sink, or tub. Press down on the handle, deflating the head of the plunger and creating a tight seal all around the edge. Then . . .

Pull against the clog. This might be counterintuitive, but the best way to unclog a drain is to pull up firmly on the plunger rather than pushing down. Look at it this way: That clog has stacked up in your drainpipe over weeks and months of accumulating material. It already has resisted considerable downward force from the water that hits it every day. So upward force—that is, your pulling the plunger up—has a better chance of clearing the obstruction by "unstacking" all that debris. If the clog persists after several strong pulls on the plunger handle, alternate firm pulls with firm pushes. "It's a lot like rocking your car back and forth to get it out of a snow bank," says Chuck McLaughlin, a plumber in Glenside, Pennsylvania.

Stand back. When you give that plunger an exuberant yank, think strategically about where you are standing and where the resulting splash might land. If you're successful at unclogging that drain, then you might just be pulling a fount of yucky debris up into the air. Many a mortified homeowner has splattered his entire front with this unmentionable gunk.

Block the Escape Routes

If you're using a plunger to unclog your kitchen sink, there are a couple of factors you will need to take into account, depending on how the plumbing is set up. First, if you have a double sink in your kitchen, remember that the drainpipes for the sinks are connected down below in the cabinet. Also, if you have both a dishwasher and a garbage disposal, there's probably a drainage tube leading from the dishwasher into the main compartment of the disposal. You don't have to have a PhD in hydraulics to see where this is going: You could stand all day over the sink pumping with your plunger, wondering why you're getting nowhere with that drainpipe clog. The answer is simple: The pressure that *ought* to be pulling and pushing at the clog is getting diverted through the path of least resistance—out the two drainage channels mentioned above.

There are easy fixes for this, and you may have to use both—again, depending on your setup:

Stop up the second sink. Take a damp rag and press it into the top of the drain of one of your two kitchen sinks. Hold it there with one hand while you push and pull on the plunger over the drain in the second sink with your other hand. Similarly, you can stop up the overflow opening in a sink or tub to preserve the drain-cleaning suction that you need.

Disconnect the dishwasher drain. Open the cabinet under your sink and find the flexible tube that runs from your dishwasher into the garbage disposal. There's probably a clamp holding the tube in place against the side of the disposal, and this clamp will be easy to remove. Pull the tube away from the disposal, and find something to plug up this opening. McLaughlin carries a special cap and clamp designed for such openings, but a cork, dowel, or anything else that will stop up the hole will do in a pinch.

With one or both of these temporary fixes in place, you should be able to plunge away at that sink clog with full force. When you're done, remember to remove the rag from your sink, to remove the stopper from the side of the disposal, and to reinstall the dishwasher drain tube.

Are You Chemically Dependent?

Now, you're a clever person. Which means that by now you're having a thought along these lines: *In a book titled* How to Cheat at Home Repair, *why can't we just pour chemical drain opener down the pipe and be done with it?*

There are a few good reasons that the typical household chemical drain openers are not advisable. For one thing, the chemicals involved are extremely powerful and could easily damage your skin, eyes, and lungs. (If you're going to ignore me and use them anyway, wear long sleeves, rubber gloves, goggles, and perhaps even a respirator.) If the chemical doesn't succeed in unclogging your pipe, then you're in quite a bind. You have harmful chemicals sitting in your pipe, and you don't dare use a plunger or a plumber's snake to remove the clog. Splashing those chemicals all around would be too dangerous. (If you want to hear a plumber whimper and groan, invite him over to get you out of that mess.)

Even if a chemical drain opener does get the water flowing through your drainpipe again, the picture is not as rosy as it might seem, says plumber McLaughlin. Usually, such chemicals do not totally remove the clog in your drain. Instead, they burn a small hole through the clog, the water starts flowing again, and the chemical gets washed down the drain with it. It will not be long before that hole gets filled up with new debris, and the process starts all over again.

Oh, you've probably learned by now that I'm holding something

When We Feast, Plumbers Toast

Pop quiz: What day of the year is the busiest for plumbers? Answer: In America, it's Thanksgiving, according to a survey by ServiceMagic.com. If you aren't American, your household is going to be most vulnerable on any other feasting occasion in which the extended family descends upon your home.

What does feasting have to do with plumbing? Plenty. First, when the table is being cleared, you have lots of well-meaning helpers dumping inappropriate food scraps into the garbage disposal. So just as you're getting ready to serve dessert, the sink is stopped up. To make matters worse, you have a large crowd of full-bellied people making an unusual number of, um, deposits into your toilets. Kids, in particular, tend to overuse toilet paper. So toilets often get stopped up, too.

So make sure you supervise anyone using your garbage disposal on feast day. Raymond VinZant of Roto-Rooter uses this rule of thumb for what should *not* go into the disposal: Any food that does not float. These dense items include carrots and rice, two foods that are notorious for making a gummy mess inside your pipes. Other problem materials—some of which *do* float—include grease, bones, eggshells, cornhusks, and potato skins. For the scraps that you do allow in the disposal, grind them up in small batches rather than stuffing the compartment full.

As for the bathroom, give the visiting kids a briefing on what can and can't be flushed down the toilet, and warn them to go light on the toilet paper, particularly if your throne gets stopped up easily.

clever back. Right you are, smarty-pants. I actually *can* offer you some off-the-shelf relief—and no, it has nothing to do with whiskey. McLaughlin swears by a drain cleaner that uses natural enzymes and bacteria to break down biologically based materials such as hair, grease, food scraps, and soap film. The product comes as a powder that you mix with lukewarm water in a bucket. Pour it into your clogged drain and let it sit for six to eight hours. (Overnight is ideal, since people aren't likely to run water and interfere with the process.) Under the right conditions, the bacteria will double in number every thirty minutes and will make a meal of the stuff that's clogging your pipe.

The enzymes and bacteria, marketed under the name Bio-Clean, work even better used as a preventive measure, plumber McLaughlin says. Upon first use, you apply the cleaner every night for a week, and then taper off the use until you're applying it once a week. This use will return your drainpipes to like-new condition, rather than leaving behind remnants of the clog. Also, contact with this cleaning agent isn't harmful. The stuff is only sold by plumbers, so ask yours about it. He'll sell you a two-pound can, which will last you a year, for around $55 and give you further instructions for its use.

Alternatively, you could attack the hair directly. If you think hair is the main obstruction clogging your bathtub drain, try this trick recommended by James Dean of Lewiston, Maine. Pour down the stubborn drain a couple tablespoons of the hair-dissolving lotion that women use on their legs (Nair is one brand). Wait a few minutes and rinse with water.

When Plunging Gets You Nowhere

If your bathroom sink is draining slowly or is totally stopped up, there's a good chance that the culprit is just a few inches (several cm) down the drainpipe. And there's a good chance that the culprit is a wad of hair that has wound itself around the stopper mechanism down there.

If using a plunger didn't free up the obstruction, no problem— we'll have the drain cleared out quicker than you can say "shave and a haircut." Go below the sink and find the rod that's sticking into the back of the drainpipe. When you open and close the drain, the lever action you exert on this rod pushes the stopper up and down. The hair clog may have collected around the bottom of the stopper, or it may have collected against the lever rod itself. In any case, loosen the nut that's holding the lever rod in place, using pliers if necessary, and pull the rod out just enough to free up the stopper.

Standing over the sink, lift the stopper out. If hair comes with it, that's great. Shine a flashlight into the drain to see if there's any more hair caught against the rod. If there is, get some coat hanger wire, bend a little hook into one end, and fish the hair out. If other debris is visible against the sides of the pipe, use a bottle brush to pull it out. Slip the stopper and the rod back into place, tighten the nut again, and then go tell your family members that everyone gets a buzz cut from here on out.

Your Backup Plan: Springing a Trap

If your bathroom sink drain is still sluggish, we'll just move a few more inches down the pipe to find relief. We're going to take apart the trap—that curvy piece of drainpipe under the sink. This is a common spot for clogging hair and other disgusting stuff. It's also the spot where your wedding ring rests—if you're lucky—when it falls down the sink drain. I know, taking apart the trap under a sink sounds scary because you're actually dismantling a functioning pipe. But in truth, this is about as simple as plumbing fixes get.

1. First scout out the situation and gather your tools. If there's a cabinet under your sink, open it up and pull out of the way all the stuff you store under there. Look at the pipe that runs from the sink drain down, loops up again, and disappears through the wall. No, the original plumber didn't miscalculate. That J-shaped piece of looping pipe is called the P-trap (because somebody decided it looked like a P, turned on its side). The curvy part is designed to hold water, which will block sewer gases from backing up into your house (doesn't that give you a whole new level of respect for traps?). See those two nuts holding the J-shape to the other two pipes? You're going to need two wrenches or two sets of channel-lock pliers to turn them. (If your trap is plastic, you might be able to remove the nuts with your bare hands.) Get a bucket, too. And you'll want a tool for removing debris

from inside the trap—an out-of-commission toothbrush or a piece of coat hanger wire will do.

2. Put the bucket under the trap. Use one of the wrenches or pliers to hold the trap steady (some old traps can break easily), and use the other wrench or pliers to loosen the two nuts at either end of the trap. With your hands, pull the trap away from the other pipes and turn it upside down over the bucket. Use the old toothbrush or wire to pull the wad of hair out of the trap. Put the trap back into position and retighten the nuts. Throw the debris in a trashcan.

Let a Snake Attack It

What if none of the approaches described above frees up your sink drain—not plunging, not pulling out the drain plug, and not removing the trap? Is it time to call the plumber? Not quite yet.

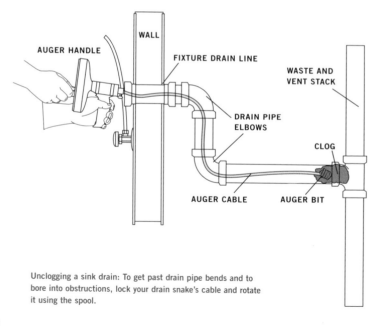

Unclogging a sink drain: To get past drain pipe bends and to bore into obstructions, lock your drain snake's cable and rotate it using the spool.

Rings and Drains Don't Mix

You're cleaning or doing some messy food preparation, so you take off your ring and set it on the counter near the sink (mistake number one). And you neglect to cover the drain hole (mistake number two). The next thing you know, your ring has disappeared down the drain. The smartest thing you can do, says Roto-Rooter man Raymond VinZant, is turn off the water immediately. If you're lucky, your ring will come to rest in the trap, that easy-to-dismantle, J-shaped piping below the sink. If water has washed your ring beyond the trap, your plumber will need to use a fiber-optic camera to locate it and then cut the pipe. The bill for that probably will be more than the value of the ring. So never place your ring near an open drain.

There's still one easy little trick remaining—the use of a handy tool called a drain snake (also called a hand auger by more serious-minded people).

The typical hand-cranked (nonpowered) drain snake has a cable about twenty-five feet (7.5m) long encased inside a covered spool. (There's also a type that uses an open spool with no exterior casing, and I only recommend this design if you like spritzing yourself with drain slime as you retract the cable.) Combined with its grip handle, it looks a bit like a model of the original starship *Enterprise*. Which is appropriate, since this tool is going to take you where, apparently, no one has gone before—into the drainpipe that passes through the wall under your sink. You're going to feed this cable into that pipe to reach the clog that has formed beyond your sink's trap. The spiral tip of the cable will either snag the clog and pull it out (in the case of hair) or burrow through it (in the case of soap buildup).

There are two basic operations that you perform with the drain snake. Hold the tool in one hand by the grip. Now take note of the little boltlike device at the front of the tool, where the cable emerges. That's your lock. Loosen the lock when you want to feed more cable into the drainpipe, and tighten the lock when you want to spin the cable using the spool crank (which helps you get past bends in the pipe and ultimately allows you to burrow into the clog).

Remove the sink trap as described above, and if possible remove the extra bit of pipe (the trap arm) that leads up to the wall. Feed the cable in until you meet resistance. Pull several more inches of cable out of the spool so you have some "slack" to work with, tighten the lock, and turn the crank clockwise as you apply forward pressure. This will help you worm past a bend in the pipe. Then unlock the cable and continue to feed it in. Continue this procedure until you meet a persistent obstruction—that's the clog. Turn the cable to drive its spiral tip into the clog. As stated above, if the clog is hair, you should now be able to drag it right out of the pipe. If the blockage is thick gunky stuff like built-up soap, turn the cable to drill through the clog a few times, then retrieve the cable. Reassemble the trap and the trap arm, and then run hot water down the drain to soften and flush out the rest of the soap.

Getting a Handle on Faulty Faucets

A dripping faucet might seem like a minor matter, but there's actually some urgency involved. In a conventional washer-based faucet, the most common cause of a leak is deterioration of that little rubber doughnut inside. Replacing this washer is easy at the outset—and only costs a few cents. If you let the dripping continue for months, however, an odd thing happens: Those tiny little water molecules, driven by the pressure of your plumbing, will erode metal parts inside the faucet mechanism. What was originally a thirty-minute job is now soaring in time and cost—and could very well grow beyond your comfort range for repair work. So when your classic "compression" faucet still dribbles after the handles are twirled shut, jump on this job right away.

Now, the cheating-est way of dealing with drippy faucets is this: The next time you have a plumber at the house, have him replace every washer in every faucet—even the spigot outside, says

Replacing a faucet washer: With the faucet handle removed from the spindle, use a wrench to loosen the bonnet nut and then lift the stem out of the seat.

Lupberger, the home improvement expert for ServiceMagic.com. What's the point? Most washers in your faucets are probably several years old anyway, meaning they don't have much life left in them. You'll get your entire house caught up for relatively little money, and you won't have to pay any additional house-call fees, since the plumber was already there on another job. Also, because faucet washers come in a boggling number of different sizes, you will save yourself several trips to the hardware store, trying to find the right match. Most plumbers will have the correct washers in their trucks.

Okay, you were hoping for a little more advice than simply "hire a plumber." No problem. Fixing a washer faucet is usually extremely easy. Here's how to stop the drip on your own.

1. Figure out which faucet handle you need to work on. Feel the water dribbling out—if it's warm, you need to repair the handle on the left as you face the sink. If it's cold, you need to repair the handle on the right. Turn off the appropriate water supply valve. If you're not sure about the water temperature, there's no harm in replacing the washers in both handles—just do them one at a time so you don't get parts mixed up.

Is the Pressure Getting to You?

If you have noticed a distinct drop in the water pressure you're getting from your faucets and showerheads, don't call the plumber just yet. I'm going to potentially save you a few hundred dollars right here. Roto-Rooter's Raymond VinZant says the likely reason for that drop in water pressure is that your fixtures have become clogged with mineral deposits from your water.

Modern faucets come with a screenlike device called an aerator on the tip. Use channel-lock pliers to remove all the aerators in your home. Turn them over to dump out the flecks of mineral. If the gray deposits are clinging to the aerators, pour a couple inches of white vinegar into a cup and drop the aerators in. After they have soaked for a few hours, brush the deposits with a decommissioned toothbrush.

Follow a similar routine for a clogged showerhead. Showerheads are easy to remove (see instructions elsewhere in this chapter). Set the face of the showerhead into a bowl of white vinegar for a few hours and then brush to remove any remaining flakes. If you're reluctant to remove your showerhead, here's a clever cheat: Fill a plastic bag with white vinegar. Pull the bag up around the showerhead, thus immersing the showerhead in the vinegar. Secure the bag in this position with wire or twine, and leave it overnight.

2. Use a screwdriver to remove the screw from the top of the faucet handle. (If you don't see a screw there, pry off the decorative cap with the point of a knife and look again.) Lift the handle off. If it's stuck, slide the flat blade of a screwdriver under the handle for a little prying help.

3. Underneath you'll find a ridged vertical spindle that the handle sat on top of, and at the base of that spindle a bonnet nut. Use a wrench to loosen this nut and lift the stem assembly out of its little metallic pit (the seat). If the stem won't lift out, turn the spindle to free it up.

4. Turn the stem upside down. You should find a screw holding the little

rubber washer in place. Remove the screw and pry the washer out of its seat. These washers come in two shapes—flat or "beveled" (that is, tapered on the side)—and they also come in a zillion sizes. So you can either buy an assortment pack of twelve to twenty washers at the hardware store and fish around for the right size, or you can take the stem into the store for a replacement. Whichever path you choose, get an exact fit.

5. Reassemble everything. Secure the new washer with the screw. Smear a little heatproof grease over the new washer, set it back into the seat, and tighten the bonnet nut. Set the handle onto the spindle, fasten it down with its screw, and if it had a decorative cap, snap that back into place.

Switching Seats

Now, if the plumbing gods are smiling on you, you won't be seeing the inside of that faucet for a few years. On the other hand, as you've come to expect with home repair, there may be complications. For instance, as mentioned above, sometimes inner parts of the faucet mechanism can get pitted or eroded. When you have the stem removed from the seat, examine the seat for damage to the metal. For instance, you might find a channel gouged into the seat that will keep a leak flowing even when you have installed a new washer. (Plumbers call this . . . well, what they call it isn't really printable, but just imagine an arcing stream of water combined with lowbrow humor.)

The seats of many bathroom and kitchen faucets are replaceable, and this added task (which you would do right after step 4 above) is probably well within your skill level. You can pick up a seat wrench from your hardware store or home store and use that to remove the seat. Or use this plumber's trick, says Raymond VinZant of St. Paul, Minnesota, who serves as the Ask-the-Plumber expert for Roto-Rooter: Put a wide, flat-bladed screwdriver down into the square or hexagonal hole in the bottom of the seat, and then clamp a wrench onto the handle of the screwdriver to help you turn it. Take the seat to your hardware store or home store to find a match.

And mention of replacement parts brings us to one other potential complication that you'll want to know about, VinZant says. Astoundingly, there are some five thousand different faucets in use. This is because models get upgraded year after year by the manufacturers, new models are released, companies get bought and sold, and the faucet specifications change. So if your regular stores don't have replacement parts for your faucet, you may very well find yourself scrounging through the world of vintage faucet replacement parts. And even when you do find a supplier who stocks such parts, you may be shocked to discover that the new parts cost more than an entire new faucet.

In which case, the official *How to Cheat at Home Repair* tactic is: Call a plumber and tell him to replace your old faucet with a shiny new one. In fact, I'm giving you permission to jump straight ahead to this tactic without even taking your faucet apart—if you know your fixture is at least fifteen years old and its exterior appears to be in rough condition. With this approach, you'll have a faucet that looks much nicer, has a warranty of five years or so, and will be in service longer than the one you have now.

Bubble, Bubble, Toilet Troubles

If you can hear water running in the tank of your toilet and you see little ripples on the surface of the water in the bowl, you have a leak that can waste more than one hundred gallons (378.5l) of water a day. For some reason, water is seeping from the toilet tank and into the bowl. First, you need to employ a high-tech maneuver known in cheat-at-home-repair circles as "jiggling the handle." You see, there's a rubber stopper in the bottom of a conventional toilet tank that fits over the valve opening. When you flush the toilet, the stopper lifts up, releasing a tank's worth of water into the bowl. Once the tank has emptied, the stopper claps over the valve and allows the tank to refill.

A Dye-agnostic Test for Your Toilet

I f you want to find out whether your toilet is leaking, here's the simplest way. Lift off the tank lid and put five drops of food coloring into the tank water. Declare the toilet off-limits, so no one in the family adds his own "coloring" to the water. Come back fifteen minutes later and look in the toilet bowl. If the coloring has seeped into the bowl, either the float that shuts off the intake to the tank is malfunctioning or the rubber stopper at the bottom of the tank needs to be replaced. Add this trick to your MBO (Maintenance by Observation) portfolio.

However, sometimes gremlins cause the stopper to close incorrectly, leaving a gap that water can escape through. When you jiggle the toilet handle—yes, you move it up and down lightly a few times without actually flushing—you're hoping that the mechanism inside will cause the stopper to reposition itself and stop the flow. If that fixes the leak, thrust both of your fists into the air above your head in a Rocky-like victory salute—and then go resume your nap.

If the toilet gods are cranky and the leak keeps flowing, you probably need to make repairs on one of two items: the float ball or the valve stopper. Don't despair—these are two of the easiest jobs on the planet.

First remove the top of your toilet tank and set it in a safe place. Check whether your toilet tank operates with a float ball, an egg-shaped orb floating on the surface of the water at the end of a lever rod. This device is supposed to shut off the intake of water when the tank is full. Try bending the lever arm downward just a little bit so the float ball sits lower and will therefore cut off the water intake sooner. That might be all you have to do! If that doesn't solve the problem, turn off the water supply to the toilet and twist the float ball off the lever arm. Give the float ball a shake. If you hear water sloshing around in there, it's leaking and isn't buoyant enough.

Tampon Advice Won't Wash

Tampons are notorious for collecting in the main drain that carries waste away from the house, plumbers say. So, ladies, no matter what the package says about your tampons being "flushable," throw them in the trash, not down the toilet.

Take it to the hardware store or home improvement store for an identical replacement, twist the new one into place, and turn the water supply back on. Done.

The Flapper Is a Snap

Well, you're done unless your finely honed diagnostic skills tell you that the flat ball wasn't the problem. That is, the toilet is still running. This means the most likely culprit is the rubber gizmo at the bottom of the toilet tank that's supposed to hold the water in the tank until you command the commode to flush. These stoppers generally come in one of two forms: a flapper (which looks like a rubber jar lid that hinges over the valve opening) or a tank ball (a rubber bulb that settles into the valve opening).

Here's how to fix a malfunctioning flapper or tank ball:

1. First, turn off the valve that feeds water to your toilet, and then flush the toilet. As a result, water will flow out of the tank and it won't fill back up again. Then look down into the tank and identify which kind of stopper you have:

   ◇ If it's a tank ball, you'll find that a thin rod with a threaded tip is set into the top of the ball. Unscrew the rod and remove the tank ball.

   ◇ If it's a flapper, remove the chain that lifts it up and then remove the flapper from the overflow tube. (It's either secured to the overflow tube by two punch holes that fit over two little posts, or it has an opening that slides down over the overflow tube itself.)

2. To put a crowning touch on your repair job, clean any mineral deposit or other gunk out of the valve opening at the bottom of the toilet. Otherwise, you might not get a thorough seal when you're done. Besides, no matter how finicky you are about housecleaning, there will never be another time when you're inspired to clean up this obscure little spot. Any abrasive scrubbing tool will do the job—a scrubber sponge, sandpaper, or steel wool. If there's stubborn mineral deposit, saturate a paper towel with white vinegar, pack it against the buildup, and let it sit for fifteen minutes to break it down. (Tell your family to leave the toilet alone in the meantime.) Then scrub.

3. Now take your tank ball or flapper to the hardware store or the home improvement store to buy a replacement. Slide the new part into place, reassemble the flushing mechanism, and use a little trial and error to make sure the apparatus lifts the stopper sufficiently when the handle is pushed down (it's simple to adjust). Then turn the water valve back on.

Congratulations—you're feeling like a king restored to his throne!

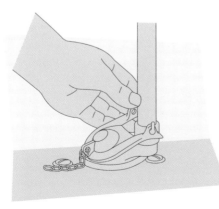

Repairing a leaky toilet tank: A replacement flapper in your toilet tank will either attach to small posts on either side of the overflow tube or it will wrap entirely around the overflow tube.

A Happier Flapper

Did you ever touch the flapper that covers the valve at the bottom of your toilet tank—and find a slimy black smear on your hand? That's an early warning sign that the rubber is disintegrating and will need to be replaced soon. Plumber Chuck McLaughlin says flappers turn brittle over time, lose their flexibility, and therefore lose their ability to form a good seal. For some reason, the problem is particularly pronounced with the flappers that come factory-installed in new toilets, he says. Chlorine in the water will accelerate the breakdown of a flapper. So if your water is treated with chlorine, or if you use chlorine treatments in your toilet tank, try this sneaky trick: The next time you buy a flapper, inspect the packaging and buy one that says it's made of a chlorine-resistant material. No more slime monsters in the toilet tank!

Septic Tank Savvy

Most houses these days are hooked up to sewer lines that will carry waste away. If you have a septic tank, however, there are a few key maintenance issues that you're going to want to know about.

Test your toilet paper. Never put anything down your toilet that's not totally dissolvable. Even your toilet paper can gum up the works if you're not using the right kind, so make sure your toilet paper dissolves rapidly, VinZant says. (Some will dissolve in six seconds, and others will take as long as ten minutes.) Look for a brand of toilet paper that promises on the label to break down rapidly. Scott Paper Co. is one of the major makers of quick-dissolving toilet papers. You also can run this test: Fill a jar halfway with water, drop in one sheet of your toilet paper, seal the jar, and shake. How quickly does it dissolve?

Outsmart the wind. There's a ventilation pipe poking out of your roof that releases gases that would otherwise build up in your septic tank. When you flush your toilet, that sewage flows into your tank and displaces air that gets pushed up the vent pipe and out into the air. All goes along swimmingly until you get a wind moving twenty-five to fifty miles per hour (40–80kmph), which can create enough air pressure on the top of your vent pipe to force sewage back into your house and bubbling up into your tub or sink. You don't have to experience that too many times before you're ready for a permanent solution. Which is: Have a second vent pipe installed, this one poking up on the opposite slope of your roof. No matter how hard an ill wind might try, it won't be able to blow into both pipes at the same time.

Look down the pipe. Sometimes a bird will take a liking to your septic tank ventilation pipe—particularly when it's emitting yummy warm gases in the winter. So it's not uncommon to get nesting debris and even hapless birds stuck down your vent pipe. This impedes the air-flow, which—as explained above—impedes the sewage flow. Now, I

OOPS!

Stalking a Nighttime Mystery

A homeowner called Raymond VinZant, Roto-Rooter's Ask-the-Plumber expert, to do some detective work. Apparently the customer's toilet was leaking in the middle of the night. First off, VinZant flicked on his trusty flashlight and shone it around the sides of the toilet. Any liquid would cause a telltale reflection. He did find traces of water running off the rear of the toilet base, but it wasn't emanating from any of the usual spots—not from the tank, not from the supply line, and not from around the base of the toilet.

"So I asked her, 'Do you have any little boys? This water looks yellow,'" he says. The mother's face turned red as she admitted that her son was potty training. He had been getting up in the middle of the night to use the toilet, but he was too short to get a direct shot at the bowl. VinZant checked the fixture over for any other possible leaks and, finding none, billed the woman for the service call.

Flushed with Embarrassment

Plumbers shake their heads and weep when they start talking about the things they have had to extract from toilet drains. Toothbrushes, bottle caps, dental floss, toy boats, jewelry, cell phones (talk about a toilet ring!), and even tennis balls. We know one Chicago plumber who was hired to unclog the toilet of an elderly gentleman who claimed to have no idea what might be snagged down his drain. The plumber cleared the drain and returned the offending item to the embarrassed customer—a set of false teeth.

Veteran plumbers have a few preventive suggestions if you want to keep your flushes unimpeded and save yourself a humiliating call for repair:

◇ Make a quick survey of the surfaces surrounding your toilet—counter, shelves, and the top of the toilet tank—and make sure that no small objects are permanently positioned within three feet (91cm) of the big bowl. Hummel figurines seem just compelled to make a swan dive into the "pool" below.

◇ Remove loose objects from your pockets before you sit down to use the toilet. When you stand up, cell phones, iPods, penknives, money clips, and coins love to slide out of your pockets and into the bowl—sometimes without your knowledge.

◇ If you have young children in the house, supervise their bathroom visits. The little darlings just love to watch objects circle the big whirlpool and disappear.

know what you're thinking, and no there's no way to put a cover on your vent pipe without inviting some kind of blockage (ice and snow, for instance). So the best you can do is add a quick visual inspection of your vent pipe every few months to your MBO (Maintenance by Observation) checklist. Get up on the roof, shine a flashlight down the vent (it's an open pipe sticking up one foot from the shingles), and look inside. If you spot blockage, feed your hand-operated twenty-five-foot (7.5-m) drain snake down the pipe and pull the debris up.

Tricks of the Trade

Here are some general insider tricks for working with plumbing materials. Any one of these could save you buckets of grief.

Handle nut goes against the grain. If you have never learned the expression "Righty tighty, lefty loosey," here's the story behind this handy mnemonic device: Virtually all gizmos that tighten by turning—including jar lids, screws, nuts, and plumbing features—are secured by turning to the right. And, of course, they loosen by turning to the left.

However, there's one big exception to this rule lurking right in your bathroom. We know one plumber who chuckles every time he has to repair a snapped toilet handle for mystified homeowners who tried to force the handle's nut—the one inside the toilet tank—in the wrong direction. Why would the nut that holds the toilet handle in place be threaded opposite from the rest of the plumbing universe? Because otherwise, flush after flush, the force of the handle would work to loosen the nut. The easiest solution was to give that nut reverse threading so that each flush only serves to secure its grip. The same thing is done with some bicycle parts when the force of a rotating shaft could unscrew a fastener attached to it.

Turn with two wrenches. Anytime you're loosening or tightening one piece of plumbing against another, secure both pieces with a wrench—one wrench providing the turning power for one piece of plumbing and the other wrench steadying the second piece of plumbing. At first blush, this may sound obsessive and namby-pamby. But failure to do so could damage your plumbing and make a big mess.

Here's an example: Say you're removing an old showerhead in the bathroom. You fit a wrench onto the base of the shower fixture and turn counterclockwise to twist it off. The threads are corroded, however, so it doesn't turn easily. At the same time, that turning force is getting transferred along the pipe (called the shower arm) that emerges from the wall to feed water into the showerhead. Inside the wall, there's a connection that bears the brunt of that turning force, and it snaps. You'd better check your watch—because it's Call the Plumber Time.

The simple preventive measure is a technique that plumber Chuck McLaughlin calls "holding back." He would simply hold the shower arm steady with one wrench while he turns with a second wrench on the showerhead. This ensures that all the twisting force goes right where you want it—onto the connection between the showerhead and the shower arm. To prevent plumbing damage, make "holding back" your standard operating procedure anytime you're tightening or loosening two pieces of plumbing that fit together.

"It's always a good habit to use—and there's no harm in it," McLaughlin says.

Seal your joints. Anytime you join one piece of plumbing to another, the connection is secured by turning a threaded "male" piece onto a threaded "female" piece. Those threads won't necessarily hold back the full force of water under pressure, however. So plumbers use this trick to fill in any voids between the threads and fully seal the joint. Wrap the threads in Teflon tape or brush them with the liquid sealer called pipe dope (both sold at hardware stores) before you fasten them together. Of the two materials, Teflon tape is faster and less messy to use.

Handy caulk talk. Caulk is one of those anonymous heroes of the plumbing world, the innocuous little material that steadfastly fills up the little gaps and makes sure that water flows where you want it to. The classic use for caulk is all around the bottom of your shower wall where it meets the bathtub. Here are some tips for using caulk, courtesy of Kropnick and other handy folks:

◇ **Before you caulk anything, make sure the spot you are filling is absolutely bone dry. Dab at the corner with a towel, follow up with a**

Freshen Up in the Shower

Maybe your showerhead is corroded, maybe it has gathered more mineral deposit that you can remove, maybe you want a water-saving model, or maybe you just want something fancier—the option for pulsing massage settings, for instance. Whatever the reason you're ready to replace the showerhead, rest assured that it's an easy way to add sparkle to the bathroom.

There are as many types of showerheads as there are types of bath soap. But whichever kind you choose, the replacement process is pretty much the same. (Do consult the instructions that come with your new fixture for any details that might be particular to your model.)

Here's how install your spanking-new fixture:

1. With the water faucets turned off, secure one pipe wrench to the shower arm, the pipe extending out of the wall, to make sure it doesn't twist as you remove the showerhead. Clamp another wrench around the base of the old showerhead and turn it counterclockwise one-quarter of a turn. At that point, you probably can remove the old showerhead with your hands. Wrap the threads on the end of the shower arm in Teflon plumber's tape or brush it with pipe dope to provide a good seal.

2. Still holding the shower arm steady with a wrench, twist the new showerhead into place with your other hand. Then use a second wrench to tighten the new fixture a little.

Now put on your sunglasses and admire your gleaming new shower area.

hair dryer, and wait patiently until there's no trace of moisture. This will ensure a good bond.

◇ You also can ensure a good bond if you remove all the old caulk before you lay in a new bead of caulk. A sharp-bladed putty knife is great for scraping up old caulk.

◇ Check the label, and make sure you're using a siliconized latex caulk.

It will remain flexible and will not harden up, thus becoming a pain to remove in the future.

◇ Applying caulk without making a mess takes a little practice. You will be squirting it out of a tube or a caulking gun. Try to apply a bead that's big enough to seal the seam but not so big that you have a lot of excess. To press the caulk into place and provide that smooth finishing touch, Kropnick likes to run his finger along the bead, pressing it into place as he goes. If this turns out to be too messy for you, wrap a plastic grocery bag around your hand and press the caulk into place with your plastic-covered finger. When you're done, throw the bag away—no handwashing necessary!

Set your tank lid on carpet. Anytime you're doing work inside the toilet tank, resist the temptation to set the lid on the bathroom counter or across the toilet seat. A toilet tank lid is surprisingly fragile and may break if you knock it to the floor. So when you remove one, set it onto a carpeted floor. If there's no carpeting handy, set it gently in an out-of-the-way spot where no one will kick it or step on it.

From the "Ounce of Prevention" Department

Okay, it's not nearly as sexy as repairing a leaky toilet or vanquishing a clog in the sink. But performing a handful of maintenance chores and inspections will head off tons of heartache and expense. Not having to make repairs at all is the most delicious kind of cheating-at-home-repair.

Here's the plumbing inspection routine recommended by sources who included Reggie Marston, president of Residential Equity Management Home Inspections in Springfield, Virginia:

Check sinks every six months. Inspect all the sinks in your home every six months. Get a flashlight with a big, strong beam. Fill each sink with water up to the overflow drain. Use the flashlight to inspect the underside of the sink, paying careful attention to the drain and the water supply connections. Then pull the stopper, letting the water drain out, and check the pipes underneath again for leaks. While you're at it, operate the faucets and watch for leaks around the handles.

Check toilets every six months. Flush every toilet and make sure the tanks refill and then shut off. If they don't, consult the toilet repair section in this chapter. Also, apply some gentle side-to-side pressure on the toilet to see if it rocks. If it moves a little, you might just need to retighten the bolts securing it to the floor. If it rocks a lot, talk to your plumber about replacing the wax seal that's underneath the base of your toilet.

Check under fixtures every six months. Go down to the floor just below every tub and toilet in the house and look up. See any signs of water or staining on the ceiling? If you do, there's a leak in one of the fixtures above that needs repair.

Operate shutoff valves every three to four months. Locate every water valve in your house, shut them off, and turn them back on again. This includes the individual shutoffs for each plumbing fixture, the main shutoff for the house, the exterior faucet, the line to your refrigerator's icemaker, the supply line to the water heater, and any other valve that regulates water. Why go through this exercise? When valves aren't used regularly, they seize up and are useless in an emergency, Marston says. If you encounter a valve that won't turn, spritz it with a little WD-40 lubricant and try it again. If it still won't close, have your plumber replace it.

Check the water heater valve twice a year. You'll find a valve with a lever handle high on the side of your water heater. Hold a bucket under the valve, push the valve open, and let it snap closed again. If you get a short blast of hot water from the valve, that's good. If the handle is seized up or if you don't get that blast of water, have a plumber replace it immediately. This gizmo keeps your water heater from blowing up if its thermostat goes on the fritz.

Flush the water heater once a year. Drain a quarter of the water out of your water heater, says Kropnick. This will remove the debris that

Water, Water Everywhere? Find the Shutoff Valve!

Ask any pro what a homeowner should do first in the event of a plumbing emergency, and the answer will always be the same: Turn off the shutoff valve. With the source of water stopped, you will have time to tinker with a repair or wait for the plumber to arrive.

That all sounds perfectly simple, but there are a few matters that you should consider before you turn another page in this book. First, do you know where the main shutoff valve is—the device that will stop the feed of water to the entire house with one flick of the wrist? You absolutely have to know this, says "Handyman Scott" Kropnick, because it's the all-purpose response to any plumbing disaster. *Hint:* This valve is probably near the front of the house, right where the main water supply pipe enters the building. Go find it right now.

While you're at it, make sure your main shutoff valve is easy to get to— you don't want to have to move two tons (1,800kg) of storage crates in order to find it when a burst pipe is filling up the basement. *And an equipment note:* The most reliable, easiest-to-use type of shutoff is the lever-handled style. If you have another type, talk to your plumber about replacing it the next time he's at your house for another job.

builds up in the tank, reducing its efficiency and costing you money because of wasted energy. Be careful when you do this, because the water, naturally, will be hot. Locate the drain valve near the bottom of the water heater. The valve is usually too low for you to be able to slide a bucket underneath, so attach a hose to the drain fixture and let the hose empty into a bucket. Check the gallon (liter) size of your water heater so you will know when you've emptied a quarter tank's worth (you'll probably need to empty about ten gallons [38l]). Check the temperature of the water coming out with a cake or meat thermometer. If it's above 125 degrees Fahrenheit (52ºC), turn the temperature setting down.

Once you have a handle (ha-ha!) on the main valve, here's another consideration that will save you wheelbarrow loads of grief: Is there a separate shutoff valve for every plumbing fixture in the house—including the tub, sinks, toilets, washing machine, and dishwasher? It's extremely handy to have shutoffs—for both the hot and cold water lines—that control the feed to every fixture. For instance, if your toilet goes berserk, you can kill its water supply in seconds by twisting the shutoff that's right there beside it. You don't have to run to the main shutoff valve and, conveniently, you don't have to shut off the water for the entire house while the toilet is brought under control. New houses are typically built with individual shutoffs, and many older houses don't have them—or only have a few. So, once again, talk to your plumber about installing them everywhere they might conceivably be needed.

Now, I know what you're thinking: If you have shutoff valves for every fixture in the house, why do you need a main shutoff at all? Because those individual shutoff valves are going to need repair some day, and then you *have* to shut off water to the whole house.

Replace washer hoses every three to five years. Replace your washing machine's supply line hoses with a set of the modern, superstrong braided hoses, available at home stores. Wrap each hose with a small piece of duct tape and write the date of installation on it so you can keep track of how old they are. Between washes, turn off both supply valves for your washer (you'll need to train family members to turn them back on before starting a load). If one of your hoses bursts when you're not there, you're going to have a nasty flood.

Check anything touching your pipes. At least once, take a look at every inch of copper pipe in your home, and make sure no other metal is touching it. If you have metal ductwork rubbing up against a copper pipe, for instance, the copper will corrode and eventually leak. If you find ductwork touching your pipes, slide a piece of nonconductive material like tarpaper between the two. Reinspect your pipes anytime a building project might create new metal-to-metal contact.

Investments that Protect Your Plumbing

Don't faint, now. We're going to talk about some moderately large expenditures—but they will pay for themselves over time because you'll avoid having to make repairs and you'll save energy. It's been a few minutes since you memorized all of the wisdom in chapter 1, so the Materials on a Program (MOP) philosophy is worth mentioning again. That is, you don't need to shell out cash for these improvements right away. Just put these items on your mental checklist for the future, and buy them when the time is right. When you do, some significant repair hassles are going to evaporate—which is why we call this cheating.

Take a hard look at water softeners. It's funny how we can become blind to an ongoing annoyance in our lives. For instance, lots of homeowners ignore the havoc that hard water deposits wreak. You know—that hard, milky-looking buildup that destroys appliances, festoons your shower door with gray crust, clogs up the showerheads, interferes with detergents, and leaves an unappetizing tinge on glassware and dishes. Installing a water-softening system will change the entire plumbing landscape in your home, says Kropnick.

Water softeners work by various mechanisms and have a variety of options for automation of the process. But basically they draw your water supply through a mineral tank that chemically strips out the calcium and magnesium that creates the crusty film. If you're considering buying one that adds sodium to the water (they often do), check with your doctor to make sure that won't aggravate any medical conditions you have. There's an option that uses potassium chloride instead of sodium, although it's more expensive to operate. Also make sure you have a clear understanding of the maintenance required for your machine—some systems demand more hands-on attention than others.

Heat your water only when it's needed. Start researching "on-demand" water heaters, which don't expend any energy on heating water until you turn on the tap and "ask" for it. On-demand water heaters (also called "tankless") come in gas or electric versions, and are becoming increasingly popular as energy prices rise, says Roto-Rooter's Raymond VinZant. When you turn on the hot water tap, an on-demand heater first runs that water through small channels in a radiator, warming it up. Conventional water heaters hold water in a large tank and heat that water well before you need it. The problem with that method is that the appliance has to keep the water hot around the clock whether any water gets used or not—a waste of energy.

Your inquiring mind will want to know whether an on-demand water heater can keep up with the hot-water needs of your household. VinZant says they deliver the goods admirably and you probably wouldn't experience any shortage of hot water unless you had two people taking hot showers at the same time, plus a hot wash running in the laundry room. On-demand water heaters tend to cost more than the conventional variety, but they will pay for themselves through energy savings. And speaking of savings, ask your accountant whether buying such a unit qualifies you for a tax credit.

Scope out your main waste line. Hire a plumber to inspect the waste line that connects your home to the sewer line under the street out front. (Right when you buy a house is a great time to do this—unless the mortgage company sucked up every spare cent you have.) This report might cost you an extra $200, but knowing when you might have to replace this line is a powerful bit of knowledge. If you know how much longer the pipe is likely to last, you will be able to have it replaced on your schedule rather than on an emergency basis, and you'll be able to fit the procedure into the family budget.

What's the big deal about waste lines? Roughly 70–80 percent of homes have a drain system that was built in the 1930s or 1940s, says Raymond VinZant, the Ask-the-Plumber expert for Roto-Rooter. This pipe might have been made of cast iron, clay, or even a wood fiber-and-tar material called Orangeburg, which is particularly vulnerable to damage from roots.

For this kind of inspection, you will need a plumber who can snake a fiber-optic camera into the waste line. Look for a service like this under "camera inspection services" in the yellow pages.

Become a Wise Buyer

When you see a handsome car cruising down the street, you subconsciously add that model to your "Someday I'm gonna buy that" list. You do the same thing with suits, shoes, sound systems, and furniture. So why not plumbing fixtures, too? No kidding. Plumber McLaughlin says that one secret of homeowner happiness is to be an observant consumer well before you need to replace these items in your home.

The best way to do this: Take notes while you travel. Good hotels tend to keep their plumbing fixtures up-to-date, so when you're on the road you are likely to be exposed to a wide range of the latest fixtures. Every time you come across a fixture that impresses you with its looks or functionality, jot down the name of the manufacturer and a description of the fixture. The next time you have to replace the bathroom sink, you won't have to hem and haw about what appeals to you.

For instance, McLaughlin has one customer who returned home from a trip to Disney World. This traveler was so impressed by the new "pressure-assisted" toilets in his hotel, that he had the plumber replace every toilet in his house with that style. In this design, a plastic tank gets pressurized by the home's natural water pressure. When the toilet is flushed, it delivers the water at a full fifty-five pounds per square inch (25kg/6.5cm^2), almost a violent flow of water. It uses no more water than a conventional toilets, but blasts the bowl nice and clean.

Pick Your Flush

I t's not the kind of thing you bring up at church, but I know you've had this thought: You urinate, you push the toilet flush handle, and you say to your-self, *Gee, does it really require all that water just to wash a little pee-pee down the sewer line?* The answer is no, it doesn't. The innovative dual-flush toilets allow you to choose how much water you expend on each flush—either a con-ventional 1.6 gallons (6l) when you have some solids to flush down, or half that amount of water if you're only flushing liquid. A Canadian study showed that homes using dual-flush toilets consumed as much as 32 percent less water than homes using conventional "water-saving" 1.6-gallon (6l) toilets—which can translate into a savings of thousands of gallons of water per year.

Dual-flush toilets are unfamiliar to many Americans. They've been popular for more than a decade in Europe, Australia, Japan, and other countries. Brands include Caroma and Toto.

Here are some other simple buying habits that will help plumbing repair go more easily.

Rely on a tape measure, not your memory. There are few mistakes that waste more time in home repair than the failure to measure. Plumbing is no exception, says home improvement expert David Lupberger. One of the most common goofs: A homeowner who buys a replacement faucet set, only to get home and discover that her sink is predrilled with faucet holes eight inches apart rather than four inches apart (or vice versa). So check and recheck your meas-urements, and write these measurements down. Never depend on your ability to remember measurements or "eyeball" the size of materials you need to buy.

Stick to the famous brands. When you buy plumbing fixtures, choose the well-known brand names, says Lupberger. *Examples:* American Standard, Kohler, Moen, and Delta. The top brands may not be the

PLUMBING REPAIRS: PUTTING WATER IN ITS PLACE

least expensive, he says, but these companies have been in business for a long time because of their high-quality goods.

Buy fixtures in your home country. Sure you're a sophisticate, a world traveler. But if you visit some foreign land and fall in love with plumbing fixtures that just can't be found back home, keep your wallet in your pants until your sanity returns, says VinZant. Here's the problem: If you ship plumbing fixtures back home, there's a very real chance that the foreign plumbing threads will not match the threads in use where you live. Sure, all is not lost, because your plumber (when he's done chuckling to himself) can probably contact the manufacturer of your new fixture and order "transition fittings" that will help everything connect properly—a process that will cost you more money and a couple of weeks' delay. But you really have to ask yourself: With the astounding variety of sleek and exotic-looking fixtures available to you right here at home, why do you need to complicate your life by jerry-rigging a foreign model to fit into your abode?

Stick to classic colors. When you're choosing new fixtures for your bathroom, resist the temptation to buy your toilet, tub, or sink in exotic colors, says Kropnick. Colors for such furnishings go in and out of style quickly, so sticking to classic white or bone (off-white) are good bets. If one of your fixtures breaks, it will be easier to find a match in the right color. And besides, some of the dark trendy colors are harder to keep clean.

Let your plumber buy his own parts. A natural part of doing your own plumbing repair is going out to a hardware store or home improvement store to pick up the parts you need to do the job. Your do-it-yourself exuberance might even lead you to buy your own parts—but to call a plumber to install them. Your reasoning: You'll save time (the plumber won't have to check out the job at your house and then go to the supply house for parts) and you'll save money (by avoiding the plumber's markup on parts).

Well, nice try, but that approach has a few inherent problems. A little background: Indeed, the plumbing parts that you can pick up

Are They Laughing Behind Your Back?

Cleavage on the human body is often considered an alluring feature. Unless it happens to be on a guy's backside when he's bending over in the kitchen making a plumbing repair. Anatomical scientists call this condition "plumber's butt." So the plumbing chapter is an appropriate place to mention a cure for this malady.

The problem, of course, is the fact that the bottom edge of your shirt rides up your back when you bend over. The solution: Wear shirts with a tail that's a few inches longer than you typically get with everyday clothing. If you wear conventional white T-shirts and you're of average height, just buy from the "tall" display rack in your department store rather than the regular size. For T-shirts in a variety of colors, styles, and fabrics, the Duluth Trading Company (www.duluthtrading.com) offers a line of "Longtail" shirts that are three inches (7.5cm) longer than the conventional cut. One variety comes with gift packaging, a small white plastic bucket with a label that reads, "Crack Spackle."

at retail stores are typically less expensive than the parts that your plumber gets from a professional supply house. The reason is that retailers work hard to keep their prices down, and the manufacturers—even the famous-name ones—comply with this by producing parts for the do-it-yourself market that aren't as durable as the professional-grade stuff. This all works out nicely when, following *How to Cheat at Home Repair* policy, you confine your do-it-yourself fixes to modest projects in which lighter-gauge materials will often suffice. It works out fine, too, when you hire a plumber for the big jobs and let him buy his own parts—you get more durable parts and professional workmanship on the significant jobs where it will count most.

However, here's what can happen if you insist on buying retail parts and telling your plumber to install them: If a plumbing part fails and gushes water into your home all day while you're at work, your plumber is going to say that you're responsible because you provided the defective parts. Had the plumber acquired the parts, the work would have been backed by a manufacturer's warranty and the plumber's insurance. Even if you don't have a disastrous flood in your home, a failed part is going to cost you more time and money if you supplied it to your plumber. That's because the plumber will charge you for an extra house call when he has to return later to make the repair all over again. And *you're* the one who will have to take the failed part back to the store for a refund.

It's true that your plumber is probably charging a markup on parts that he gets for you from a supply house, but if you've done a good job of selecting a reliable professional (see chapter 13), the added cost should be modest. Think of the extra cost as insurance. And besides, consider how the plumber is going to feel if you're nickel-and-diming him and forcing him to work with less durable parts than he's accustomed to. Do you really want someone working on your house under those conditions?

SO NOW YOU know the wisest, sneakiest ways to tame the water that we invite into our homes—incredibly easy fixes for the most common plumbing problems, smart investments to make in preventive maintenance, and cutting-edge technology that will strip some worries and hassles out of your life forever.

Walls, Floors, Doors, and Windows

LET'S TALK ABOUT THE EASIEST WAYS TO CARE FOR THE BASIC STRUCTURES THAT MAKE A ROOM A ROOM—THE WALLS AROUND YOU, THE CEILING ABOVE AND THE FLOOR BELOW, PLUS THE PORTALS THAT ALLOW THE EBB AND FLOW OF PEOPLE, PETS, FRESH AIR, AND LIGHT. SADLY, THESE FEATURES OF THE HOME ARE EASY TO TAKE FOR GRANTED—UNTIL THEY START TO SHOW SIGNS OF NEG-LECT AND ABUSE. HERE'S A COLLECTION OF INCREDIBLY SIMPLE FIXES THAT WILL KEEP YOUR ROOMS LOOKING AS HANDSOME AS EVER, SNEAKY WAYS OF MAKING THE GRUE-SOME TASK OF PAINTING A BREEZE, AND SOME LIFESTYLE ADJUSTMENTS THAT WILL KEEP GRIEF AND HASSLE AT BAY FOR YEARS TO COME.

How the Pros Slash Painting Time to a Minimum

I look forward to painting the rooms of my house the way I look forward to colonoscopies. How could any homeowner of sound mind enjoy the messy, fumy, grueling work of applying paint to acres of wallboard and trim? Fortunately, this is a realm where the *How to Cheat at Home Repair* philosophy pays off in spades. Here's a collection of sneaky tricks for whittling the time and frustration of interior painting to a bare minimum. A particularly jaunty paintbrush salute goes out to two painting pros who shared their secrets: Ed Waller, the co-founder of the CertaPro painting company who swears that he's the "fastest painter in the world," and Dean Bennett, an architect, contractor, and builder based in Castle Rock, Colorado.

Prep the Room to Avoid Hassles and Messes

You already know that a room needs to be prepped for painting before the first splotch of latex touches a wall. You want to protect the stuff that *shouldn't* get paint on it, you want to clear away obstructions that will slow you down, and you want all the right tools within easy grabbing distance so you don't have to search all over the house for equipment in the middle of the job.

All these are excellent goals, but the problem is that many people put much more effort into the preparation process than they have to. One of the biggest time-wasting practices, says Bennett, is the habit of using "painter's tape" to mask every edge that a paintbrush or roller might come near—including window glass, baseboards, and trim. In some rooms, that masking mania alone will take hours. And painter's tape doesn't even do its job very well. Inevitably, some paint will seep underneath the tape, discoloring the spot that you thought you were protecting. And then when you pull the tape up, it often rips up swatches of your tender new paint along with it—meaning you have to paint that area all over again.

Here's a telling fact, says Bennett: Despite the name *painter's*

The Cure for Wall "Cavities"

You were oh-so-young. Overwhelmed with the logistics of moving out of your first apartment and desperate to get that damage deposit back from the landlord. But what about all those nail holes marring the walls where you had hung framed posters all around the apartment? You wracked your brain to think of some pliable substance that would plug those holes and came up with—toothpaste!

Well maybe you got your damage deposit back after all, but in truth toothpaste is not a good choice of patching material for holes and cracks in your wall, says builder Dean Bennett, of Castle Rock, Colorado. Here's the problem: There's a lot of moisture in toothpaste, and as it dries it will shrink, cracking any paint layered over it. Lightweight spackling and painter's caulk are designed not to shrink, making the patch job invisible under the paint. Besides, repairing a wall with toothpaste doesn't make economic sense either, says Bennett. "A tube of caulk costs a dollar," he points out. "A tube of toothpaste costs a lot more."

tape, professional painters rarely stock the stuff in their own trucks—because it wastes their time and they know how to do a good job without it. So toss your painter's tape into the trashcan, Bennett says, and instead follow these two practices to get the orderly look you're after:

1. **Take down everything that's removable.** Before you open the first can of paint, remove all switch plates, outlet covers, and hardware from the room. Remove all pictures from the walls and park them in a safe spot in another room. Pull any nails or picture hangers out of the wall. Save all hardware in one small plastic container so it will be easy to find later. Of course, when you reinstall these items, they will be free of the telltale streaks of paint that's the sign of a sloppy painter.

2. **Learn to paint in a precise line.** This is the kind of brushwork that allows you to dispose of your painter's tape. When you need to paint a precise line—say, on the wall just above a baseboard—get enough paint in the brush to create a nice bead along the side of the brush as you drag it along that edge. That beaded side will give you the straight line you're looking for. Don't attempt to paint a straight line with the tip of the brush—that's impossible. Use a trim brush to do this detail work (the type of brush with a "beveled" tip—cut at an angle, as opposed to cut flat and straight across). Hold the trim brush's narrow handle in your hand, much as you would a pencil. Slowly draw the tip of the brush down the line where the two different surfaces meet, being careful to let the bead of paint in the brush drag along the straight line.

Getting good at this precision painting requires just a little practice, Bennett says, but the technique will shave hours off your painting job. Be fearless, and repeat this mantra to yourself: "There are no mistakes in painting." With a damp sponge on hand, you can quickly and easily mop up stray brushstrokes if you slip up. If you do happen to get a smudge of paint onto window glass, don't fret. Once all painting is done, you can razor the errant paint off in seconds. (Pick up a handled, single-edge razor at your hardware store.)

With your painter's tape now safely retired to the trashcan, here are some more room-preparation tricks for speed-painting a room's interior. On your mark, get set . . .

Clear the room. Ed Waller's number one rule for speedy painting is to move as much stuff out of the room as possible. Carry all movable furniture to an adjacent room so it won't be underfoot, forcing you into constant detours as you try to work. If closets need painting inside, pull every single item out and pile all of them on the nearest nonmoving furniture (perhaps a bed or couch), and then cover those items with a drop cloth. If there's a china cabinet in the room, transfer everything in it to the dining room table, cover the table with a drop cloth, and don't go near the table during the entire paint job.

Cover everything that remains. Use cheap plastic painter's drop cloths (1.5–2 mil, or 38–50 micron, plastic works fine to wrap every other not-to-be-painted object that remains in the room—tables and shelves, for instance). (A mil is 1/1,000ᵗʰ of an inch, the standard thickness measurement for plastic sheeting.)

Paper the floor. Now cover the floor thoroughly as well—but this time not in plastic, says Waller. That's too slippery to walk around on. Instead, cover the floor with kraft paper, which you can buy in large rolls in the painting section of your home improvement store. Use masking tape to secure the sheets of kraft paper so they don't shift while you work and expose the floor to dribbles. This way you can cover a room's floor in no more than five or ten minutes.

Use a fast-drying filler. Part of prepping a room for painting is filling in any cracks and nail holes, of course. Make sure the filler you use doesn't slow you down with a long drying time. Whatever you do, don't use drywall compound to patch cracks in the room you want to paint—that stuff has to dry overnight. There are two classic, inexpensive alternatives, says builder Dean Bennett. Both of these products are quick-drying and ready to paint within twenty minutes or so.

◇ **Lightweight spackling.** This stuff comes in a little white tub. Apply it with a putty knife or even your finger.

◇ **Painter's caulk.** This latex material comes in a tube made to fit in your caulking gun.

Waller's favorite wall-patching material is even speedier: Durham's Rock-Hard Water Putty. This is a powdered filler that you mix with water, and it will dry within five or ten minutes. And if that's not quite fast enough for you, Waller offers this secret to accelerate the process even more: The product dries still faster when you use hot water to mix it.

When you're filling cracks and nail holes, keep a damp sponge handy and use it to smooth out your patch job if there are any rough spots that would leave a visible impression through the paint.

Seal Your Caulk with a Screw

You patched up a few nail holes with a fresh tube of painter's caulk, and now there's enough goop left to service every house in the neighborhood. What do you do with it—store it in the pantry, where it will harden to stone? No, here's builder Dean Bennett's trick: Drive a galvanized screw or a galvanized nail into the tube's open tip. That will prevent the caulk from drying out, and since the metal is corrosion-resistant, it won't discolor the caulk. If you have no galvanized screws or nails, regular metal will do—but later you will need to squirt out the rust-discolored caulk before you start your new patch job. Unless, of course, rust happens to be the hot new decorator color that year.

Once it's dry, give the filler a quick sanding to smooth it out. Unlike some kinds of wall-patching materials, these fix-it-fast products do not require a coat of primer before you paint.

Now for the Actual Painting—You're on a Roll!

Now let's look at the task of actually applying paint to the wall. As creatures of habit, we're prone to repeating the same time-wasting mistakes again and again. Here are some tools and techniques that will ease your way and restore your sanity.

Pick up a multitasking assistant. Interior painting, by definition, is a series of tricky, confounding situations. To keep stress at a minimum, says Bennett, pick up a gizmo that the pros like to use, the device typically called a painter's all-in-one tool or multitool. Such tools are packed with more functions than a Swiss Army knife. These features include a sharp point for clearing out cracks in your drywall, a curved edge for squeegee-ing paint off a sodden roller, a scraper edge for chipping up flaking paint, a putty-knife edge, a prying edge for opening paint cans, and a teardrop-shaped hole for grabbing the heads of nails and lifting them out of the wallboard.

Heck, they probably sell one that will make sushi, too. This is definitely a tool to have around when you want to project that "I know what I'm doing" image.

Slather on some sunscreen—even at night! Sure, we're talking about inside work. Nevertheless, before you start applying paint to wall, give any of your exposed skin a light coating of sunscreen. Why? Because your face, hands, arms, and legs will inevitably get dripped on and splattered by paint during the job. If you leave these splatters in place for a few hours, it will take quite a bit of skin-scrubbing to make you presentable again. However, when you have the forethought to apply sunscreen before you start painting, any paint spots will slide right off your slick skin when you give it a quick soap-and-water rinse.

"Cut in" with one coat. The process called "cutting in" is actually the most time-consuming part of painting a room. This is when you first

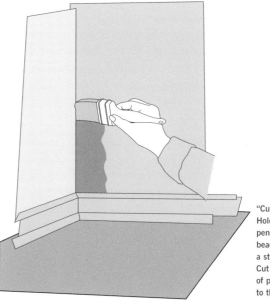

"Cutting in" a corner: Hold your trim brush pencil-style and use the beaded paint to create a straight vertical line. Cut in with a thick layer of paint and feather it to the side.

apply actual paint to the wall, brushing it on along those edges and borders where your paint rollers can't cover reliably—where wallboard meets window frame, doorframe, baseboard, or electrical outlet, for instance. With most paint colors, cutting in will do nicely with just one thick coat, says painting exec Ed Waller (the possible exception being dark colors, such as deep red or green, which may require two coats). Use as big a brush as you can manage comfortably. When you're painting up against a corner, position the edge of the brush parallel to the corner and hold the brush handle pencil-style. Slather on the paint thickly, and feather it (drawing lighter brushstrokes out to the side) toward the open wall where the paint rollers will overlap it later.

Ready to roll? Do it twice. At first blush, this may not sound like advice for speedier painting, but it is. When it's time to roll paint onto the open walls and ceiling, don't try to get away with one coat. Rolled-on paint may look nice and thick when you first apply it, but that's because it starts out ten mils (a quarter of a millimeter) thick. However, it dries to half that thickness, and small voids inevitably appear as the water in the paint evaporates and the coating left behind shrinks. So patience will pay off here. Roll on the paint, wait the prescribed drying time listed on the can, and roll again. That's much more efficient than realizing a day or two later that you have a patchy paint job—and that you have to go through all that paint-job setup a second time.

Leave your extension pole attached to the roller. You probably have learned to use extension poles for reaching your paint rollers to ceilings and high spots on the wall. For the best economy of movement, says Waller, just leave your pole permanently affixed to the roller handle during the entire painting job. This will eliminate a lot of the bending, stooping, and reaching that are inevitable when the pole isn't attached. A two- to four-foot (61–122-cm) pole is ideal for roller-painting a room with an average-height ceiling, although you may find the fancier aluminum telescoping variety convenient if you have higher ceilings.

With paint rollers, think big. When you're buying materials to paint your interior walls, buy the bigger paint rollers—the eighteen-inchers (45.5cm) instead of the regular nine-inch (23-cm) kind. Make sure you buy paint pans that are wide enough to accommodate the larger rollers, too. Painting goes twice as fast with the larger rollers, says Bennett. Because they hold more paint, you spend less time returning to the pan and dipping the roller again for more paint. Also, make sure you buy roller handles that accept the threaded end of an extension pole.

Line your paint pan with plastic. Pouring paint directly into your aluminum paint-roller pan is a recipe for a number of kinds of grief. Getting the pan totally clean again hours or days later will be impossible. The dried-on paint will soften the next time you use the pan and break off into annoying little flecks floating around in your new paint. And woe unto you if you try to switch paint colors—the old paint will bleed into the new, altering the color. The simple solution to this dilemma: When you buy a paint pan, also buy several of the molded plastic liners that are made to fit inside that particular pan. Just pop the liner into the pan, pour the paint into it, and throw the liner away at the end of the day. Cleanup problem solved!

Before you dip your brush or roller into the paint, get it damp. The fibers in a paintbrush and paint roller will draw up paint and release it better when they have been dampened in water first. If you dip your brush or roller into the paint dry, the paint will pull the fibers together and not transfer to the wall as readily—which means you will find yourself taking more trips to the paint can or roller pan. And who wants to work harder? So before you start painting with a brush, rinse it lightly in the sink, hold the brush handle between both hands and rub back and forth to spin off the excess water. To dampen a roller, hold it under the running tap briefly, and then squeeze with your hands down both sides to wring out the excess.

Pass up the conventional painter's ladder. Sure, your classic five-step ladder, with the fold-down paint can shelf near the top, may be emblematic of interior paint jobs. However, they're not actually the ideal tool for giving you extra reach—not in most conventional interior rooms anyway. The problem is that they're oversized for the job at hand, and they become a bulky hassle because you have to move them around frequently. Waller's favorite device when he needs some extra elevation: the smaller hoop-style two-step ladder, the kind with the rounded handle across the top that makes it grab-and-go easy to move around the room.

Make painting a two-handed job. With a little practice you can learn to paint accurately with both your left and right hands—whether you're using a brush or a roller, says Waller. The advantage to doing this: You will find yourself moving your ladder around half as often, since you will be extending your reach in both directions instead of one.

When you cool it for the day, freeze your brushes and rollers. A lot of indoor painting jobs are involved enough that they need to be spread over more than one day. So keep a container of plastic wrap handy while you're painting. When you need to take a break and resume painting another day, just wrap your brushes and rollers in plastic and put them all in your freezer. When you're ready to paint again, pull them out and let them thaw at room temperature. You'll find your brushes and rollers still moist and ready for action.

When painting's done, throw it all away. When many homeowners are done with interior painting, they leap into the gruesome task of cleaning the paint off the rollers and brushes, as well as folding up all the plastic drop cloths—a process that's guaranteed to leave you speckled in flecks of paint from your hair right down to your sneakers. If that sounds like you, the official *How to Cheat at Home Repair* technique will save you a ton of grief: Throw it all away. Yup, stuff the brushes, rollers, paint-pan liners, and plastic drop cloths into a garbage bag and haul it all out to the garbage can. Cleaning those tools is virtually impossible, and they will inevitably bleed some old paint into your new paint if you try to use them again. Besides, these tools are relatively cheap—chalk their cost up to the price of any home paint job.

Bag that balky roller. Anyone who has roller-painted a room has run across this classic quandary: The spring-loaded bracket that fits inside the roller gets stuck in place, seemingly fused inside the roller by dried paint. So how do you extract the roller—without splattering the entire room, and yourself, with paint flung off the recalcitrant roller? Here's Bennett's trick: Grab a plastic supermarket bag and insert the roller inside it. Also, just to contain any potential mess, stand over a large sink, perhaps the utility sink in your laundry room. With the bag around the roller, you can safely grab the roller in one hand without squishing paint all over yourself. With your other hand, grab the wire frame of the roller mechanism and pull it away from the roller. If it slides free, lucky you—rinse the thickening paint off the bracket and throw away the roller itself. If the two parts are hopelessly stuck together, drop it all into the closest trashcan (conveniently, the roller is already covered in plastic to prevent added mess).

Paint: It's the Little Things That Count

Paint is such a staple in a homeowner's life that it's hard to imagine that there could be any true innovations in the stuff. After all, we only ask of our paint that it cling to the wall, last a long time, and look pretty. Now, though, the science of nanotechnology (designing materials at the molecular level) has entered the field of house paint. Such paints are made up of tiny particles that spread more easily and dry into a finish that's more complete, harder, tougher, and longer lasting, says builder Dean Bennett, of Castle Rock, Colorado. The Behr brand pioneered nanotech house paints, but you can expect competitors to emerge as well. Part of the *How to Cheat at Home Repair* philosophy is to embrace laborsaving technology, and nano-paint will pay off for years to come.

Add Years to the Life of That Paint Job

How long does your living room paint job last? Do marks and scratches accumulate so heavily that the room feels trashy after five years? Don't go zipping over to the paint store just yet. Painting is a backbreaking, time-consuming task—which calls for some powerful cheat-at-home-repair tricks. Here are some techniques that will help you double or triple the life of that paint job—without wetting a brush again or opening another paint can.

First, understand the finish choices. I know, your brain is already numb from our choice-crazy society. (Paper or plastic? Tall or grande? Chocolate or swirl?) But when it comes to picking the paint finish for the walls of your home, don't leave your decision making to the flip of a coin. The kind of finish you choose will actually affect the amount of home maintenance hassle you have to endure in the future, says Bennett. Here's what you need to know:

◇ **Flat paint.** You often find flat wall paint in new homes, because builders know that it leaves no sheen to highlight imperfections in the wall. There's a downside, however: You can't clean marks and smudges from a wall painted in flat paint without messing up the color. Your only choice is to repaint. So cross flat paint off your shopping list permanently.

◇ **Eggshell.** This is the great, basic finish for interior walls. It has just a slight sheen, and it will stand up to gentle cleaning.

◇ **Semigloss.** The classic hard-and-shiny scrubbable finish that's perfect for kitchens and bathrooms.

There's one more choice to make about your wall paint. Oil-based or latex? The official *How to Cheat at Home Repair* reply is "latex." Oil paint is much too stinky and a nightmare to clean up afterwards, while latex cleans up easily with soap and water.

Even with a good, durable paint on your walls, they won't be

For a Lasting Paint Job, Go Dark

Have you ever stood in the center of a newly painted room, only to shake your head in despair when you realize that you're doomed to paint these surrounding walls every year or two? You feel like Sisyphus, forever pushing that boulder uphill. Next time around, do yourself a favor. Choose darker colors for your walls, which will show fewer of the scuffs and smudges that persuade you (or your spouse) that it's time to repaint. Darker, show-no-dirt colors are particularly important in high-traffic areas, especially if you have children and pets in the house.

immune to the occasional scuff, scratch, and finger smudge. The good news is that these flaws are easily cured, and you can have a fresh-and-clean looking room in no time without repainting—which, of course, is what cheating at home repair is all about.

Use mild abrasive to fill in gouges. You were moving a table in the dining room and the corner scratched into the wallboard. Surely that requires repainting! Never fear, says "Handyman Scott" Kropnick of Blue Bell, Pennsylvania. It's easy to mix up a mild abrasive that will soften the surrounding latex paint enough to fill in the scratch invisibly. Find a pure white cotton rag (diapers work well). Dampen the rag under the faucet and sprinkle a small spot lightly with powdered cleanser, such as Ajax or Comet. (*Hint:* Kropnick keeps a container of powdered cleanser in his truck with all the holes but one taped off, so he gets minimal flow when he pours and he can better control the amount he's using.) Now gently rub the moistened cleanser against the mark on the wall, working it in a small circle until the paint softens. The mark will lift, and the liquefied paint will settle into any gaps. Dab with the cloth to smooth out the finish, and rinse the rag in the sink. The repaired spot will look darker than the surrounding paint at first while it's damp, but it will

WALLS, FLOORS, DOORS, AND WINDOWS

121

Get Hooked on a Nail-Free Hanging System

When you want to mount an object on the wall, often the only solution involves gouging a hole in the surface—which, of course, adds a little repair job to your to-do list sometime in the future. But it doesn't have to be that way. Victoria Higgs, an inventor in Adelaide, Australia, is a big fan of the newer puncture-free hook systems (she uses 3M's Command hangers). To fasten such hooks to the wall, you first clean the spot with rubbing alcohol, put an adhesive backing on the hook, and then press it into place for half a minute. After an hour, the hook has bonded to the wall and is ready to use. The hook is easy to remove from the wall without leaving any damage or residue—just pull on a stretchy tab at the base of the hook and it all pops free. The hooks come in a variety of sizes, some of them capable of holding several pounds (1–2kg or so). Maybe your days of patching nail holes are gone forever!

dry to the natural color. This technique will work to clean marks on woodwork, too.

Sponge away smudges. Cleaning up finger smudges, the kind you find around switch plates and doorknobs, is a simple matter of gently applying cleaners you already have around the house. Pour warm water into a bowl, add a squirt of dishwashing liquid, and dip a clean sponge into this solution. Dab at the smudges until they dissolve and you can wipe them up. If you want a little more cleaning power, spritz a clean sponge with ammonia-based cleaner and rub gently.

Erase those mistakes. Pick up a pack of those stiff-white-sponge cleaning tools known as "magic erasers," available in supermarkets and discount stores. Dampen one with warm water, and rub lightly at the mark. The superfine abrasive material will loosen and lift scuffs and smudges. In all cases, rub very gently so that you don't damage the paint color. After all, the whole point is to extend the time until you have to paint again—so clean with a light touch.

Streamline your picture hanging. You can buy all manner of contraptions for hanging pictures on your wall, but in most cases such hardware is a needless expense, says Bennett. You can do virtually all your picture hanging with cheap, conventional nails. "Nails do just fine—and they're almost free," he says. For smaller pictures, all you need is a small finishing nail. Drive it into the wall at a thirty-degree angle, and leave about a half-inch (13mm) protruding to catch the hanging wire. This method will do the least damage to

Break the Wallpaper Habit

If you're a fan of *How to Cheat* books, you've learned that now and then I take a beloved tradition and declare it a woeful waste of time and energy. A number of crazy things are done in the name of home improvement, and one of the most ill-considered embellishments is wallpaper. Now, don't pout. I know you adore the pattern you chose, and the colors set just the right tone, and a nicely papered room can look oh-so-sophisticated. But the truth is that, in terms of the hassle factor, wallpaper introduced into a home has on balance a negative impact rather than a positive one. You're going to have to live with the look of that wallpaper for years or even decades, and when you do get tired of it, removing it from your walls will be a nightmare of lung-busting steaming or slathering of chemicals. (Resist the temptation to paint over wallpaper, by the way—it will bubble up and create a mess, unless you use a specialized lacquer that's a fumy pain to work with.) Life throws enough hassles at you, so be kind to yourself and cross wallpaper off your future-projects list. If solid-color walls bore you, explore stencils to add some graphic interest to your kitchen or dining room.

WALLS, FLOORS, DOORS, AND WINDOWS

your wall. For pictures that are a little heavier—say, frames that are two feet by three feet (61cm x 91cm)—drive a drywall screw into the wall at the same angle. For hanging even heavier items, pick up an item called a drywall anchor. This consists of a large white plastic screw that sets into the wall, and then you drive a second screw into the plastic (leaving the screw head protruding).

Flooring: Minimizing Hassles Underfoot

As a cheat-at-home-repair enthusiast, you want your floors looking great for a long time—to forestall the time when you need major work done on them, such as refinishing or outright replacement. Your success at this will hinge largely on what kind of flooring you choose and your commitment to a mopping-and-vacuuming routine.

Now, quit rolling your eyes. Over the long haul, floors that are kept clean simply look better for years longer. Tiny little grains of dirt that collect on hard flooring (such as wood, vinyl, and laminate) will grind away at the finish and damage it, and when you leave those same particles in your carpet, they tear at the fibers with a scissoring action. So first let's discuss how to prevent the need for floor repair. Honest—establishing a few simple habits is a lot easier (and less expensive) than the hassle of selecting new flooring and having it installed.

◇ **Vinyl.** Ideal for the kitchen, bathroom, and laundry rooms, vinyl is just about the easiest kind of flooring to care for. Vacuum quickly, and then mop—usually, all you need is a sponge mop and a bucket of warm water. For a tad more cleaning power, add one of the cleaners available at the supermarket.

◇ **Hardwood.** Vacuum and use a disposable mop system regularly to keep damaging grit off the floor. Put down throw rugs in the high-traffic areas. This is particularly important if you have pets that run around the house. Watch for spots where your animals whip around corners and then dig their nails into the floor to keep from sliding—those are definitely spots for throw rugs, says Dean Bennett, the builder based in Castle Rock, Colorado.

◇ **Laminate.** There's usually a material inside this kind of flooring that's similar to particleboard, which means that it can be ruined by water. So laminate probably isn't a great choice for the kitchen or laundry room. But it's a fine choice for any living areas where you don't allow water balloon fights. When you mop it, use a slightly damp mop so there's not enough water on the surface to seep between the cracks.

◇ **Oh yeah . . . carpet.** In many ways wall-to-wall carpeting raises the level of repair and maintenance woes in your home. I call it an Anxiety-Inducing Luxury (AILment). Dust can't hide on a hardwood floor, for instance, but it can burrow out of reach between carpet fibers. On vinyl, a gravy spill is a quick sponge-up job, while on a carpet it can cause cardiac arrest. If you don't feel right about your home unless you have cushy fibers under your tootsies from baseboard to baseboard, then at the very least commit to two ongoing practices: a thorough, deep vacuuming at least every week, and a policy of immediately blotting up any spills, dribbles, and stains.

Hard Floors: The Easiest Duty

If you're a hard-floor enthusiast, here are some tricks for making your flooring last a long time and touching it up quickly when it acquires the occasional scuff mark. Just a handful of simple habits will pay off big-time in preserving your sanity.

Stop dirt at the door. The more you prevent dirt from entering the home, the less damage your hard flooring will suffer and the less mopping and vacuuming you'll have to do inside. So keep damaging dirt in its place—that is, out in the yard where it's supposed to be—by placing good shoe-scouring mats both directly outside and inside every entrance to your house. Look for a tough synthetic nap, as opposed to the natural-fiber stuff that degrades and sheds debris all over your stoop. Make sure every family member knows

WALLS, FLOORS, DOORS, AND WINDOWS

the drill—shuffle the bottoms of your shoes directly against each mat when you enter the house. And speaking of family, taking the mats outside and smacking the accumulated dirt out of them once a week is a great job for your teenager.

Quick-mop the grit once a week. The most efficient way to protect your ceramic tile and hardwood floor is to just fill a bucket with warm water once a week and give the floor a quick damp mopping. (Unless some youngster decided to make mud pies in the family room, you probably can do without cleaner in the water.) Or better yet, use one of the mop systems that offer moist, disposable mopping pads for an even faster once-over. This will prevent buildup of grit that will grind against the floor as family members walk around.

Flush your mop water. When you pour dirty mop water into a sink, you're inevitably going to get some gritty sediment left behind. A better trick: Pour the water into the toilet, which, after all, is designed to get rid of solid stuff, right?

Mop up immediately. If water spills on hardwood or laminate flooring, mop it up right away so it doesn't seep between the cracks and cause swelling or other damage.

Give those legs a lift. Drop by your home store and load up on protective pads to set under the legs of any furniture or appliances that rest on your hard flooring. Not only will this will prevent dents and scratches, but it also will prevent the transfer of rust from metal parts in the legs to your ceramic or vinyl tile.

Raise throw rugs to an art form. Embracing the advantages of hard flooring doesn't mean you'll never have cushy carpet fibers beneath your feet. Liberal use of throw rugs not only helps you protect your floors but also provides a lot of decorating flexibility. Move your throw rugs around periodically so sunlight doesn't etch their shape into your wood floor. Take your throw rugs outside and shake them vigorously once a week so they don't built up dirt and grit, grinding it against the floor. If one of your throw rugs seems to slide too easily against a hard floor, secure the edges with some double-stick rug tape, available in the carpet section of your home improvement store.

Get a Light Once-Over for That Hardwood Floor

When you hire a company to refinish your hardwood floor (that is, sand it and apply new coats of that hard, clear finish called polyurethane), you're going to enjoy that gleaming new floor for at least five or ten years. However, there's a simple way to gain all that satisfaction for just a fraction of the hassle and expense, says builder Dean Bennett. When your floor starts looking hopelessly scratched and marked, tell your floor person that you want a "screening" for your hardwood floor, not a full refinishing. Screening a wood floor means sanding it once over lightly, and then adding one new coat of polyurethane. Screening will give you that like-new look for another five years. The process generates less of that dust that wafts into every nook and cranny of your house and, because the job is easier to do, you can expect screening to cost half of what a full refinishing would cost, Bennett says.

Rub out floor scuffs. The sneakiest way to remove scuff marks from a hard floor is to simply use a pencil eraser. As the eraser accumulates grime, rub it against your jeans to clear up a fresh spot of eraser to work with. If the eraser trick doesn't quite do the job, here are some other ways to spiff up a vinyl, hardwood, or laminate floor with gentle abrasion:

◇ Go to your bathroom drawer or cabinet and pull out the nail polish remover, also known as acetone, says Jeff Bishop, technical advisor to the Institute of Inspection, Cleaning and Restoration Certification. Dribble the acetone onto a white cleaning cloth, and rub at the scuff mark to remove it. Try this on an inconspicuous part of your floor to make sure the acetone doesn't affect the finish of your floor.

◇ Pour a tablespoon of baking soda onto a saucer and add enough water to make a paste. Use a clean cloth to gently rub the paste against the scuff mark, and then wipe it up with a damp sponge.

◇ There's another mild abrasive hiding right in your medicine cabinet: Nongel toothpaste. Dampen a cleaning cloth, smear on some toothpaste, rub it gently against the scuff mark, and wipe it up. And one more easy approach:

◇ Those stiff-foam "magic erasers" available in the supermarket will make quick work of floor scuffs, too. Just moisten one with warm water and rub gently.

Carpet: Easy Going on the Softer Side of Life

Gosh, are you still pouting about the things I said about carpeting above? If you have checked your family's genealogical records recently, you will find that I am not your mother. If your home doesn't feel like home without carpet, then follow your heart. I'm going to help you anyway—with some corner-cutting tricks for repairing carpet, protecting it, and keeping maintenance hassles to a minimum. Friends again?

Buy carpet with built-in protection. The number one secret to an angst-free life with wall-to-wall carpeting is buying the right kind to begin with, says Paul Pearce, the London-based international vice president for the Institute of Inspection, Cleaning and Restoration Certification. The carpet industry has made enormous strides in recent decades in developing high-tech stain- and wear-resistant fibers. So for the sake of your sanity, welcome nothing else into your home. Look for nylon carpeting produced by a well-known brand such as Stainmaster—"as nearly maintenance-free as they come," Pearce says. Now, if you have older carpet that's in reasonably good shape but has less built-in protection, there's no sense in emptying your bank account for new carpet for a few more years. This is where the Materials on a Program (MOP) philosophy comes in: At the right time in the future, buy the materials that will make your repair and maintenance life easier. In the meantime, take to heart the tips and shortcuts in the following list, which work equally well for carpeting old and new.

Attack spills immediately. Think of it as a reflex action: When your carpet suffers a spill, smudge, or some other insult, you whip out your cleaning implements and attack the problem right away. The longer you wait, the more opportunity the filth has to settle in and damage carpet fibers.

Vacuum like clockwork. Jeff Bishop, also an executive with the Institute of Inspection, Cleaning and Restoration Certification, has a formula for ensuring long life for your carpet: "Vacuum, vacuum, vacuum," he says. "Get the soil while it's on the surface—before it sinks down into the pile." Deep in the carpet, dirt is beyond the reach of many conventional vacuum cleaners, and it will grind away at carpet fibers, damaging them. So vacuum at least weekly.

Never rub at a spill. When you spill something onto your carpet, don't panic. One of the biggest mistakes that homeowners make is to start scrubbing frantically, says Pearce. That abrasion can permanently damage carpet fibers. For any liquid spill, blotting with white cloth towels or white paper towels will solve the problem.

Attack notorious, nonoily stains with white vinegar. Most carpet owners live in dread of stains from coffee, soft drinks, tea, red wine, and the like. Fear not. Pearce has a tried-and-true tactic for eliminating such stains. The secret lies in the use of white vinegar, which breaks down tannins and reduces the chance that a stain will remain behind.

1. Get up as much of the moisture as you can quickly. Blot with white cloth towels or white paper towels. If there's excess moisture, a wet vac will help, too.
2. Mix in a spray bottle one ounce (28g) of white vinegar and three ounces (85g) of water, then spray the mixture onto the stain.
3. Blot again with fresh towels, as described above, until you have removed all possible moisture from the carpet.
4. Place six to eight thicknesses of fresh white paper toweling over the stain area, top it with a dinner plate, and add further weight, such as a stack of books. Leave it all in place overnight.

One Builder's Spot-Busting Secret Weapon

As a builder and contractor in Castle Rock, Colorado, Dean Bennett has seen many a messy carpet and has tried many ways of cleaning them up. So I put him on the spot (so to speak) and asked for his number one solution for cleaning up tough dribbles and blotches on carpet. His answer: Put this stuff in your arsenal—a spray bottle of Stain Extinguisher made by Chem-Dry. It's intended for tough spots on colorfast carpet and upholstery. To clean a spot, you spray the product onto the grime, give the liquid time to penetrate, blot with a clean towel, let it dry, and then vacuum. Stain Extinguisher also makes a good prespotter for difficult laundry stains. "Man, it works so much better," Bennett says.

You may have to work a bit harder to acquire Stain Extinguisher. Some home improvement stores carry it, you can buy it from Chem-Dry carpet cleaning professionals, or you can order it over the Internet (conduct a search on the product name).

Blot rubbing alcohol onto oily spots. To get oil, grease, or even tar out of your carpet, the solution lies no farther than your bathroom cabinet—rubbing alcohol, says Pearce. Moisten a clean white rag with rubbing alcohol and blot at the spot to dissolve it and draw the stain into the rag. As the rag absorbs the offending material, switch to a clean part of the rag, apply more rubbing alcohol, and blot again. (Note that, despite the term *rubbing alcohol*, you're blotting only—not rubbing at all.)

The solution for mud: Wait it out. Mud tracked onto your carpet is probably the simplest of messes to clean up, says Pearce. Just bite your lip and leave the smudge alone. Trying to clean up the mud while it's still moist will just spread the grime hither and yon. Instead, let the mud dry out and then vacuum over it with a machine that has a good beater bar. The mud will crumble into particles and get sucked away instantaneously.

Keep your vacuum up to snuff. Dirt particles left in your carpet long term will shorten its life and dull its appearance. So it behoovers you (sorry) to use a vacuum cleaner that performs well. This means selecting a machine with good suction and a robust beater bar that loosens dirt, and changing the filter bag frequently.

Give your carpet little vacations. Don't let sun blast through the windows onto your carpet for hours at a time—close the blinds now and then to reduce the chance of fading. Move your furniture around from time to time to reduce that chance of permanent indentions in the carpet and to change traffic and wear patterns.

Snip away that burn spot. You wake up the morning after a cocktail party to the dreadful discovery of a cigarette burn on your plush carpet. Arrg!—a permanent blot on the décor! Well, calm down—there's a way out of this. With a little judicious scissor work, you can disguise that woeful souvenir of your merrymaking. Start with a pair of small, sharp scissors (the kind you buy at drugstores are ideal). Lie on your tummy so you can see the burn spot clearly while you work. Carefully snip off the blackened tips of each carpet fiber, trying to remove no more material than necessary. If you're lucky, you won't have to cut down deeply. This may leave a slight depression in the carpet. If so, snip just a little from some of the surrounding fibers as well to disguise the divot. When you stand back from the repair job, you'll find that offending spot nicely camouflaged. Then do this:

1. First, gather a few items: You'll need a utility knife, some double-sided carpet tape from your hardware store or home store, and a round metal object that just fits over the offending spot on your carpet. This disk could be a jar lid, a tin can, or a round cookie cutter.

2. Press your metal circle over the spot of damaged carpet. Using the circle's edge as a guide, reach the tip of your utility knife down to the fabriclike base of the carpet and cut. Slice between the carpet fibers, not over or through them. Lift up the circle of damaged carpet.

Wine Stain Cure Is All Wet

Many people swear by the "like dissolves like" principle when it comes to eradicating a red wine stain on carpet. That is, pour a little *white* wine over that red splotch, and then blot it all up. No, no, no, says Paul Pearce, the London-based international vice president for the Institute of Inspection, Cleaning and Restoration Certification. The problem is that the white wine will leave a sugary residue behind that will attract even more dirt. (Yes, you could say that your carpet will then have a "hangover.") Instead, attack a red wine stain with Pearce's white-vinegar technique described on page 129.

Permanent damage? Give your carpet a transplant. What happens when, despite all of your stain-fighting efforts, you realize that your carpet is permanently damaged—right in a highly visible spot of your home? Time to drain your bank account for fresh new wall-to-wall? Oh, ye of little faith! With a little transplant surgery, you will have that carpet looking its best in no time.

3. Now you need to create a patch. If you have leftover carpet from the original installation, just follow the same procedure to cut a fresh-and-clean patch in precisely the same size. If you don't have leftover carpet, cut your patch from an inconspicuous area of the floor—perhaps a spot that's permanently covered by heavy furniture, or a spot in the back of a closet. If your carpet has a pattern to it, make sure your replacement patch will continue the pattern correctly when it's laid into place.

4. Use scissors to snip pieces of the double-stick carpet tape and fit them against the flooring. Then lay your new patch into place and press down firmly.

Note: At some home stores and on the Internet, you can find a patch-cutting tool that will perform this same "surgery." It consists of a cylinder with a knife edge around the bottom, which cuts through the carpet when you twist it in your hand. Some have replaceable blades and a sturdy pivot pin in the center to help you along. One variety of this patch-cutting tool is especially designed for carpets with long, loopy fibers and will resist snagging fibers and causing an unsightly "run."

Your Squeaky Floor Is Crying for Support

Got a squeaky floor in your living room that's driving your whole family nuts? Under certain conditions, a squeaky floor is so easy to fix that you'll look like a hero after only a couple of minutes' work. But first let's take a look at why floors squeak in the first place. The problem is that in certain spots the support under your flooring isn't as firm as it should be. When you walk on such spots, the flooring materials sag, rub against each other, and make those mousy sounds. The most frequent culprits in this lack of support are the heavy beams running under your floor called joists, says "Handyman Scott" Kropnick, based in Blue Bell, Pennsylvania. In any spot where a joist is warped, it's allowing too much give in the flooring above it. You have the best shot at an easy fix, then, if you have open access to the joists—say, if your basement ceiling is not covered and the joists above are exposed.

So here's how to squelch the squeak in just minutes.

1. Get an assistant to stand in your living room on the squeaky spot and walk in place to keep that annoying racket going while you go to the basement to watch the ceiling.

2. Slip on safety goggles and a dust mask. (Flooring is notorious for gathering dust, and the work required for this job is sure to loosen debris that will fall straight into your face.) When you see the spot where the subflooring or floorboards are pressing up and down, mark it with a pencil.

3. Tell your assistant to stand aside.

4. Use a small hammer to tap a couple of slim pieces of wedge-shaped

wood (called shims) between the joist and the flooring. This will eat up the gap that allows the floor to bend, and it will squeak no more. If you don't have any wood scraps that would make good shims, you can buy them premade at lumber stores or hardware stores.

Here are some other possible culprits when it comes to squeaky floors, and ways to fix them:

Firm up a cracked joist. Besides being warped, there's another reason that a joist might be causing your floor to squeak. If there's a substantial crack in a joist, it may sag slightly every time someone puts weight on that part of the floor, causing the squeak. In such a case, adding shims between the joist and the flooring won't help, because the joist will still sag where it's cracked. The cure is to shore up that crack by "sistering" a supportive block of wood—perhaps a two-by-four—along the side of the joist at the cracked spot to prevent the sagging. This would make an "easy enough" project for you, or an item for your handyperson's next visit. For a minor crack, one two-by-four secured along the joist with long drywall screws will provide enough support to stop the sagging. For a more serious crack, place supporting two-by-fours on either side of the joist, drill several holes through all three pieces of wood, and tighten them together with long bolts.

To silence a squeaky floor, tap a shim between the subflooring and the joist that allows it to sag.

Floored by a Marble-Cleaning Mistake

"**H**andyman Scott" Kropnick knows a fellow fix-it man who decided to clean a customer's beautiful marble-floored foyer with (what else?) a conventional floor cleaner. But the hapless worker discovered the hard way that the finish on marble can actually be quite delicate. The cleaner etched a filmy haze into the stone, and it was going to cost hundreds of dollars to replace.

Fortunately, Kropnick had the solution that bailed his colleague out. If you're in a similar fix, go to your home store and ask for a marble restoration product. This stuff allows you to eliminate haze by rubbing in a restorative liquid (and you won't need powered polishing tools). The directions will walk you through surface preparation, application, and drying time. For mild abrasion, you'll be using such materials as a sanding sponge or 0000-gauge steel wool to polish out the haze.

When you buy marble restorer, be prepared to match your marble's finish with the appropriate product. Some marble restorers are for the not-very-reflective finish called honed, and others treat the highly reflective polished finish.

Or attack squeaks from the top down. What if you have no access to the joists underneath a squeaking floor? Say you have a carpeted second-floor bedroom with a squeaky floor, and in the living room below, well you just don't quite feel like smashing up the ceiling to work with the flooring above. In that case, go to your home center or browse the Internet for a squeak repair kit for carpeted floors. Such kits give you the tools you need to drive a screw through the flooring into a joist below, binding the flooring and joist together to stop the squeak. Then you snip the top of the screw off below the carpet. A couple of things you should know about this approach:

◇ Driving a screw through the floor and into the joist below requires knowing where the joist is when you can't even see it. So first understand which way the joists are running under that particular floor. In your basement, look up at the underside of the first floor and note which way the joists run. Let's say they happen to run north–south. Now here's the trick: On the next floor up, the joists will run in the opposite direction, perpendicular to those on the floor below—east–west in this hypothetical case. That's how home construction typically goes.

◇ A wall in your home will usually sit on a joist, and joists are spaced a fixed distance apart, often 16 inches (45cm), depending upon where you live and the age of your home. (To check, go to your basement, and measure the spacing of those overhead supports.) So a tape measure running from a wall out onto your squeaky floor will help you pinpoint the spot where a joist lies.

◇ Just as you might knock against a wall to locate a stud inside it (listening for that sound change from a hollow thud to a dense thunk), you can locate a joist even through carpet by knocking against the floor. The end of a screwdriver handle is a good tool to bang with.

Key Strategies for Simple Door Repair

We don't ask much of our doors. Keep the weather out. Keep us secure. Give us some privacy. But despite being simple mechanisms, our doors sure fall prey to a mind-boggling array of maladies with annoying regularity. The good news is that by using just a few quick repair tricks and adopting some preventive habits, you can have all your home's doors back in the swing of things in no time.

Give that sticky doorframe a whack. Why do doors sometimes stick inside their doorframes? Often the reason is that doors are installed while the wood is dry, says builder Dean Bennett. When humidity sets in, the door and doorframe swell, eating up the narrow gap of space that had once allowed the door to swing freely. The common solution is to physically reduce the size of the door by planing or sanding down its sides to create more of a gap. The problem with that solution is that during times of low humidity, your door will dry

A Slippery Solution for Sticky Door Syndrome

Don't have the time or the tools to free up that annoying door that consistently sticks in the doorframe? Here's a sneaky way around the problem: Give the top and side edges of the door a rubdown with bar soap to lubricate it. The door should open and close smoothly. A first-class cheat, bar none!

out again and an oversized gap will appear between door and frame. And besides, your cheat-at-home-repair sensibilities have quickly identified that approach as a lot of bother as well.

So before you set about planing and sanding, take the sneaky approach to loosening up a sticking door, Bennett says. Find a piece of scrap wood and a hammer. Analyze where the door and frame are sticking and which way the frame would need to move in order to open up more of a gap between the two. Set your scrap wood against that part of the doorframe and give it a few good whacks with the hammer. The frame will shift ever so slightly and will suddenly accommodate that door. Hey—not a shred of sawdust to sweep up!

Still sticking? Thin the paint. If your door still sticks after you've tried to tap the doorframe back into place, the next culprit to attack is buildup of paint over the decades. The cure is a simple project of removing those paint layers from the doorframe and the door until you have restored the minute gap around the entire perimeter. Attack the built-up paint on the door (top and sides) as well as the inside of the doorframe. You should be able to accomplish this easily without taking the door off its hinges. Pick your weapon: A scraper, a sander, or a heat gun. The next time you paint that door, remember to take it easy and apply only a thin coat.

Firm up the hinges of your sagging door. When a door is hanging out of kilter, it's often because the screws supporting one of its hinges have ripped up the wood they are driven into and they no longer

WALLS, FLOORS, DOORS, AND WINDOWS

grip the wood firmly. Open the door and inspect the facing plates of each hinge to figure out which one(s) are a little loose. The problem may lie on the doorframe side or on the door itself. We're going to use a clever little trick to rebuild the wood so the screws will hold to it firmly.

1. Leave the door open and prop it into place by sliding a folded towel under its lower edge.

2. Remove the screws from the loose side of the problematic door hinge. Fold the hinge closed to get it out of the way.

3. Collect several skinny wooden sticks—wooden matches with their heads snipped off are ideal, and wooden toothpicks work fine, too. Dip each stick in wood glue and slide them into the loose-fitting screw holes. Leaving a little excess stick protruding from the holes is fine. When each screw hole is packed with glue-covered sticks, clip off the excess stick ends with wire snips, shears, or a utility knife. Allow the glue to dry. Now drive the screws back into their newly tightened holes. (If it helps, drill a narrow pilot hole to get each screw started.) Your firmed-up hinge will now hold that wayward door on the straight and narrow.

Tighten up the pins in that ghostly door. Sometimes a door seems to be possessed—unaccountably, it swings open or closed without your prompting. Time for an exorcism? No, we're just going to make those hinges a little more resistant to slight imbalances and breezes. Remove the pins from the door's hinges, and mark them so you'll remember which pin belongs in which hinge—it's better not to mix them up. (You might need the help of a screwdriver to pry the top of the pin up, pliers to grasp the head of the pin, and perhaps a hammer for gentle tapping and persuading.) Now take those hinge pins outside. We're going to bend each of them ever so slightly. One by one, lean each pin at an angle so that it's supported by two hard surfaces—say, the sidewalk underneath and a stone to the side. Give each hinge pin a whack with your hammer in order to bend them just a little. (*An alternative:* Secure the pin in a shop vise and hit it to the side with a hammer.) Tap the pins back into their original hinges. Now slightly bent, they will put up more resistance to the turning of the door. No more ghosts!

Don't let those hinge pins wander. Now and then you need to remove a door in your house—perhaps for a repair, or perhaps because your new refrigerator will never fit through the entryway unless you get the door out of the way. In any case, make sure that each hinge pin (those vertical rods that hold the two halves of a door hinge together) are returned to the very same hinge they started out in, says "Handyman Scott" Kropnick. Why? Because hinge pins develop a wear pattern that makes them work best in their comfortable original "homes." Switching them back and forth randomly will lead to fit problems in the future. So when you pull hinge pins from your door, mark the pins numerically so you will be able to match them with their original hinges correctly. Or just pull out a scrap of newsprint and lay the pins on it in order, top to bottom, so you can later install them in their proper places. The paper will prevent the oily grime on your hinges from rubbing off on your floor or furniture.

Hassle-Proof All Your Locks

When a door lock fails you, you're in for a miserable time indeed. You may find yourself burglarizing your own home just to get inside. If the balky lock is on your car door, you have to enter by the passenger door and crawl over to the driver's seat every day until you can get the car to the shop. Putting together a little lock-care kit will whittle such hassles out of your life, says "Handyman Scott" Kropnick. Gather the following two items in a plastic bag and hang the bag up in a convenient place—say, your tool pegboard in the garage, in the shed, or on your back porch. Wherever you store this kit, make sure a frozen lock won't prevent you from getting to it. (*Hint:* The glove compartment of your car isn't a great idea.)

◇ **A container of lock lubricant.** This one's your maintenance tool. At least once a year, squirt lubricant into each home and automobile keyhole, and then insert your key and turn it a few times to spread the lubricant around. Carry a tissue with you to wipe up excess. You have a few choices of lubricant: a tube of powdered graphite, a product such as Lock-Ease that provides graphite in liquid form, or a spray lubricant like WD-40.

◇ **Lock deicer.** This product is your get-me-out-of-a-jam tool. If you're bamboozled by a frozen-stiff lock on your car, ski rack, garage door, house, or padlock, use a scraper to chip off any ice covering the keyhole, and then squirt the lock deicer inside. This chemical will thaw the lock and get its innards moving again. Once you have the lock working smoothly, add a squirt of the lock lubricant mentioned above. The deicer may have washed away some of the original lubricant, and it's a good idea to replenish it to prevent more moisture from collecting inside the mechanism.

Hunt down the source of lock friction. Is the key in your door lock getting hard to turn? Don't ignore this—that repeated grinding of your house key back and forth is putting wear and tear on lock and key alike. First do this simple check: Make sure that the problem does not lie with the alignment of the lock's deadbolt with the strike plate in the doorframe. Just open the door and turn the key back and forth so that the deadbolt extends into the open air. If the mechanism *still* gives you a lot of resistance, then the alignment of the deadbolt is not the problem—you need some internal lubrication. Take the lubricant of your choice from your lock-care kit (described above), set the nozzle against the keyhole, and squirt. Hold a tissue or paper towel under the keyhole to catch any spillover. Put the key back in the lock and work it back and forth to spread the lubricant around.

But what if your lock is hard to turn only when the door is closed? Then you know that the deadbolt that slides in and out of the side of your door is scraping against the strike plate in the door-

Door Damage: The Key Question

You may wonder if your home is plagued by poltergeists—you know, those troublesome ghosts that play tricks on you. How else would you explain, for instance, a rash of doors that no longer fit properly in their frames but just rattle when you try to close them? Builder Dean Bennett of Castle Rock, Colorado, has seen that syndrome many a time, and his first question for the perplexed homeowner is: "Do you have teenagers living in the house?"

You see, there's something about teen temperaments that often leads to the slamming of doors. And door slamming loosens the brad nails that hold doorframes in place. This creates an unusually large gap, meaning that the door fails to settle properly into the frame. If you study the edges of the frame, you probably will be able to detect a line of paint around the outside edge that will indicate the original position of the wood. Set a piece of scrap lumber against the wayward frame and tap it back into place with a hammer. Then have a talk with your teenager about easing up on the doors.

In a similar vein, Bennett says, a lot of mysterious furniture damage is attributable to younger, rambunctious kids. For instance, he discovered that one customer's boy was using his open dresser drawers as a staircase—and then he was diving from the dresser top onto his bed.

frame. Chances are, your door has settled a little. First take a look at the door hinges to see if they have loosened, and then firm them up as described above. If your hinges are tight as can be, the other easy fix is to simply reposition the strike plate so its hole allows the deadbolt in and out without scraping, says builder Dean Bennett. Watch the deadbolt as you turn the key and determine whether you need to raise or lower the strike plate. Use a screwdriver to remove the strike plate from the doorframe. Using a wood chisel and a small hammer, tap out a new depression in the wood for the strike plate (you're probably shifting the strike plate $1/16$ inch [1.6mm] or so). Drill new pilot holes for the strike plate screws, and drive the screws

WALLS, FLOORS, DOORS, AND WINDOWS

into place to secure the strike plate in its new position. Now your deadbolt should slide in and out freely without that metal-to-metal friction.

Looking at Ornery Windows in a New Light

Time is rarely kind to windows. For such a stalwart, highly visible feature of the home, they sure have a ton of vulnerabilities—glass cracks, screens rip, paint gums up the works, and icy air creeps in around the frame. Sure, a window replacement company will gladly install glimmering new insulated substitutes—for several hundred dollars apiece. But the truth is that you can actually happily coexist with the cantankerous old windows in your home. A few simple and inexpensive procedures will change your entire outlook, if you'll pardon the term.

Free your stuck window with a gentle tap or two. If you have a window that won't budge in the window frame, first make sure there are no devices that are intentionally holding it in place. Release the latch holding the top and bottom halves of the window together. Also, scan the window frame to make sure there are no other security devices that would restrict the window's movement. For instance, some wood-frame windows have a long nail set into a drilled hole that passes through the frames of both window halves, locking them together. Also, window air-conditioners typically come with hardware that locks a window into place so the appliance won't fall outside. If there's no such intentional obstruction and the window still refuses to budge, the problem is probably that paint seeped in around the edges of the window and fused it into place. The solution is simple, says "Handyman Scott" Kropnick, although it requires a gentle touch. Get a hammer, a putty knife, and slide on protective goggles (no kidding—sharp little paint chips are gonna fly). Set the blade end of your putty knife against the gap between the window and the outer frame and tap lightly (remember, you're working around glass) to break the dried-paint seal. Work your way down each side and across the bottom. Now your window should slide up and down freely. If any ridges of wayward paint remain in the way of your window, use a paint scraper or sandpaper to finish them off. Next time you paint windows, go light on the brushwork, okay?

Put some glide in the slide. If you have old windows that are "double-hung" on a rope-and-pulley mechanism, you may find them difficult to push up and down. Usually, this requires just a simple fix. You probably have paint that has built up over the years in the channels that the window sash slides up and down in. So resist the temptation to dismantle the entire window to get at the internal mechanics, and try this easy tune-up instead. All you need to do is take a narrow paint-scraping tool and clear out the channels that guide each side of the window frame. (Wear protective goggles and a filter mask for this.) Then give the pulleys on each side a spritz of spray lubricant. Now your newly tuned-up window should slide up and down easily.

You say your double-hung windows still need help? Before you let anyone talk you into spending hundreds of dollars per window for new replacements, talk to your handyman or a window repair company about overhauling your old one. (This is a HIRE situation—if the job is Hard, Important, Rarely done and Elaborate, pay a pro to do it.) For them, it's a simple matter to disassemble the window frame and touch up the pulley and weight systems inside.

Toss your old window latches. As discussed elsewhere in this chapter, one of the preliminary steps for painting an interior room is removing and setting aside all hardware and switch plates. If you have old-style double-hung windows in the room, here's a good habit that will slice an ongoing annoyance out of your life: When you remove the metal window latches (those swiveling devices that secure the top and bottom window halves into place), throw them away. Why? Because it's probably been several years since you replaced them, and their metal tends to fatigue and break. Which means they're providing zero security and letting your heating and cooling escape because the window is no longer snug. Your old window latches are probably on the unsightly side, too, from paint drips, scratches, and corrosion. So this is a great opportunity to drop by the hardware store and pick up a gleaming new set that will work with your new color scheme and provide a professional-looking touch to your new paint job. Removal of the old latches and installation of new ones is a simple matter of driving a few screws.

Clear out those clogged weep holes. Walk around the inside of your house and take a look at all your windowsills. Toward the outside edge of the sill, probably just under the storm window, you should find a few holes that angle downward toward the outside. Keeping these weep holes free and clear is important because they drain off condensation and other moisture that would otherwise damage your windows and walls. Let them weep now, or *you* are going to weep later. The problem is that weep holes can get clogged with dirt, leaves, or dead bugs—and occasionally a well-intending home-owner will mistakenly caulk them closed, not realizing how important they are. As you survey your sills, carry along a long, thin nail, a stiff wire, or a straightened-out paper clip to open up any obstructed weep holes. If you simply cannot find weep holes at the bottom of one of your windows (maybe they were thickly painted over), fit a ⅛-inch (3-mm) bit onto a power drill to bore two or three holes through the wood or aluminum frame, says Kropnick. Gotta do it—they're not optional.

Plug up the arctic airflow. If you have an old window that seems to pump cold air into your home during the winter, a simple caulking job will keep you comfortable and lower your heating bills. Buy a tube of exterior weatherproofing caulk from your hardware store or home improvement store. The paintable kind is helpful in case you find yourself painting that window later. On a warm and dry day, go outside and use a scraper, a putty knife, or a screwdriver to remove any debris from between the leaky window frame and the side of the house. Use a knife or shears to snip a quarter-inch (6mm) off the tip of the caulking tube, and set it into your caulking gun. Insert the tube's tip between the window frame and the house's siding, and lay a bead of caulk into the gap around the entire perimeter. To

Wipe Out Caulking Accidents

Caulk is drippy, gooey stuff. Working with it inevitably involves unexpected plops and splotches. If you wipe them up right away, no problem. If you leave these little messes too long, they'll become a permanent fixture. The easiest way to clean up caulking accidents is to carry a damp rag with you while you work and wipe the drips up as you go. Caulk is water soluble, so moistening a rag with tap water works just fine. Squeeze the rag out so it's not dripping wet, and just tuck it into a belt loop or a pocket of your tool belt where it will be handy.

ensure a good seal, it helps to press the bead of caulk into place. Many people just use their index fingers, although that can be a tad messy. *Alternatives:* Use a popsicle stick, cover your finger in a scrap of plastic grocery bag, or smear a little dishwashing liquid on your finger so the caulk won't stick to your skin.

A brush-up for teensy holes in glass. Is there a ne'er-do-well with a BB gun in your neighborhood? Well, no matter why you might have a teensy hole punched into the glass of one of your home windows, here's the sneaky solution. Brush the hole with clear nail polish, allowing a small bead of the liquid to collect in the fracture. Wait for the polish to dry, and then add a little more with the applicator brush. Keep this up (dabbing and drying) until the hole is entirely, invisibly filled. (*Note:* Don't use this trick on automobile glass, since it could interfere with official repair techniques the pros use. Car glass and home window glass are two different species.)

For minor window cracks, find a great cover-up. Got a small crack in one of your home's windows? Replacing a windowpane is, well, a pain. But with this simple trick, you won't even care about that crack. Drop by your home improvement store and review the menagerie of glass-tinting films available—thin sheets of Mylar you can apply to the inside of window glass to filter light, reduce heat,

WALLS, FLOORS, DOORS, AND WINDOWS

145

or provide a decorative touch. Depending on the type of film you choose and the position of the cracked window, you may be able to disguise the flaw completely. At the very least, the film will prevent loss of heating or cooling through the crack.

For small screen holes, a little needlework. To fix a tiny hole in a metal window screen, get a sewing needle and use it to push the strands of the screen back into place. If the strands of screening were merely shoved aside when the hole was created, this may be all you need to do. If strands were broken, use the needle to line up the broken ends together as you close up the hole. Then brush at the strands lightly with clear nail polish, let it harden, and reapply as necessary to bond the broken ends together again.

For larger screen holes, a patch and a stitch. To repair a large hole in a metal screen, buy a piece of screening made of the same material. Cut out a patch that's one inch (2.5cm) wider that the hole in the

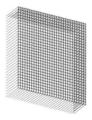

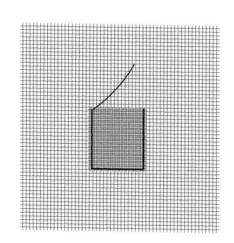

Create a one-inch (2.5-cm) fringe around the edge of your window screen patch and form it into the shape of a box lid. Slide the patch through the damaged screen, fold the edges flat, and stitch with fine nylon thread or fishing line.

screen on all sides. Now create a half-inch (13-mm) fringe around the perimeter of your patch by removing the strands of screening that are interwoven side to side. Fold the remaining fringe at right angles to the patch, so that the entire piece is in the shape of a box lid. With the fringes pointing toward the torn window screen, position the patch over the hole and push the strands of fringe through the screen until the patch is flush against the hole. On the opposite side of the screen fold all the fringes flat against the screen to hold the patch in place. To further secure the patch, use a sewing needle to stitch fine nylon thread or fishing line in and out around the perimeter of the patch.

Revive that lazy shade. Do you have a window shade that just seems to have lost its enthusiasm? You pull it down, and no matter how you jerk it or pull it, the shade just won't roll itself back up? This is an easy matter to remedy. One end of the shade should be round like a pin or nail, and the other end should be a flat piece of metal that can slide in and out of its slot-shaped bracket. Just lift the shade out of its brackets, roll the shade completely by hand, and then set the shade back into the brackets. Now, when you pull the shade down, the spring inside the core of the shade gets fully wound. It should have enough tension to snap the shade back into place when you're ready.

IT FEELS PRETTY liberating, doesn't it—knowing that you can keep the walls, floors, doors, and windows of your home in great repair with such a minimum of effort? That's what cheating at home repair is all about: establishing a peaceful and sane relationship with the things you own, mastering those possessions rather than having them enslave you, and making lifestyle choices that will make homeownership easier and easier for years to come. You'll have no trouble finding ways to spend the time you've saved. Frolic with the family, improve your backhand, read a classic—or try something that's even a little, well, off the wall!

Appliances:
When the "Household
Help" Go on Strike

FEW THINGS PROMPT THE GULP PHENOMENON (GIVING UP LOGIC PREMATURELY) LIKE HOME APPLIANCES. THEY HIDE MYSTERIES WITHIN THOSE CASINGS AND CABINETS. APPLIANCES HAVE CONTROLS LABELED WITH OBSCURE, INVENTED WORDS—IF THE CONTROLS ARE MARKED AT ALL. THEY COME WITH BOOK-LENGTH OPERATING INSTRUCTIONS AND UNFATHOMABLE PIECES AND ATTACH-MENTS. MANY HAVE BOTH WATER AND ELECTRICITY FLOWING THROUGH THEM, AND YOU HOPE LIKE HECK THAT THEY'RE KEEPING THE TWO WELL SEPARATED.

In the face of that kind of intimidation, when an appliance doesn't behave the way you hoped it would you can be forgiven if your first thought is a frazzled, "It's broken!" But don't forget that you took a pledge in chapter 1, a commitment to free yourself from panicky snap judgments that lead to unnecessary service calls or the purchase of replacement appliances you don't need.

Here's a collection of super-easy appliance fixes that will spare you a call to the repair company, some procedures that will keep your appliances humming happily for years longer, and some simple upgrades that may help prevent disastrous damage (and thus more repairs) to your home. And as you have come to expect, there's a passage that will get at least a few of you angry with me—the observation that virtually all small appliances are as disposable as facial tissues.

Refrigerators: Keeping Your Cool

We are food-dependent beings. That's why they say the kitchen is the heart of the home—we naturally gravitate toward it. And by extension this means that a well-run refrigerator, protecting a lot of our food, is awfully important to the well-being of our family.

Here are some valuable tips for keeping your fridge in tip-top shape:

Reconsider the kitchen layout. Think about it: Refrigerators are made for cooling and stoves are made for heating. So when you put them side by side, do they resolve their differences amicably? No. The fridge has to work harder to stay cool when it absorbs all that heat from your stovetop and oven. This runs up your electric bill and puts more strain on the refrigerator's compressor. You have the same situation if your refrigerator is near a heating vent. If your floor plan allows, find a new place to park your icebox.

Pack both compartments. Don't be miserly with your refrigerator—keep it well stocked. When you have plenty of food in the freezer compartment and the refrigerator compartment, the appliance have to work as hard to keep the interior cold. An overworked, sparsely furnished unit will need repair much sooner than one with a full belly. What if you'd rather not stock that much food in the freezer? Easy, says Dave Donovan of Atco, New Jersey, an electrician who writes for Doityourself.com.: Fill a jug or two with water, and add those to the freezer compartment. If you ever need more room in the freezer, a space-filling jug will be the first thing to toss out. In the same vein, establish a rule among your family members: Don't open the refrigerator door until you have decided what you're looking for. Standing at an open refrigerator door while you try to make up your mind is a waste of energy. Both these tricks will save electricity and prevent wear on your refrigerator.

Keep the surrounding air flowing. The coils on the outside of your refrigerator depend on good air circulation to transfer heat and do a good cooling job, says Donovan. So to give your icebox a power boost, pull the bottom grill off the front of the refrigerator, and vacuum up all that dog hair and dust. Then put the brush attachment onto the vacuum cleaner and suck up the dust covering the coils on the back of the appliance, too. (This is a heck of a lot easier to do, by the way, if you set your refrigerator on a pair of appliance rollers, which will allow you to move that hulking machine with a gentle pull.) Do this quick vacuum job every three months. The machinery in a dust-free refrigerator will not have to work as hard and therefore will last years longer, Donovan says. You'll save on electric bills as well.

Straighten the door. Take a second to examine how your refrigerator door hangs. Is it perpendicular to the floor, or does the side of the door with the handle on it hang down a little bit? If the door is hanging askew, the rubber seal is not holding the cold air inside the appliance efficiently, says Donovan. Which means your refrigerator is working overtime and wearing itself out minute by minute. Usually, a refrigerator door is drooping only because the screws holding the door's hinges in place have loosened. Tighten them up with a screwdriver and check the door's alignment again.

Dislodge that drippy glacier. Finding little pools of water collecting inside the refrigerator can be really perplexing—especially if your refrigerator has no automatic icemaker or water dispenser (and therefore no water supply line). Here's where that water is probably coming from: glacier melt. No kidding—if you have a freezer-on-top kind of refrigerator, there's a wide, flat block of ice built up behind the walls of your freezer. It has built up there because the drainage tube in the bottom of your freezer got blocked up by an errant frozen pea or something. This tube is supposed to drain off moisture and feed it into a pan under your refrigerator, where the water will evaporate. But since the tube is blocked, moisture builds up in the freezer, creates an ice dam, and excess water seeps into the refrigerator compartment below. Here's how to fix it:

1. Unplug your refrigerator for safety. Then transfer everything in your freezer to either another freezer or a cooler.

2. Remove the screws that hold on the plastic back and floor of your freezer. This should expose the ice dam. Get an enormous sponge, a bucket to squeeze excess water into, and a hair dryer. Melt the ice with the hair dryer, and mop up the water as you go along. Resist the temptation to chip at the ice with a sharp object, since it's easy to puncture the interior walls of the freezer. When the ice is gone, look for the little drain hole and clear any stray food away from it.

3. Pour some hot water into a measuring cup and dribble it into the freezer's drain hole. This will help melt any remaining ice in the tube.

4. Remove the panel on the bottom front of your refrigerator, find the drain pan, and empty it if necessary.

5. Reassemble the freezer walls, return your frozen food to its rightful place, and plug the freezer cord back in.

Drinks taste funny? Fix it fast! Pop quiz for owners of refrigerators that have automatic ice cube makers and water dispensers: When is the last time you changed the water filter in your fridge? Now, because

No Juice for the Fridge?

The circuit breaker governing your refrigerator trips off. You check all the electrical devices on that circuit, find nothing to be concerned about, and reset the breaker. And the circuit snaps off again a few minutes later. What kind of gremlin is at play here? Oddly enough, it all depends on the age of your refrigerator, says Dave Donovan an electrician who writes about home repair. If your refrigerator is five or six years old, its compressor is probably going bad and that is causing a spike in voltage. Get your appliance repairperson involved. If your refrigerator is only a year or so old a compressor problem is unlikely, so recheck the other devices that are plugged into the same circuit. If you don't uncover the culprit, have an electrician check the circuit.

One more thing you will want to know about refrigerators and electrical circuits, Donovan says: Newer homes typically have a circuit dedicated solely to the refrigerator and the microwave oven. In older homes, your refrigerator may even be sharing a circuit with an adjacent room—your living room, for instance. In that case, if you're scouting around for misbehaving electrical devices you will have to broaden your search a bit. You did thoroughly map out your circuit panel when you read chapter 4, didn't you?

I am psychic, I am going to tell you something about yourself. All of you who answered "What water filter?" have noticed that the water and ice provided by your refrigerator tastes funky. That's because modern refrigerators that have water hooked up to them include a water filter concealed somewhere in the appliance's cabinet. That filter needs to be changed every three to six months, says Scott M. Brown of New London, New Hampshire, who does business as "Samurai Appliance Repairman." This is more than a nicety. Once the filter gets clogged with impurities, the water flow slows down, and bacteria can breed in the cartridge. This fouls the taste of the water—and could even make you sick, Brown says.

APPLIANCES: WHEN THE "HOUSEHOLD HELP" GO ON STRIKE

So if you've been ignoring your refrigerator's water filter, stop by your appliance store, pick up a set of replacement filters, and establish a reminder system for yourself. On most units, you can find the water filter either behind the bottom grill or near the top of the interior fridge compartment.

Spray the ice cube tray. If your icemaker keeps jamming up, it could be because the cube-making tray clings to the ice. Take the tray out, spritz it with cooking oil, and use a paper towel to wipe the oil into a thin layer. Then reinstall your newly nonclingy tray.

Whipping Up Solutions for Stoves and Ovens

After the refrigerator, your stove is stop number two along the food chain. Let's make sure everything goes smoothly all the way to the dinner plate. A lot of people are surprised by how easy the most common stove repair jobs are.

Pop in a new burner coil. Has one of the coil-type burners gone permanently cold on the top of your electric stove? We'll get you cooking in no time, says electrician-writer Dave Donovan. First, make sure the stove is off and cold, and turn off the appliance's circuit at your home's electrical panel. Below the surface of the prob-

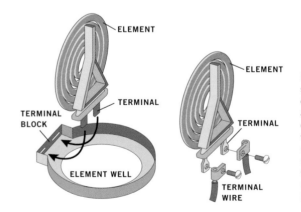

ELEMENT

ELEMENT

TERMINAL

TERMINAL
BLOCK

TERMINAL

ELEMENT WELL

TERMINAL
WIRE

In newer electric stoves, a burner coil can lift up and slide freely out of its electrical connection (left). In older stoves, the electrical connection may be secured by screws (right).

Your Oven's Ups and Downs

You probably thought that when you turn on your oven and set the controls for 400 degrees Fahrenheit (204.5°C), the appliance obediently warms itself to that temperature and stays there. Not so, says "Samurai Appliance Repairman" Scott M. Brown. And this may account for some mysterious behavior of your oven—say, when some delicate cookies get overbaked.

The temperature that you order up on your oven's controls will actually be the *average* baking temperature, not the literal, continuous baking temperature. When an oven warms up, many models will overshoot the target by as much as eighty degrees (27°C). Then it will cool down and undershoot the target by the same amount before it starts warming up again. This seesaw heating may be fine for a dish that bakes for hours, but could account for those cookies that got too brown around the edges.

Buying an oven thermometer isn't going to help you much in achieving more precise baking, by the way. Such thermometers don't react to temperature changes very quickly and essentially are giving you an average reading as well. If you're a finicky chef, you may just have to invest in one of the high-priced ovens. The high-end ovens also heat in seesaw fashion, but their deviation from the target temperature tends to be narrower, giving you more precision.

lematic burner, you will see where the two ends of the coil disappear through a hole in the side of the drip pan to make the electrical connection that heats the burner. When you pull the burner up and away from that electrical connection, two terminals will come away with the burner. (On older stoves, you may need to loosen a couple of screws to release the burner terminals from the electrical wires.) Take the burner with you to a home improvement store or hardware store, buy a replacement burner in the same size and style, and slide it into place when you get home. Restore the stove's power and test the new burner. If the burner still doesn't work, the stove has a more

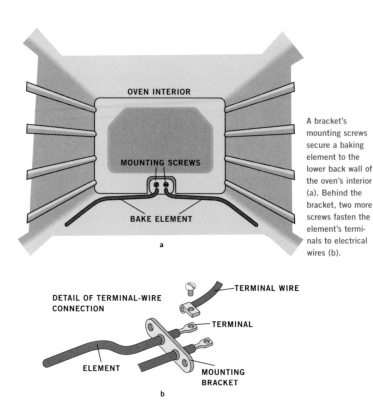

A bracket's mounting screws secure a baking element to the lower back wall of the oven's interior (a). Behind the bracket, two more screws fasten the element's terminals to electrical wires (b).

serious problem that's beyond your control—probably a broken switch—which means a call to your appliance repairperson.

Oven baking element: Big and easy. An electric oven's baking element may be one of the more imposing features of your kitchen (you know—it's that big, scary black hoop near the bottom of the oven that glows red when you turn it on). But changing a broken heating element isn't a lot more complicated than changing a light bulb.

1. Make sure the entire stove is cold, and shut off its circuit at your home's electrical panel. Pull the racks out of the oven so you have working room, and then find the spot where the broken element is

Reset Your Lazy Microwave

You press START on your microwave oven, it obediently hums and whirs, but
when the "cooking" is done the food inside is as cold as ever. Time to haul
your microwave to the curb and buy a new one? Not so fast, says Dave
Donovan of Atco, New Jersey, an electrician who writes for Doityourself.com.
Microwave ovens have a thermostatlike device that can trip occasionally. When
that happens, the appliance is capable of making all its usual noises, but the
cooking action is disabled. Here's the fix that will save you a repair bill or a
whopping replacement fee: Pull the microwave oven's electrical cord out of the
outlet, wait for thirty to sixty seconds, and then plug it back in. In the absence
of a live electrical source, the machine will reset and behave itself.

secured to the back wall of the appliance. Use a screwdriver to
loosen the screws on the mounting bracket there, and pull the element a few inches (several cm) toward you.

2. You will find two electrical wires secured to the element by screws.
Before you loosen those screws as well, make sure the wires won't
fall back through the hole in the back of the oven and out of your
reach. Otherwise, you'll have an awkward time fishing them back out
with a piece of coat hanger. (So clip clothespins to each wire. Or use
a couple of those clips you seal potato chip bags with. Or use a strip
of electrical tape to wrap around each wire to form a "flag" that's too
big to fall through the hole.) Now loosen the screws that secure the
element to the wires.

3. Take the element with you to your home store or hardware store so
you can be sure you're buying a replacement in the right size. Pay
particular attention to the spacing of the terminals on the element
so you're sure they will fit through the back of the oven.

4. Back home, slip the new element's terminals through the two holes
in the mounting bracket, and screw the terminals to the wires. Then
remove from the oven the clips or tape that you used to keep those

wires from falling through the hole in the back (you don't want a smoldering surprise when you turn the oven on). Tighten the screws that secure the mounting bracket.

5. Restore power to your oven and turn it on for a test run. If your oven still won't heat up, the next-most-likely culprit is the oven's control mechanism—which means a call to your appliance repairperson.

The Cleanup Crew: Dishwashers and Disposals

And now for the kitchen cleanup department—your dishwasher and garbage disposal. These two appliances are more than neighbors in your kitchen. In most kitchen arrangements, they're physically connected. Usually that works out well—but not always, as we shall see.

Empty your dishwasher's "swimming pool." Is your dishwasher retaining water? That is, do you find a little pool in the bottom of the cabinet when the machine has finished its cleaning cycle? What could be wrong: A broken pump? A fouled-up timer? Settle down, says repairman Scott M. Brown, proprietor of Fixitnow.com. Most likely, the problem does not lie inside your dishwasher at all, but fourteen inches (35.5cm) away from the appliance—yup, right next door, under your kitchen sink. You see, most dishwashers are not set up to transfer their wastewater directly into a drainpipe. They pour their wastewater into the garbage disposal hanging under your kitchen sink, and then the water flows out the disposal's drain instead. When all goes well, this is a simpler plumbing configuration than having separate drainpipes for each appliance. Fortunately, when dishwasher and disposal aren't playing well together, the solution is simple as well.

Open the cabinet that's below your kitchen sink and find the flexible plastic tube that leads from your dishwasher to some spot on the side of your garbage disposal. With both appliances securely off (that is, turned off at both the electrical panel and the control switch), remove the clamp that holds the hose to the disposal. Right inside the little entry hole on the disposal, you probably will find a buildup of

Clamp Down on Inferior Dishwasher Connections

If a drainage hose has ever slid loose from your dishwasher and caused a flood in your kitchen, you'll agree that a firm connection is fairly important. There are two such drainage hose connections, one under the dishwasher and the other at your garbage disposal in the cabinet under the kitchen sink. The clamps that secure these connections typically come in one of two styles: a spring-loaded clamp or a ring-style compression clamp with a screw on the side for tightening. The compression clamp provides a far more secure connection, says electrician and fix-it writer Dave Donovan. So if you have the spring-loaded style, switch to compression clamps at the first opportunity. If you don't see them stocked where you buy replacement drainage hoses at your home improvement store, pick up a set in the hardware section.

slimy flecks of food that were pushed there by your dishwasher and flung there by the disposal. Your dishwasher was trying to empty its water but couldn't get past this blockage. Use a dowel, a pen, or some other slender object to pull the gunk out. While you're at it, extract any buildup from the end of the dishwasher hose as well. Reattach the hose securely to the garbage disposal, and then run your dishwasher through a short cycle to make sure it's emptying OK now.

Change that wayward drainage hose. One of the most common dishwasher malfunctions is leakage—a scary little tide of water creeping out onto your kitchen floor. Fortunately, the most common cause of such leakage—a crack or loose connection in your drainage hose—is easy to fix, says fix-it writer Dave Donovan. But your first priority is to find out for sure where the leak is coming from. Grab a flashlight. Lie down on the floor in front of your dishwasher, pull the wide access panel off the bottom of the machine, and shine the light around until you spot the drip. You'll see the plastic drainage hose, which carries off the wastewater—usually snaking into the cabinet under the kitchen sink next door. There, it connects to your

APPLIANCES: WHEN THE "HOUSEHOLD HELP" GO ON STRIKE

garbage disposal. If water is dripping from some middle part of the hose, then it's cracked and needs to be replaced. If the water is dripping from the spot where it connects to the dishwasher, you may get away with resecuring that connection if the opening of the drainage hose is in good shape. Here are the steps you need to follow:

1. Turn off the dishwasher, then go to your electrical panel and kill its electrical circuit. Use a sponge mop and old towels to sop up any water on the floor.

2. Disconnect the drainage hose from your dishwasher (it's probably held in place by a spring-loaded clamp or a ringlike compression clamp with a screw on the side for tightening). If the hose is cracked, disconnect it from your garbage disposal, too, and pull it out. If the hose is in perfect condition and its connection to the dishwasher was merely loose, push it firmly back into place and reset the clamp. (And "advance token," as they say in Monopoly, to step 5.)

3. If you have to replace the drainage hose, take it with you to the hardware store or home improvement store. Dishwasher drainage hoses are fairly standardized, but you want to be sure you get a good match. If taking the hose with you isn't practical, at the very least measure it so you will know you're getting the right length.

4. Back home, slide the new drainage hose into place and securely clamp the connections to the dishwasher and the disposal.

5. Turn the dishwasher's electrical circuit back on. Start up your dishwasher to run it through a test cycle. Lie down with your flashlight in hand to watch under the appliance for any more leakage. If no drips appear, then replace the access panel, stand up, and do your victory dance.

Cap off broken dish rack tines. When the tines on your dishwasher rack snap, the heat and moisture they endure every day puts the exposed metal on a fast track to corrosion. Not only will your dishwasher suddenly look rather down-and-out, but those broken tines can scratch your dishes and transfer rust stains to them as well. The

Quit Feeding Your Dishwasher

Ignore what salespeople and advertisements imply about how a dishwasher can cope with food scraps. Even the fanciest dishwasher will never win a food-grinding competition with a garbage disposal. To help your dishwasher drain properly, scrape dishes completely and give them a quick rinse under the kitchen faucet before sliding them into the dishwasher. Otherwise, food particles eventually will clog up the appliance's drainage system and you'll start to see water left behind in the bottom of the dishwasher at the end of a cleaning cycle. If this happens, slide the bottom dish rack out so you can reach the bottom of the dishwasher. The drain is usually toward the back on the right side. Slide your hand all around the area and pull out any food scraps and other gunk you find. If the problem persists, see "Empty Your Dishwasher's 'Swimming Pool'" on page 158.

millionaire's solution to the problem is to order an entire new rack for the appliance (at a cost approaching the typical car payment). In an old dishwasher, that's a dubious investment. The sane approach: Pick up an inexpensive dishwasher rack repair kit at your home improvement store, hardware store, or over the Internet, says Mike Kozlowski of Hoffman Estates, Illinois, director of product quality and support for Sears Home Services. Such kits typically include vinyl caps that you can slide over the shaft of a broken tine and a small bottle of brush-on liquid vinyl. Make sure you're getting one that's a good color match for your dishwasher rack and that you're getting enough slide-on caps to cover all your rusty tines. One note of caution, says Kozlowski: When a tine breaks in your dishwasher, make sure you find the separated piece and toss it out right away. Otherwise, that bit of metal could get sucked into your dishwasher's pump and jam it, requiring a costly repair call.

Get your disposal out of a jam. You flip on the switch for your garbage disposal and all you hear is a humming sound—clearly the broccoli trimmings down in the darkness are not being ground up at all. Or perhaps you're getting no sound whatsoever out of the appliance—it just seems to be dead. Repairman Scott M. Brown says the cure is so simple that he now handles the job over the telephone when a flustered customer calls.

The problem is that something not-grind-uppable fell into your disposal—most likely a penny, a screw, a toy car, the base of a small candle, or a similar object. The grinding blades jammed on the object. Eventually, the disposal's overload switch activated, killing power to the appliance. All you need to do is *safely* extract the offending hard object and reset the disposal. Here's how:

1. Kill all power to the appliance. Turn the disposal's switch to OFF. Then go to your circuit breaker (or fuse) panel and turn off the circuit that governs the garbage disposal.

2. Open the cabinet below your kitchen sink. Get a flashlight and an Allen wrench. (That's one of those L-shaped bars that fits into a hexagonal socket. If you're a wise and organized sort, you have an Allen wrench stored under your sink—the one that came with your disposal.) The actual garbage disposal is that enormous metal casing hanging right under the sink's drain. Find the hexagonal socket on the bottom of the casing, fit the tip of your Allen wrench into the slot, and wiggle the wrench back and forth. This motion will shift the jammed blades inside the disposal and free them up. However, the object that jammed them will still be inside the disposal.

3. So stand up and shine your flashlight down in the maw of the disposal to see if you can spot the object that jammed your chopper blades. Reach in carefully, feel around if necessary among those broccoli bits, pull the hard object out, and decide which family member needs a lecture. If the object broke during its encounter with the grinding blades, make sure you have extracted all the parts.

4. Now look again at the bottom of the garbage disposal's casing. You will probably find a red button that has popped up—that's the overload switch that killed power to the disposal. Push the button back

in. Then go to your electrical panel and restore power to the disposal's circuit. Return to the kitchen and turn on the tap at the sink. Flip the disposal on and wave good-bye to the broccoli trimmings (with your hands at a safe distance, of course).

Grind away that rising tide in your sink. Is there a disgusting tide of murky water, studded with flecks of food, rising out of your kitchen sink's drain? Don't have a heart attack. This is probably another situation in which you simply need to impose good dishwasher–garbage disposal relations. Someone in your household probably shoved food scraps into your garbage disposal and forgot to grind it up. Then you turned on the dishwasher. As we learned above, dishwashers and garbage disposals usually share the same drain system. But when there's unground food blocking your disposal's drain, the wastewater being pumped over by the dishwasher has nowhere to go but up into your sink. (Yuk!)

If you see this happening, don't panic—just turn on your garbage disposal, which will grind up the food that's blocking the drain. That scary rising water will recede. Then turn on the faucet for a few seconds to wash away any food bits that settled onto the bottom of your sink. Wait until you get that free-spinning "all's clear" sound from your disposal before you shut it off. Next time, make sure there is no unground food sitting in your disposal when you start up your dishwasher.

Playing Spin Doctor for Washers and Dryers

There's something so ho-hum about clothes washers and dryers. They beg to be ignored. You can load them up, punch a few buttons and walk away. Ensconced in a remote part of the house, they chug away at their jobs with little supervision whatsoever. However, *completely* ignoring your washer and dryer is a big mistake. Let's look at a few fixes, upgrades, and wise habits that will keep your laundry room a stress-free zone. At least until you find that rip in your child's best pants.

Mystery leak? Check the drainage hose. If your clothes washer seems to have sprung a leak onto your laundry room floor, don't panic just yet. One of the likeliest sources of the leak is an inexpensive, easy-to-replace feature—and you don't even have to open up that hulking appliance cabinet to get to it. Grab a flashlight and lean over your washing machine to look at the back. You'll find the drainage hose hooked to the back of your washer and leading to a nearby drainpipe. Drainage hoses are made of hard plastic with accordion-style sections. Tiny cracks can develop in the valleys between those sections, meaning that water will trickle onto your floor every time the washer empties its wastewater. So run your flashlight over the drainage hose, and feel with your hand as well. If you detect moisture, replace the hose.

Turn off the clothes washer and unplug its electrical cord (no sense in mixing water and electricity, right?). Move the washer enough that you can get access to the hose hookup at the back. Then simply loosen the screws that secure the connection to the washer and pull the hose off the machine. Take the old hose to your hardware store or home improvement store to find the right match. Push the new hose's opening onto the washer's wastewater outlet, tighten the connection's screws, and feed the other end of the drainage hose into the drainpipe. While you have the washer pulled out, mop up any water remaining on the floor behind the appliance (you don't want to mistake that water for new leakage). Push the washer back into place, plug it in, and run a load of laundry to test your handiwork.

Get flood insurance for your washer. Think of your clothes washer as a ticking time bomb. Actually, a water bomb. Why? Because your washer is fed hot and cold water through two rubber hoses that are under perpetual pressure from your home's plumbing system. Think about it: Your garden hoses eventually wear out and burst. What will happen when your washer's hoses burst inside the house? If you're not around at the time to shut off the water, the resulting flood could do unspeakable damage to your home. That's why a few precautions are in order:

◇ **Replace your ordinary rubber supply hoses with the kind that are reinforced with braided stainless steel. Think of the extra cost as prudent flood insurance. Installing them is not much more complicated than hooking up a garden hose.**

◇ **Install a new set of supply hoses every year, just as you change the batteries in your smoke alarms. When you install new supply hoses, wrap a piece of masking tape around the upper end of each hose and write the date of installation on the tape so you will know at a glance how old your hoses are.**

◇ **If you check the spot where your washer's supply hoses connect with the plumbing, you will find two shutoff valves (one for hot water and one for cold). Train your family in this new habit: Shut off both valves when the washer is not in use. If that's not workable, at the very least shut off those valves when you go on vacation. (Just imagine how deep the water could get when a burst hose has been dumping water into your house for several days.)**

Give your failing dryer switch a boost. Has your clothes dryer left you high and . . . well, wet? You toss your damp clothes inside, close the door, press the start button—and nothing happens? You could have a simple switch problem. Open the door of the dryer and inspect the inset area that the door fits into. You will find a small button-style switch. When the switch is pushed in, the dryer thinks the door is closed and ready to operate. When the switch is out, the dryer shuts off because it thinks the door is open. The problem is that when such a switch starts to wear out, it may fail to complete the electrical circuit even when the dryer door is closed. So use scissors or a knife to cut out a square inch (6.5cm^2) of corrugated cardboard. Position the cardboard on the inside of the dryer door where it will press against the switch when the door closes. Tape it into place. Now when you close the door, the cardboard will give the switch that extra push it needs to close the circuit and get your clothes tumbling. Yes, you'll want to get a new switch installed—but you'll be able to get your shirts dry in the meantime.

Pull out the lint filter. Sadly, there really are people in the world operating clothes dryers who consider cleaning off the lint filter to be a finicky nonnecessity. Eventually a mattress-thick layer of lint covers the entire filter screen, and the dryer's airflow plummets to a trickle. The machine can't readily get rid of its water-saturated air, so it takes eons to dry clothing. This is an enormous waste of energy and time, so after every one or two laundry loads, pull out the filter and scrape off the accumulated lint into a trashcan. I know, I know—*you* happen to be a laundry room smarty-pants, and *you* are shaking your head at how obvious that advice is. But there's more you can do to increase your dryer's efficiency that you haven't thought of: Find a bottle brush with a long handle at your discount store or home improvement store, and hang it on a hook near your dryer. Every three months, while you're removing lint from the filter, also slide the brush down into the slot that the filter fits into and pull out any loose lint that has collected inside. Otherwise, this loose lint will continue to accumulate invisibly inside your dryer and create a drag on its efficiency.

Check the vent connection. The other oh-so-common blockage to a dryer's airflow involves lint, too. Getting to the source of the problem is only slightly less convenient, but when you accomplish this fix, you're going to feel like a hero. First, make sure your dryer is off and unplug it. Your dryer probably backs up to a wall in your laundry room. If so, pull the appliance about a foot (30.5cm) away from the wall (you need to be able to reach the spot where the dryer vent connects with the back of the dryer). Remove the vent from the back of the dryer. Put on a work glove, reach into the opening of the vent, and pull out any lint you can find. Now look into the opening on the back of the dryer where the vent hooks up, and pull out any lint you see in there, too. If you have harvested a sizable wad of lint in this procedure, then you have just restored much of your dryer's effi-

Costly Private Lessons

Are you a brand loyalist when it comes to major appliances? Perhaps there's one and only one brand of clothes washer that you ever buy—and you get the same model every time you buy a new one? Pay careful attention and don't assume you know everything about your new washer when the delivery truck drives off, says Mike Kozlowski of Hoffman Estates, Illinois, director of product quality and support for Sears Home Services. A scary number of service calls involve customers who *think* they know how their new appliances work—but new features that were added to the model baffle them, and they think their new appliances are defective. Kozlowski has had customers call in repair people because they didn't understand a new wash cycle, didn't realize that a special high-efficiency detergent was required—and were even flummoxed by the difference between a front-loading washer and a top-loading version.

Paying for a service call is an awfully expensive way to learn the basics of operating your new appliance. Kozlowski's advice: Assume your new model has a new feature or two and read the owner's manual and care guide before you start pushing buttons.

ciency. But you're not quite done, because there's one more crucial—even lifesaving—factor to consider . . .

Size up the vent itself. While you still have the dryer pulled away from the wall, study this hidden part of the vent that carries air away from your dryer. Is it crushed or bent? Often a homeowner will inadvertently smash the lower part of the vent when he slides the dryer into position against the wall, says Brown. A misshapen vent will reduce airflow because it's narrower, and the irregular surfaces inside the crumpled vent also will more likely snag lint—slowing the air even more. So bend the vent back into its proper shape before you reconnect it to your dryer and push the appliance (gently this time!) back into place.

When Hype Swirls Out of Control

The manufacturers who make stoves, clothes washers, and dryers really know how to push your buttons, if you'll pardon the expression. The fanciest appliances have sleekly designed electronic control boards with digital displays and pressure-point buttons ensconced under heavy plastic—all worthy of the International Space Station. Surely these high-end electronic displays are technological marvels compared to the frumpy old turn-and-twist knobs and individual push buttons that you still find on less expensive models.

Think again, says appliance repairman Scott M. Brown of New London, New Hampshire. The glitzy-looking electronic display boards are often cheaply made and are prone to failure, he says. What's more, they add easily $200 or more to the cost of the appliance—just because they're an extra "feature" that the salespeople can pitch to you. So the next time you buy a major appliance, resist fashion and glitz. Invest in function: For reliability, nothing beats the good old mechanical knobs and push buttons, Brown says.

Now, here's the lifesaving factor: Many people have flexible plastic or corrugated metal dryer vents, especially on older dryer installations. Not only are these styles particularly susceptible to crushing, but they're also a fire hazard. If you have one, replace it immediately with smooth, four-inch (10-cm) sheet metal venting. The details of this little job will vary depending on what path your vent takes to the outside, but it's not much more complicated than playing with a kid's Tinker Toy building set. Whether you do this job yourself or add it to your handyperson's to-do list, here are some basics you should know:

◇ You can buy segments of smooth (don't get a corrugated kind) four-inch-diameter (10-cm-diameter) sheet metal dryer vent from your home improvement store. You also will need some elbow joints for any turns that your vent takes. So before you buy materials, whip out your tape measure and map out the total length and shape of your vent.

◇ Joints between segments of the vent are done with a simple male-female connection, sliding the narrow end of one segment into the wider opening of the next one. Make sure the, um, "maleness" is always pointing in the direction of airflow so that little ridge between segments inside doesn't collect lint. Secure these connections with three-inch (7.5-cm) aluminum tape. Don't use screws (which also will snag lint inside the vent). Also, don't use duct tape (despite its name) or masking tape—both are fire hazards in this situation.

◇ Make sure that your vent really does lead your dryer's jungle-moist air outside the house. Dumping dryer air into an attic, a crawl space, or another interior room will create damaging moisture problems inside your home.

The Sad Reality of Throwaway Small Appliances

When your toaster broke in the olden days, you would drive it over to your friendly appliance repair shop, where a technician would replace its frizzled parts and return it to you in a day or two. Today, sadly, for much of the industrialized world just about any small appliance in your home has to be considered a disposable item. That is, don't even bother trying to get it repaired—even if you could manage such a thing, it wouldn't be worth the effort.

What other appliances fall into the disposable category? For starters, just about any electronic gizmo in your home that costs $100 or less: kitchen appliances, such as blenders, steamers, and coffeemakers; bathroom items, including electric toothbrushes, shavers, and hair dryers; plus a broad range of power tools such as drills, hedge trimmers, and sanders. Once a small appliance is out of warranty, even if you could eventually find a way to get it fixed (extremely rare), attempting to do so would cost you heavily in terms of aggravation (research, driving, phone-calling, packaging, shipping, lousy customer service, and months of waiting). Your time and your peace of mind are worth much more.

I know, you're a responsible citizen of the world, you hate waste, and you want to save the planet. But this book is all about preserving your sanity in a world fraught with problems, breakdowns, and quandaries. Part of the *How to Cheat at Home Repair* strategy is to make the easy fixes yourself and to hire out the hard ones to experts who will save you grief and hassle. Fixing a broken toaster falls into neither category. Even if in some fantasyland there were a way to repair it, getting it done would make no economic sense— the time and energy you would invest in the repair would far outweigh the value of the toaster.

On this score, you deserve some guilt relief. It's not your fault that small appliances around us are essentially disposable, so there's no need to wallow in guilt about throwing away the broken ones. You didn't design them, manufacture them, or establish the world's economic structure. You *will* feel better, however, if you do your part to rein in the culture of hyperconsumerism, and these strategies will help you preserve your sanity while dealing with throwaway appliances:

◇ Buy only the small appliances that are true workhorses in your life and have multiple uses or at least crucial uses. Avoid single-function appliances that will sit in the pantry or garage unused for months at a time.

◇ Quit giving small appliances as gifts unless the recipient specifically asks for that item. (How many unused gifts do *you* have stuffed in a closet?)

◇ Reward the people who make excellent small appliances. Before you buy one, research what the most reliable model is. Check consumer magazines, and ask your friends about their favorites. Consider the money that you pay for high-quality goods to be a vote for the good guys.

◇ If an appliance is still under warranty, don't consider it a throwaway. When you buy a small appliance, stuff the receipt, the owner's manual, and the inside packaging into the box and store the box on a shelf in your basement or garage. If the appliance has a warranty, mark the warranty's expiration date on the box. If there's no warranty, write the date that's one month in the future. Most stores will let you return an appliance with its original packaging after a week, and you might be able to shame a manufacturer into replacing a broken appliance within a month (but you'll have to ship it to the company). When a date you marked on one of these appliance boxes has expired, file the owner's manual and throw away the rest.

◇ Don't hold onto a broken small appliance out of some vague notion that it will be useful someday. If you're going to buy a new one in the identical model, there may be a couple of parts and accessories that are worth holding onto. Otherwise, throw the entire thing into the trash and don't give it another thought. And, no, nobody will give you money for a broken appliance at a yard sale.

◇ When you decide that a small appliance is broken, make really, really sure that it's broken. Stories abound of consumers who thought appliances were defunct when the owners were actually misusing the controls. Use your analytical skills (a kind of savvy you can only achieve once you've read *How to Cheat at Home Repair*) and be sure to read the appliance's manual—sure, it sounds pollyanna-ish, but you might just find some valuable information in there. The "I never read manuals" folks are throwing money away.

IF YOU'RE LIKE the average homeowner, you read this chapter and now have a checklist of quick and easy projects that will increase the efficiency of your appliances and head off repairs. You also know exactly what to do when the most common malfunctions occur. I hope that by now you view your appliances in a different light—less like mysterious hulks that behave erratically sometimes, and more like helpful coworkers who need some tender loving care on occasion.

Basements and Attics: The Neglected Nooks and Crannies

IT'S HARD TO HAVE A HEALTHY HOME WITHOUT A HEALTHY BASEMENT AND ATTIC. WHEN THE TOP AND BOTTOM FLOORS OF A HOUSE ARE NEGLECTED, THERE'S A CASCADE EFFECT THAT WILL LEAD TO DAMAGE IN OTHER PARTS OF THE BUILDING AS WELL. IN THE CHEAT-AT-HOME-REPAIR TRADITION, WE'RE GOING TO IDENTIFY INCREDIBLY EASY FIXES THAT WILL HAVE A MAJOR IMPACT ON THE WELL-BEING OF YOUR HOME, REVEAL SOME WOEFULLY COMMON MISTAKES AND MISCONCEPTIONS, LOWER YOUR UTILITY BILLS, AND ADD A FEW CRUCIAL ITEMS TO YOUR HANDYPERSON'S TO-DO LIST THAT WILL KEEP YOUR HOME IN TIP-TOP SHAPE, SO TO SPEAK.

A Sea in Your Basement?
A Whole Raft of Solutions

The most wrenching repair issue in the basement has to be persistent leaks. So we're going to wade right into the subject fearlessly. First, let's establish whether you even have the credentials to say, "My basement leaks." If every three years you find a six-inch-wide (15-cm-wide) puddle in your crawl space, then I am sorry to say that you have no standing in the leaky basement community. However, if once a year you have to mop up about three gallons (11.5l) of water in your crawl space, you have just barely made it into the club. Nevertheless, the stalwarts of the leaky basement community look down their noses at you because whenever it rains hard for several hours in a row, they can float rafts in *their* basements. For them, every wet basement episode is a nightmare of lugging possessions to high ground, squeezing sponge mops, hauling buckets, and blotting with towels—a backbreaking process that goes nonstop for hours on end.

I'm guessing that it's not really a club you aspire to. So the next time "the surf is up" in your basement, let's try a few tricks that just might get your membership revoked. You can save yourself an enormous amount of miserable labor just by instituting a couple of simple procedures during a hard rain. There are more powerful remedies, too, if you're willing to invest in a few gizmos and modifications to make this nightmare go away.

Don't wait to be surprised. If you have a leak-prone basement, a hard rain that has been falling for hours should throw you into red-alert mode. At least once an hour, make two simple checks:

◇ **Outdoors, are the gutters still moving the rainwater away from the house efficiently, or are they overwhelmed and spilling water against the foundation? True, you might have to throw on a slicker and actually walk around in the rain in order to inspect all your downspouts.**

However, sixty seconds of squishing around the yard is far preferable to hours of sopping up water in the basement if you are caught off-guard. If you find a gutter that's gushing water against your foundation, fix it then and there. If you can safely manage it, yes, haul out the extension ladder and pull any clogging debris out of the offending gutter. At the very least, spread out a tarp on the ground under the splash zone (secure the corners with bricks or rocks) so that the water drains away from the house. It also will help if you can extend the reach of the bottom of your downspouts by slipping segments of PVC pipe or plastic corrugated drainage pipe over the downspouts' openings.

◇ In the basement, is there any trace of water pooling in the spots where leaks usually occur? If you do find a new puddle, mop it up right away and assess how quickly it replenishes itself. That will give you an idea of how serious the current leak is and what kind of equipment you're going to need to prevent the puddle from growing into a basement-wide sheet of water. After all, tending to a small puddle is much easier than trying to control an enormous one that's already soaking some of your possessions.

Now, you're going to hate me for this, but I propose that when you go to bed during a heavy rain, you should set the alarm for a couple of middle-of-the-night checks as well. A little sleep loss is much preferable to waking up in the morning to a pond in your basement.

Work with a partner. As discussed above, when you discover a leak in your basement there are two urgent issues: outside, fixing the source of the water; inside, keeping ahead of the water that's coming into the house. Unless you have perfected instant cloning, you will need a partner to handle one of the two venues. Enlist a family member if possible, or plead with a neighbor to help you out, even if it's only for twenty minutes. If there's absolutely no help available, first go outside and redirect water away from the house and for the moment forget about the growing puddle inside. There's

BASEMENTS AND ATTICS: THE NEGLECTED NOOKS AND CRANNIES

no sense in trying to mop up a free-flowing river in your basement—you'll never catch up. You have to stop or slow the source of the water first.

Keep your cleanup gear nearby. Permanently store in your basement the very best leak-fighting equipment you have. When you're surprised by a leak, you don't want to have to run all over the house—or out to the shed—to find these items. Now, some leak cleanup tools and techniques are better than others. Here are notes on various approaches, starting with the most primitive and labor-intensive, and progressing to the cheating-est strategy there is. In all cases, you will want easy access to a drain in the basement—a utility sink works well—so make sure there are no obstructions barring your access. And remember that you have to be extremely careful when you are working with any electrical device near water.

◇ **Mops, buckets, and old towels.** This is how newcomers to the leak-fighting world start out. The main disadvantage is capacity: These tools will not sop up enough water fast enough to stay ahead of a major leak. If you find yourself squeezing out towels frequently, use rubber gloves. If you do this task barehanded, your fingers will quickly soften from the moisture and the abrasion from the towel fabric will form blisters on your fingertips.

◇ **Wet vacuum.** Now you're talking! A shop vacuum that's designed to handle wet cleanups will make your basement leak battle go much more smoothly. Available at home improvement stores, many wet vacs will hold several gallons (9–12l) of water, making it easier to stay ahead of an aggressive leak. But don't forget how heavy the machine will get when it's full. If you have to empty its tank by lifting it and pouring the water into a sink, do so frequently. Before you start vacuuming up water, open your wet vac and see whether it has been used for dry vacuuming in recent history. If dirt and debris are inside, empty it into a trashcan first. Remove the air filter, too—there's no sense in getting it soaked.

Put Basement Wallboard on Stilts

A lot of the building materials used in your basement will recover nicely from a minor flood—but wallboard is not one of them. Once it has gotten soaked, you will have to replace it. So if you're finishing a basement that has a history of leaks and minor flooding, follow the example of the folks who build beach houses on stilts: Position the delicate materials above the tide and out of harm's way. Have a wide baseboard installed along the floor of your basement, with the wallboard sitting on top of it. This will keep your vulnerable wallboard several inches (7–10cm) above that pool of water spreading across the floor.

◇ **Submersible pump.** Ah, this device comes with the official *How to Cheat at Home Repair* seal of approval. Also available at home improvement stores, this small electrical pump will stand upright on your flooded floor, draw up water from around its base, and push the water through a garden hose into a drain. Store it in your basement along with any accessories you might need, such as an extension cord and a hose. You don't want to have to search around for such items in the midst of a watery panic.

Give your basement some "deodorant." Once the flow of water into your basement has stopped and the mess has been cleaned up, mop over the floor again with a disinfectant. Also, run a dehumidifier in the basement for several days to wring even more water out of the room. These measures will inhibit the development of mold and musty odors.

Seal your cinderblock. If a lot of groundwater collects against your foundation, you might find little pinprick leaks coming through the cinderblock wall in your basement. A basement wall sealer—basically a thick waterproofing paint—will at least slow down this source of moisture in your basement. You can apply the sealer with a paintbrush, but you'll be much happier with yourself if you think to cheat by using a paint roller. Layer the sealer on thickly, and watch closely to make sure none of the little pores in the cinderblock are left open. Two or three coats will provide a better seal than a single application. If you have access to the spot where the wall meets the concrete floor (if there's no flooring or baseboard in the way) add sealer to the corner and a couple of inches of floor as well. Don't kid yourself into thinking that interior wall sealer will totally solve your basement's moisture problem. If there's continual water buildup outside the foundation, the sealer will slow seepage through the cinderblock—but "nature will find a way," as they say. Ultimately, the more powerful fix lies outside: Getting water away from your foundation.

Re-grade the yard. After several miserable basement-leak episodes, you're going to be ready to throw some money at a permanent cure. If you're still getting persistent leaks in your basement even though your rain gutters are in good repair and not clogged up, the problem may lie in the slope of your yard. A properly graded yard quickly directs rainwater away from your home's foundation and off the property. If you get snowy weather, the slope of your yard also is important when that white stuff begins to melt. You can tell a lot about how well water flows away from your house just by inspecting the slope of the ground on all sides of your foundation. If you have any doubts, however, spread a tarp on various parts of the yard. Each time you lay the tarp down, pour a cup of water onto it and see which direction the water flows in. Do the same with your patio—if you discover that the patio tilts toward the house, have it rebuilt. No kidding—it's nothing but an enormous funnel pouring water against your foundation.

Re-grading your yard is not the kind of thing to attempt with a shovel and a wheelbarrow. Invite a few professional landscapers to assess your yard and bid on the job. Yes, the work will involve tearing up some of your lawn and possibly installing below-ground drainage pipes. But which would you rather do—sow some grass seed, or spend the rest of your life splashing around in the basement?

Drain it and pump it. Another solution to a persistent basement flooding problem: installing a French drain and, working in tandem with it, a sump pump. This approach also requires an investment and is best left to a contractor. It will involve jackhammering out a foot-wide (30.5-cm-wide) swath of concrete around the perimeter of your basement floor, installing a drain system in the trench, and covering it again with new concrete. This drain channels water to the sump pump, which is set into a pit in the floor of the basement. When rising water trips the pump's switch, it pushes the water outside, away from the house.

Get Peak Performance Out of Your Attic

You really don't want to have to think about your attic, do you? I mean, what's the use of having an attic—a place where you can stuff your holiday decorations out of the way and forget them for a year—if you really have to tend to the space as if it were a bona fide living space? Isn't *attic* defined as "spooky, dusty, funny-shaped, underfinished space at the top of the house"? Well, actually there are a number of benefits to be derived from this space if you just put a little effort into controlling the temperature of your attic. (Honest, it won't be painful.) There are several other simple repair and maintenance duties up there that affect the well-being of the entire house, too. Also, we'll explore an innovative, easy way to create more and better walking surfaces in a floorless attic.

Help your attic breathe. Getting plenty of ventilation in your attic will help you eliminate damaging moisture, prolong the life of your roof, and save on utility bills. So review what ventilation your attic already has, and decide if you need to add more. Decades ago, some of the folks building houses weren't aware of the importance of attic ventilation and provided woefully inadequate airflow. Supplementing your attic's ventilation is an easy job for a handyperson or roofer. Here are things you will want to know about the typical forms of attic ventilation.

- ◇ **Gable vents.** These are the louvered vents that you will find on the two side walls of a house, just under the peak of the roof. In many older homes, there is no other attic ventilation, and that is not at all adequate.

- ◇ **Soffit vents.** These are little vents on the underside of eaves, where a roof extends beyond the edge of a house's outer wall. If you have soffit vents, go into your attic and inspect the interior side of each one. Sometimes a homeowner will unwittingly cover up soffit vents with stored possessions or poorly placed insulation. Removing such obstructions will go a long way toward improving airflow in your attic.

- ◇ **Ridge vent.** This device is a great "team player" in ventilating your attic. It runs along the peak of the roof, letting the hottest (and therefore rising) air escape while cooler air enters the attic through other vents. From the outside of your house, a ridge vent looks like a row of raised shingles stretched along the entire peak of the roof.

- ◇ **Roof vents.** These are hooded plastic or metal vents that can be spaced evenly across the roof. The vent's cover deflects precipitation, and metal sheathing (flashing) works with the roof shingles to keep water flowing toward the gutters.

Tailor attic insulation according to the room's use. If you live in a wintry climate, make sure your attic has insulation that's appropriate for the way you use it. If it's not a living space in your household, just fully insulating the floor is a good idea. In the winter, with good ventilation in place, the attic will then remain cold and there will be no heat escaping through the roof. (Escaping heat is not only a waste of energy, but it will melt snow on your roof and contribute to ice dams.) If you use your attic as a living space, make sure there's good insulation all around—ceiling, walls, and floor.

Leave a ventilation gap in the rafters. Some exuberant homeowners will firmly pack their attics' rafters with insulation, from the roof's plywood sheathing right up to the interior edge of the overhead joists. That's a big mistake, notes "Handyman Scott" Kropnick. Leave a two-inch (5-cm) gap between the roof and the insulation to pre-

Supercharge Your Attic Ventilation

When your attic gets baking hot in the summer, your roofing materials age much more rapidly. Possessions you store in the attic age rapidly, too—particularly objects such as photographs, books, clothing, and decorations. Having your handyperson install an attic fan is the answer. Not only will an attic fan prolong the life of your roof and stored items, but you also will save on heating and cooling costs. An attic fan is typically positioned in the ceiling of a central hallway on the top floor of the house. It pulls air from the living spaces, and pushes it into the attic and then through the attic's ventilation to the outside. On a summer evening, this will cool the attic and at the same time pull cool evening air from the outside into your home. Choose a fan with controls that include a thermostat, a timer, and a speed adjustment. When the attic fan is on, open some windows and doors to the outside to improve airflow.

Other styles of attic fans give a boost to attic ventilation without drawing air out of your living spaces. One type is mounted on the roof and draws air through a hole in the roof. A gable-wall fan draws air through one of the side walls of the attic. It may be mounted in a hole cut through the wall, it may just replace your gable vent, or it may be mounted behind the gable vent.

vent the buildup of damaging condensation. Home improvement stores sell plastic spacers called rafter vents that will help you keep this gap free and clear if you're installing attic insulation.

Screen out the birds, bees, and bats. Pests often find their way into an attic through the gable vents (the louvered vents on either side of a pitched roof). Inspect your gable vents from inside your attic. If there is no screened barrier across the vent, or if it's damaged, buy some fine screening at your home improvement store and staple-gun it all around the vent. It will keep critters out without impeding the airflow.

When the Sky Opens—and Your Roof Does, Too

If a storm-tossed tree branch punches a hole in your roof and the rain starts trickling in, a quick cover-up will keep your home dry until roofers can make permanent repairs. Clear any debris away from the damaged spot on the roof. Toss a sheet of heavy plastic over the hole in the roof—a tarp, a sheet of painter's drop cloth, or even a shower curtain liner will do. Along the top and sides of the plastic, fold the edges over for added strength. Staple-gun the folded edges to the roof shingles. The garden club will not award you bonus points for aesthetics, but you can assure them that you have a lovely and dry interior. *A safety note:* A wet roof—and wet plastic, for that matter—can be slippery. Only attempt a task like this if you are sure-footed and confident about working at heights. Check chapter 10 for more precautions about roof work.

Poke around for rotting wood. Let's check the condition of the wood components of your roof—the plywood sheathing that lies under the roofing felt and shingles, as well as the rafters that support it all. Go into your attic with a flashlight in one hand and a screwdriver in the other, and inspect all the overhead wood methodically. If you spot patches of darkened wood, that could mean moisture is seeping through—record the location so you can study the problem from the outside. Give the rafters and plywood the occasional firm poke with your screwdriver (both wet areas and dry) to test for softening—an indication of rotting wood that will need to be replaced.

Close up open junction boxes. Check all electrical junction boxes in your attic. It's possible that, years ago, someone working in your attic neglected to reassemble a junction box after completing a job. If any are uncovered, pick up the parts you need at your hardware store or home improvement store and install them. This is one of those little tasks that might look insignificant at first glance. However, an open junction box is actually a serious electrical hazard lurking in your home. Before you work on an open junction box, go to your electrical panel and turn the appropriate circuit off.

Shed light on leaks. During the daytime, stand in the middle of your attic and turn off all the lights. Look all around you for any glints of daylight poking through the roof where it shouldn't be—a sign that a potential leak has opened up somewhere. (Don't walk around in a dark attic unless you have full flooring and there's nothing to trip over.) If you do spot such a hole, turn on the lights and use a tape measure to record its location. This way, you'll be able to find the exact spot when you're out on the roof to patch up the hole—or at the very least you'll be able to direct a roofer there.

Tame a leak with a wick. If your roof springs a small leak, you can prevent damage to your home's interior by diverting the trickle of

---

T H E   M O S T   L I K E L Y   P R O B L E M 👁

A Mysterious Attic "Leak"

Some of the storage boxes you leave in your attic are showing curious signs of damage from water droplets. However, you can find no leak in the roof that would explain them. Well, the water is probably coming from inside the house, not outside. Take a flashlight up to the attic and look for spots where shingle nails come through the plywood sheathing of the roof. Are any of the nails corroded, with the wood around them darkened? When these nails get cold in the winter, they collect condensation from overly moist air in your attic. The condensation freezes on the nails and later melts, dripping onto your stored possessions. This is an indication that your attic needs better ventilation and that humidity from your living areas is seeping in as well. Talk to a roofer about installing more roof vents (those gable vents on the sides of the house aren't enough). Also, check that insulation in the attic floor includes proper vapor barriers at the bottom (plastic or foil sheathing on the insulation itself).

water with a cloth wick that will deposit the water into a bucket. First, do a little detective work in the attic to pinpoint the source of the leak. This will help you capture as much of the water as possible, and it will also help you—or a roofer—locate the spot that needs repair on the outside. This is more easily done when the leak is active (meaning it's raining), but you might be able to find the origin of the leak in fair weather as well. Look for signs of water dripping onto the floor of the attic (or water-damaged floor insulation if it's exposed). Overhead, inspect the rafters and plywood sheathing for trickling water or moisture-darkened wood. Follow this trail to its highest point, and mark the spot for future reference.

Now make your wick. Cut a strip of absorbent cloth (old towel or diaper, for instance) about an inch (2.5cm) wide and a few feet (61–91cm) long. The length will depend on the position of the leak and where you want to place the bucket to catch the water. Staple-gun or tack one end of your wick to the source of the leak—where you know it will absorb the water as soon as it enters the attic. Then staple-gun or tack the wick down the plywood or down a rafter, flush to the wood. Let the last several inches (8–12cm) of the wick hang down toward the floor, and position your bucket under this end. When it rains, check the bucket and empty it as needed. The wick will forestall damage to your home's interior, but it's obviously not a long-term solution to your leak. Get the hole fixed as soon as possible.

Squares: The Sneaky Way to Floor Your Attic

If you have an unfinished attic that you need to walk around in occasionally (if you use it for storage, for instance) the flooring up there often presents a quandary. Attics usually start out in life with nothing but floor joists, some insulation between the joists, plus the occasional wiring, junction box, pipe, or casing of a light fixture between the joists as well. Which means that if you venture into the attic, you get to play tightrope walker, placing your feet carefully on the joists. If you accidentally step between joists, you're going to poke your sneaker through the living room ceiling below.

Perhaps over the years someone managed to haul into your attic a couple of sheets of plywood or a few planks, giving you either a small walking surface or a spot for plopping several storage boxes. You might be tempted to board the entire attic floor over, but that approach could present its own problems: It would be tough getting all that wood into the attic in the first place, and the weight of that wood could put more of a load on your joists than they were intended for—particularly when you add the weight of stored items and people walking around. Also, if you place a bunch of boards over the joists, you're giving up access to the wires, fixtures, and the like that lie below. Spreading boards around *without* nailing them down isn't a great solution either—they can shift and wobble dangerously under your feet.

As you have come to expect, we're going to cheat our way out of this dilemma, giving ourselves secure attic flooring—without any of the disadvantages mentioned above. As often happens in the cheatin' world, a relatively new innovation is going to help us out. "Modular" attic flooring is sturdy-but-lightweight plastic flooring that comes in sixteen- or twenty-four-inch (40- or 61-cm) squares. These panels have interlocking edges and you secure them to the joists in your attic with a few screws. One variety is a solid panel, and another variety features a see-through grid reminiscent of industrial catwalk flooring. You can place these floor panels in a zillion configurations—for instance, in a large rectangle, side by side across multiple joists, in a long row bridging just two joists, or in a stepping-stone pattern that leads to the parts of the attic you want access to. These panels also will work in the storage area over a garage.

Each panel is typically rated to support 250 pounds (113.5kg). On a per-square-foot basis, modular plastic flooring will cost you more than wood, but the convenience and flexibility these panels provide is worth the investment if you want to get more hassle-free use out of an unfinished attic. At this writing, modular flooring wasn't in wide distribution yet, although some home improvement stores and discount stores do carry it. To find a source, fire up your

A Breakthrough in Repair Work

"**H**andyman Scott" Kropnick had just finished a day's work in a nice home when he sent his young assistant up to the attic to retrieve a work light. The helper returned not by the attic steps but by crashing through the ceiling of the master bedroom. The young man had stepped between joists in the attic floor, where there was nothing to support his weight except wallboard. Needless to say, the job wasn't complete after all—considering the cleanup, wallboard replacement, and painting required to make things right. Not getting paid for the work stung a bit, too.

Lesson learned: Flooring in an attic is not at all reliable, so take care when you're walking around up there—particularly in low light. In an area where there is no flooring, remember how far apart your joists are (usually sixteen inches [40-cm]), and make sure you're always standing on them.

Internet browser and do a search for "attic flooring." Of course, make sure that the dimensions of any modular flooring you want to buy matches the spacing of your home's joists.

IT ALL COMES down to humans versus nature, doesn't it? When we dare to erect homes on open land rather than cower in caves, we're going to need well-managed attics and basements to withstand the assault of heat, cold, wind, wetness, and other natural forces. Now you have an edge over the average homeowner—a checklist of shortcuts, easy fixes, and common mistakes to watch out for. Suddenly your often-neglected basement and attic are no longer spooky and foreboding. Feels good, doesn't it? Another little toehold on sanity!

A Zillion Other Possessions Need Help, Too

LET'S SEE, IN EARLIER CHAPTERS WE DISCUSSED FURNI-
TURE, PLUMBING, ELECTRICITY, WALLS AND FLOORS, AND
MORE. YOU OWN A ZILLION OTHER ITEMS AROUND THE
HOUSE THAT NEED A QUICK REPAIR NOW AND THEN.
LUCKILY, I HAVE A BUNCH OF SNEAKY FIXES FOR THEM
THAT I'M ITCHING TO PASS ALONG!

CHAPTER 9

Make your counter's gouge disappear. An overenthusiastic chef has left a knife gouge in your laminate kitchen counter. Replacing the counter would be costly enough to require a home equity loan. But we're going to patch things up for mere pocket change. Go to your home improvement store or hardware store and ask for a laminate counter repair kit. Select the color that best matches your counter— you might have to mix more than one color to arrive at the right hue. Back home, clean out the gouge on your counter: Dribble rubbing alcohol onto a white cleaning rag, rub it into the scratch, and let it dry. Then squirt some of the plastic paste from your repair kit into the gouge on your counter, smooth the paste out with a putty knife, and wipe up the excess with a rag. Leave the patch alone for the drying time prescribed on the repair kit package—probably a day or so. And talk to that overzealous chef about using a cutting board next time.

Flip your cooking knives over. Your cooking knives will become dull more quickly when you store them the conventional way in a countertop stand. The problem is that their razor-sharp edges slide back and forth against the bottom of the stand's slot. Victoria Higgs, an inventor in Adelaide, Australia, has a simple fix for that: Store your knives in the stand with the cutting side up instead of down. You will find yourself sharpening knives much less frequently. Talk about gaining an edge!

Revive the sparkle in your drinking glasses. Have your drinking glasses taken on a milky look that no amount of scrubbing in the sink can cure? Don't toss them out just yet. You are probably seeing the buildup of mineral deposits from your water supply, and it's just about impervious to conventional cleaning techniques—whether you're doing it by hand or by dishwasher. But we cheaters are going to return the sparkle to your glassware with just a minute of effort per glass. Go to your supermarket or discount club and buy a large jug of distilled white vinegar (you'll be shocked by how inexpensive this is). Back home, put all your milky-looking glasses on a counter near the kitchen sink. Fill a large bowl or plastic bin with the white vinegar to a depth where it will cover a glass turned on its side. Also, keep a clean scrubber sponge and a clean kitchen towel handy. Now pull on some rubber gloves and do this to each glass, one by one: Submerge the glass in the vinegar and leave it for at least fifteen seconds. Remove the glass and rub it inside and out with the abrasive side of the sponge. Rinse the glass in the sink and dry it with the towel. If some of the mineral deposit remains on the glass, repeat the procedure and double the soaking time for the rest of your glasses.

Give squirrels the slip. To keep squirrels from scaling your bird feeder pole, give the pole a once-over with spray lubricant like WD-40, or use a cooking spray like Pam. You'll get a laugh watching the furry critters slip-sliding to the ground. And you'll be able to quit fiddling with baffles and other devices to discourage the squirrels from raiding your bird feeder.

Rub out sap spots on your car. Little pinpoint droplets of sap will cling to your car's finish through just about any washing process. Except for this trick: Park your car in the sunshine to let the sap soften. Spritz a small amount of spray lubricant onto a clean car-washing rag. Rub gently at the sap until it wipes free. Wipe again with a clean rag to remove the lubricant. Use the same procedure to remove squished bugs from your car's finish.

Free your sneakers of oily grime. If the soles of your sneakers are blotched with tar, oil, grease, or some other petroleum-based grime, go to your toolbox and pull out your can of spray lubricant (such as WD-40). Spray the soles with a thin layer of the lubricant, let it soak in for five minutes, and then wipe with an old rag.

Do your glasses have a screw loose? If the hinge screw on your eyeglasses keeps coming loose, causing the frame to come apart, here's an easy way to keep that screw in place long term: Tighten the screw using one of those teensy eyeglass screwdrivers available at the supermarket or discount store. Then brush a little clear nail polish on the top of the screw. Let the polish dry before you use the glasses again. If you lose the hinge screw altogether, here's a quick

A Cure for Unseamly Timing

Clothing hems and seams have no sense of propriety. They might decide to unravel or burst right at work, for instance. If this happens to you, grab an office stapler and head for the bathroom (you'll want privacy if you have to remove clothing for this repair). Lay the garment on a flat surface, and pull together the two strips of material that have separated. Then bind the material together with closely spaced staples. Do what you can to hide the more noticeable top bar of the staple—by making your repair on the inside of the garment, for instance. In the case of a fallen hem, staple from the inside out. When you get home and you're in a position to make a conventional needle-and-thread repair, carefully unbend the staples' prongs to remove them. The holes they leave in the fabric will be minimal.

fix that will get you by until you can buy a replacement: Tie a firm knot in a length of fishing line. On one side of the knot, snip the line directly beside the knot. On the other side of the line, cut one-half inch (13mm) from the knot. Slide the little piece of fishing line through the top of the screw hole, letting the knot settle on top of the hole. Light a match and touch it briefly to the fishing line above and below the screw hole to form a bead of melted fishing line. Let the fishing line cool, and prop those newly repaired glasses on your nose.

Lubricate your guitar strings. When you need to change the metal strings on a guitar, give the new strings a little insurance against breaking. Guitar strings typically come rolled into a circle. Lay these circles in the bottom of a bucket. Give them a coating of spray lubricant, turn them over, and spray them again. When you uncoil each string to install it on your guitar, wipe the string from top to bottom with a clean rag. Your strings will be protected from corrosion, and with less friction, they will be less likely to break as you install them.

Firm up your loose doorstop. The kind of doorstop that screws into a wooden baseboard may come loose after years of use. No, there's no need to drill a new hole and patch over the old one. Instead, just remove the doorstop from its hole, fill the hole with a crack filler that dries firmly (for instance, Durham's Rock Hard Water Putty), and immediately reinsert the doorstop. When the filler dries, the doorstop will be rigid once again. Use the same trick to firm up the grip of cabinet pulls, drawer pulls, and wood screws.

Fluff up a flattened stuffed animal. Sometimes a child's well-loved stuffed toy animal will flatten out after years of hugs. Spare yourself the trauma of trying to persuade a child that a *new* Mr. Polar Bear would be just as good. Go to a fabric store and buy a bag of polyester fiberfill. Carefully clip the threads of a seam on the stuffed animal. You will want to open up a few inches (7–10cm) of working room. If the toy animal is rather old, it may have been originally stuffed with toxic pellets. If that's the case, remove and dispose of the original stuffing and replace it completely with your new fiberfill. Make sure the fiberfill is evenly distributed inside the toy. Then stitch the seam closed again with a needle and thread. And then the best part: returning the rejuvenated toy to your child—you just might get a hug or two yourself.

Silence your rattling exhaust fan. If your bathroom exhaust fan rattles, you probably can silence the little machine with just a screwdriver. Turn the fan off. Set a step stool under the exhaust fan and remove its cover. (There may be a couple of screws to loosen, or the cover may be suspended on a spring-loaded mechanism.) Now look for the spot where the fan inside is secured to the enclosure, probably by two screws that poke through keyhole-shaped openings. Tighten both those screws to reduce the vibration of the housing. Replace the fan's cover, and turn the fan back on to test whether the noise has stopped. If not, then the side of the exhaust fan's housing may be vibrating, too. Remove the exhaust fan's cover again. With an electric drill, bore a hole through one side of the fan's housing and into the wooden joist next to it. Insert a screw into the hole and tighten it with a screwdriver. Replace the cover and test the fan again.

Redirect your drippy air-conditioner. A window air-conditioner will often drip water into the house. That's because of a common installation error, says "Handyman Scott" Kropnick of Blue Bell, Pennsylvania. Window air-conditioners are designed to tilt slightly toward the outside, so the condensation that the machine generates will drip off the far bottom edge and onto the ground. If the air-conditioner is secured by a window that slides down against it, adjusting the tilt is easy. If there's any hardware securing the window in place, remove it for the moment. (Such screws or brackets make sure the air-conditioner doesn't accidentally fall out the window.) Raise the window about a half-inch (13mm), and keep a hand on its top to keep it from rising farther. Slide your other hand under the interior edge of the air-conditioner and lift it a half-inch (13mm) to meet the window. Now visually check that the machine is tilting slightly toward the outside. If it is, reinstall the hardware that secures the window. If the air-conditioner needs even more tilt, repeat the procedure.

Winterproof your satellite dish. Does your satellite television reception deteriorate during snowy and icy months? That can happen when you rely on a small satellite dish that gets caked with snow and ice. Here's the easy fix: Once a month on a clear, dry day, give your satellite dish a quick spritz with a spray lubricant (WD-40, for example). Any snow that hits the dish will slide right off, and you'll never miss another football game on the tube due to fuzzy reception.

Give that balky disk a rubdown. If you have a CD or DVD that has started performing erratically, it's possible that dust or grime on the disk is interfering with the audio and/or video quality. To remove the dirt, dribble some rubbing alcohol onto a soft cloth. Hold the disk by the edges only and wipe gently with the moist cloth straight from the center of the disk to the outer edge. Do not use a side-to-

Sweet Solutions for a Leaky Canoe

The Boy Scout troop that I hang out with loves to canoe on a river that's sometimes rocky and shallow. Which means that the fiberglass hulls can take a beating and occasionally spring a leak. One year we discovered that one of our canoes was taking on water hopelessly fast while we still had a few miles to paddle before returning to shore. First, we stopped at a rocky bank and turned the leaky canoe over so its hull would dry in the sun. Having no official patching materials on hand, we began to scrounge among the canoeists. Finding several stretches of duct tape was easy (these were Scouts, after all), but we also needed something puttylike to mash into the crack in the bottom of the canoe. One good lad sacrificed his partly chewed bubble gum. We pressed it into the gash and then covered the newly filled crack with duct tape.

History, as we know, is prone to repeating itself. A year later we found ourselves on the same rocky bank repairing yet another leaky canoe. We had plenty of duct tape again, but this time there was no bubble gum to be found. However, one young man had in his lunch a packet of the sticky-chewy candy known as gummy bears. One of our repair crew lightly chewed the bears and "pressed them into service" on the cracked hull. Then as we had done a year earlier, we covered the patch with duct tape.

It dawned on me that this was the perfect opportunity to document the age-old question of what made the better emergency canoe patch—bubble gum or gummy candy. I made this test on identical canoes on the same stretch of river. (Okay, surely *somebody* has wondered.) Unfortunately, the age-old question remains unresolved—but for a very happy reason. Both patches held divinely to the end of the canoe trip, leaking not an ounce. So pack either one on your next canoe trip. Duct tape, too, of course.

A ZILLION OTHER POSSESSIONS NEED HELP, TOO

side or circular wiping motion. If you spot a scratch on your disk, copy it right away using a computer's CD/DVD burner. Your player might eventually decline to play the damaged disk.

Restore balance to your ceiling fan. Does your ceiling fan wobble? Your first order of business is to make sure its screws are firmly tightened. Of course, turn the fan off anytime you're working near it. Get a stepladder, and tighten all the screws you can find—particularly those that hold the blades in place, those that hold the fan housing to the rod that hangs from the ceiling, and those that hold the entire assembly to the ceiling. When you're done, climb down and test the fan. If it's still wobbling, your next option isn't much more difficult—balancing the blades through trial and error.

This time, take a marker, a small coin, and some cellophane tape up the ladder with you. Number each fan blade by writing on the top so you will be able to tell them apart later. Tape the small coin to the center (according to both width and length) of fan blade number one, and then test the fan. If the fan still wobbles the same amount, test the other blades in sequence until you find a blade that causes the fan to wobble less with the added weight. If the wobble has not stopped completely, experiment further either by adding more weight (taping another small coin beside the first one) or by moving the coin farther away from the hub of the fan or nearer to it. When you have found the weight and positioning that creates the least amount of wobble, experiment again with the other fan blades to reduce the wobble even more. Then just leave the coins taped in place—you've fixed the problem for mere pocket change!

Loosen up your fan's pull-chain. If the pull-chain switch on your ceiling fan frequently gets caught up inside the fan's housing, try this easy fix: Turn off the fan. Then squirt a tiny amount of spray lubricant into the hole where the pull-chain emerges. Pull the chain a few times to spread the lubricant around, and then turn the fan back on.

Home Exteriors

NO MATTER WHAT KIND OF CLIMATE YOU LIVE IN, COM-
PARED TO THE INTERIOR OF YOUR COMFY HOUSE, THE
OUTSIDE IS A BRUTAL ENVIRONMENT. WIND, PRECIPITA-
TION, TEMPERATURE EXTREMES, SUNLIGHT, FALLING
LEAVES AND BRANCHES, CRITTERS, AND OTHER DESTRUC-
TIVE FORCES HAMMER AWAY AT YOUR HOME'S EXTERIOR.
UNFORTUNATELY, MUCH OF THE CONSEQUENT DAMAGE
LETS THESE FORCES CREEP INSIDE YOUR HOUSE, TOO, IF
YOU DON'T PATCH THINGS UP PROMPTLY. SO IN THE *HOW
TO CHEAT AT HOME REPAIR* TRADITION, WE'RE GOING TO
TALK ABOUT QUICK, EASY, AND EVEN SNEAKY FIXES FOR
THE COMMON KINDS OF DAMAGE TO YOUR HOME'S EXTE-
RIOR FEATURES. AND AS YOU'VE COME TO EXPECT, WE'LL
ALSO TALK ABOUT SOME WIDELY PRACTICED REPAIR AND
MAINTENANCE TRADITIONS THAT ARE A BIG WASTE OF
YOUR TIME AND EFFORT.

CHAPTER 10

The High Road: Only for the Sure-Footed

Roof work is no time to test your physical abilities or balance. If the slope of your roof is too steep for you to walk on with sure footing, hand off all jobs up there to your handyperson or a roofer. Do the same if the roof in question is higher than one story, if the repair you want to make requires you to be near the edge of the roof, or if there's any other reason that you're not totally confident working on high.

Now, the very fact that you're reading this book tells me that you have an independent streak. So if you're determined to climb ladders and trounce around on rooftops, let's at least review some precautions about working up high. These aren't prissy rules you can ignore—any one of these pointers could save life and limb. Besides, I haven't yet written *How to Cheat at Hospital Stays.*

◇ Wear rubber-soled shoes that provide a good grip as you walk around.

◇ Stay away from wires on the roof. Most homes have a power line that anchors at roof level, and you could get a deadly shock.

◇ Stay off a roof that's wet, snowy, or icy—it's too slippery.

◇ If you're going to use an extension ladder for any work on your home, fully review the precautions that come with the ladder.

◇ Make sure your extension ladder leans against the house at a safe angle. For every four feet (122cm) that your ladder reaches up, the bottom of your ladder should be one foot (30.5cm) away from the wall.

◇ Firmly plant the feet of the ladder on level terrain. If the ladder's feet dig into the soil a little, that's good—but avoid soft and squishy ground.

◇ Don't carry stuff in your hands up and down a ladder. Use a tool belt, and load other items into a bucket that you can haul up by rope.

◇ Have an assistant steady your ladder while you're on it.

- ◇ **If you're using a ladder to get onto the roof, the ladder should extend three feet (91cm) above the roof's edge. Step around the top of the ladder to get onto the roof and off the roof again—don't climb over the top rung.**

- ◇ **Never stand on the top three rungs of an extension ladder.**

- ◇ **Only mount the roof from a horizontal edge, not the pitched (dormer) side of the house.**

- ◇ **When you move a ladder, always carry it parallel to the ground so you don't accidentally hit any overhead wires.**

Still determined to do some easy home repairs up, up, and away from terra firma? Here are simple cures for a roof's common maladies.

Keep your valleys sealed. Here's a quick check to make the next time you're up there. Wherever two sloping roofs meet, you should find a long stretch of flashing (a thin metal shield) that carries water away from the valley where the roofs join. In five seconds you can assess whether the flashing is still doing its job of keeping water out of your house. You'll see that your asphalt shingles overlap the flashing a little on each side. Those shingles should be bonded to the flashing by roofing adhesive to create a good seal. Wind or falling branches could break that bond—and sometimes a forgetful roofer just fails to apply the adhesive in the first place. Feel along the edges of the shingles on each side of the flashing to make sure they're firmly in place. If any are loose, buy some roofing adhesive in a caulking tube from your home store. To seal the shingles to the flashing, start at the lowest loose shingle on each side of the flashing and work your way up. Gently lift the edge of the loose shingle and lay a bead of roofing adhesive on the flashing a half-inch (13mm) under the edge of the shingle. Then press the shingle back into place. A second issue to check: Look for any punctures in the flashing (darn those falling branches), which you can fill in with gutter sealant, another caulking-tube product from your home store.

Spy on Your Roof

When damage happens to an obvious part of your house—say, to your porch, patio, deck, or siding—you will spot it immediately and fix the damage before it gets worse. Roofs don't get the same scrutiny. Wise homeowners avoid heights whenever possible, especially the kind with a pitched surface underfoot. However, the roof of your house can't be left to its own devices year after year without some kind of inspection. So here's a little trick to add to your MBO (Maintenance by Observation): Twice a year, take a pair of binoculars outside and inspect your entire roof from every side. Look for signs of wind damage, critter damage, and damage from falling branches. Look for misshapen or out-of-place shingles, moss and mildew, damaged siding, corrosion, gutters that are overflowing with debris, and any other changes in the condition of your roof. Some of these problems you might safely take care of yourself, and others may go onto your handyperson's to-do list. But if you ignore such problems for another year or two, it's a sure thing that you'll be dealing with them from *inside* your house as well as outside.

I know what you're thinking: Yes, you can do a fair amount of this "work" while lolling in your hammock on one side of the house and a chaise lounge on another.

Tune up your pipes. Those ventilation pipes that poke up through your roof are often the source of leaks in a home. Patching up a deteriorating seal is an easy job, says "Handyman Scott" Kropnick of Blue Bell, Pennsylvania. When you inspect the base of a vent pipe, you probably will find the pipe surrounded by a collar or flashing that's flush against the roof. Under that collar is a rubber seal, called a boot. This seal is supposed to keep precipitation from entering your house, but these boots deteriorate over the years and become a major source of unwanted moisture inside. If you find a seal that's cracked, crumbling, or has separated from the vent pipe, go to your home store or hardware store and pick up a container of roofer's

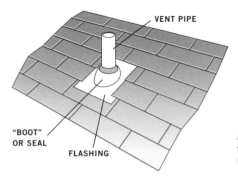

VENT PIPE

"BOOT" OR SEAL

FLASHING

A deteriorating rubber seal at the base of a roof's vent pipe is a common source of leaks.

patch (Kropnick prefers Black Jack flashing cement, available in cans or caulking tubes). Pull on a pair of rubber gloves (the roofer's patch is messy stuff). Leave the old boot in place, but pull away any old caulk or other debris around the seal. Then apply the blackjack to fill in any gaps left by the deteriorating boot. If you're using roofer's patch out of a can, apply it with a wooden paint stir, and when you're done slip it into a throwaway bag, along with your messy rubber gloves, to contain the mess.

Put a roof over your chimney. Stand in your yard and look at the top of your home's chimney. Is your chimney wearing a "hat"? That is, do you see a rectangular metal covering on it that has a solid top and mesh around the sides? Such devices are called chimney caps, and they provide a number of benefits. A chimney cap will keep birds, squirrels, and other critters out of your house. It will prevent moisture, leaves and other debris from entering, too. A chimney cap

Summertime, and the Fixin' Is Easy

A note about timing your roof repairs: Working with asphalt roof shingles—and just walking on them, for that matter—is better on warm days. Shingles bend more readily when they're warm and are less likely to break.

HOME EXTERIORS

reduces the chances of sparks wafting out when you have a fire in the fireplace, and prevents drafts from pulling chimney odors into your home.

Installing a chimney cap is easy—but first determine whether you can safely do the job yourself. If you're perfectly comfortable working on the roof, if the chimney is easy to get to, and if the chimney is well away from the edge of your roof, consider installing a chimney cap yourself. Otherwise, this one goes on your handyperson's to-do list, or you should call a chimney repair contractor.

Chimney caps come in various shapes and styles. If you're going to install one yourself, take a tape measure onto the roof and measure the size of the terra-cotta flue liner that emerges from the top of the chimney—your chimney cap will need to grab onto that flue liner, and you want to be sure that the one you buy is a good fit. Buy a chimney cap at your home improvement store. You might find them in a variety of metals, but stainless steel is best, says "Handyman Scott" Kropnick. The chimney cap will come with a tension band around the base. Follow the instructions for tightening the band around the upper edge of the flue. Don't overtighten—you don't want the terra-cotta to crack or chip.

Break up that darned dam on your roof. If you bask in a warm climate year-round, then you live in blissful ignorance of a homeowner nightmare called ice dams. They're a practical joke that nature plays in the winter. When snow accumulates on a pitched roof, warmth from the house starts to melt it and the resulting water flows down toward the lower edge, where a gutter is supposed to carry the water safely away from the house. However, many homes have a design feature called eaves, a short extension of the roof beyond the walls of the house—and also beyond the *warmth* of the house. This means that water trickling down the roof will freeze when it hits the last couple feet (61–91cm) of shingle. Ice builds up into a dam, shaped like a broad speed bump, along the edge of the roof. With no way to escape, any new meltwater seeps backwards under the shingles and finds its way into your house—perhaps flowing into the walls, perhaps dribbling down your windows, and perhaps dripping from the ceiling.

Now, there's a pricey solution to ice dams: Hire a roofer to install a warming device along the edge of your roof that will keep the water flowing into the gutter. The other path is to recognize ice dams as a chronic problem and to commit to physically removing snow from the edge of your roof every time the flakes start to build up. I know one guy who used to take a shovel onto his roof after every snowfall and push the white stuff over the edge. I don't recommend this approach because of the danger of falling. And also the danger of having your neighbors think you're a lunatic. You can do a reasonably good job clearing snow from the edge of your roof from the ground, however (if your house is two stories or less). Take a push broom or a garden rake and attach an extension pole to it with several firm wraps of duct tape. Reach the broom or rake head three feet (91cm) up the roof and pull the snow toward you. You also can buy specialized roof rakes for this purpose. Whichever tool you use, try not to scrape too firmly against your asphalt shingles; that will wear them out prematurely.

Rakes and brooms will do nothing for you if you already have an ice dam pushing a mini-river into your home. Here's an approach that requires no ladder work or sliding around on the roof. Find a few pairs of old panty hose and cut them into two-foot (61-cm) sections. Tie a firm knot in one end of each section, pour a pound or two (about 1kg) of calcium chloride (the sidewalk deicer you buy at the hardware store or home store) into the open end, and knot that second side closed, too. Depending on the severity of your ice dam, you may want to make several of these deicer bags. For each deicer bag you have created, cut a piece of thin rope eight to ten feet (2.4–3m) long and tie it to one end of the bag. Now you can toss these bags onto the ice dam and use the rope to retrieve them or position them strategically. The calcium chloride inside the panty hose will go to work melting the ice dam and allowing water to flow into the gutter where good water belongs. And speaking of the

The Sands of Time—In Your Gutter

When you're cleaning out your gutters, you find all the predictable items—leaves, sticks, and seedpods—but you also discover that there's an odd component lining the bottom of the gutter: a layer of gritty debris. Did a sandstorm blow through when you weren't paying attention? No, those granules have fallen off your asphalt shingles. If your gutters are catching a lot of this grit, the outer coating on your roof shingles is deteriorating. Your roof may not be springing leaks left and right just yet, but your shingles are reaching retirement age and it's time to start thinking about a reroofing job.

gutter, if it's also overwhelmed by ice, let at least one of your deicer bags settle right onto the gutter near the downspout to help restore proper flow. Remove or refill your deicer bags once the calcium chloride is depleted.

Make the leaves back off. If you have tall trees in your yard, keep their branches trimmed back well away from your roof. This alleviates your outdoor repair and maintenance duties in two significant ways. Leaves, twigs, and seedpods will be less likely to settle on your roof and eventually clog your rain gutters. Also, trimmed-back trees will allow more sunlight to hit your house. That will discourage the growth of mold and moss, which degrade your shingles.

Improvise a gutter-cleaning tool. Cleaning out your rain gutters isn't only about grabbing handfuls of leaves and flinging them to the ground. It also means dipping a hand into the grit and rotting muck that's been accumulating for months in the bottom of the trough. To make this job go a lot faster—and, frankly, to make it less disgusting—use a putty knife to scrape along the bottom of the gutter and lift the gunk out. Better yet, pull a narrow plastic bottle out of the recycling bin, cut the bottom off with a utility knife, and slide the bottle along the bottom of the gutter to collect the mucky debris.

Just throw the debris to the ground. Motor oil bottles are particularly well shaped for this.

Note: It's safer to clean out your gutters while standing on an extension ladder (one-story height only, please). Don't risk reaching into your gutters from the roof's edge.

The Low Road: Easy Fixes—Within Easy Reach

You might ignore the condition of a sidewalk or your front steps for years on end, but you won't get away with that when it comes to another outdoor surface: your wooden deck. Wood decks need to be sealed to protect them from weather and rot (the frequency of this appalling task depends on the type of sealer you use). You may need to stain the wood periodically, too, depending on your taste. When parts of your decking do rot, you have to pull up and replace the damaged wood. If you have kids in the house, or other folks who are prone to cavorting on the deck in bare feet, then you know the danger of picking up splinters from a wooden deck.

Well, part of the *How to Cheat at Home Repair* philosophy is to embrace technology when it offers us alternatives that handily remove repairs, maintenance, and other hassles from our to-do lists. An innovation called composite decking, made from a blend of plastic and wood particles, is one such technology. This stuff doesn't rot, requires no sealing or staining, isn't infused with toxic chemicals (like pressure-treated lumber), insects leave it alone, and it won't thrust shards of wood into your five-year-old's heel. What's more, the wood component in composite decking comes from recycled lumber that would otherwise be dumped into landfills—so you can doze on your deck and save the planet at the same time.

In 1990, researchers started experimenting with the crazy idea of blending ground-up wood and plastic, says Paul Bizzarri, vice president of innovation for manufacturer TimberTech in Wilmington, Ohio. The first application: making rot-resistant lobster traps. In the mid-1990s, startup companies began making decking from the stuff. By the end of the new millennium's first decade, about a quarter of the decks built in North America were made of composite decking, and the material was becoming increasingly popular in Europe, Australia, New Zealand, and other markets as well. Other applications for the material include fencing, house trim, window frames, doors, outdoor furniture, docks, and marina construction.

A deck built from composite tends to cost at least 20 percent more than the equivalent deck made from wood alone. The more costly varieties of composite decking are those that come closest to simulating the look and feel of real wood. And don't expect composite to have quite the structural strength of natural wood. Spans for composite deck railings, for instance, are limited to six- to eight-foot (1.8–2.4m) pieces, and the large supports under your composite deck are still going to be conventional treated wood. Here are some more points you will want to know if you jump into this innovation the next time you need to build a deck:

Attack stains immediately. Composite easily sloughs off the everyday dirt that finds its way onto a deck, but nevertheless act quickly to clean up staining spills such as ketchup, barbecue sauce, wine, and oil. Remember that there's a wood component to the decking, and that means it's still susceptible to stains. You can use standard deck cleaner (available at home improvement stores) on composite, in combination with a garden hose or a pressure washer, says Bizzarri, the TimberTech exec.

Ante up for "ultra" convenience. If you're going for your master's degree in avoiding repair and maintenance, there's an emerging decking product you'll want to consider: what the industry folks call "ultra-low-maintenance" decking. Since this stuff is pure plastic— yes, it contains no ground-up wood whatsoever—it differs from composite decking in look and feel. It resists stains, wear, and scratches. If you have to pay any attention to it at all, you can probably limit your efforts to a swoosh with a broom or a spritz with a garden hose. As often happens, you'll pay extra for the convenience, however—an "ultra-low" deck tends to cost 30 percent more than the equivalent structure made from conventional wood.

Replace rotten wood with composite. If you have a wooden deck with some persistent rotting problems in certain spots, composite decking may provide a solution, says Bizzarri. Let's say one area of your deck is moisture-prone, or it's in perpetual shade and fails to dry out enough to forestall rot. When you pull up the failing boards, take them to a lumber center, where you'll find rot-free composite in the traditional board sizes. You probably won't find an exact color match with your current wood decking; a "close enough" color will probably have to do. Using conventional wood is no better in that respect, however, since new wood stands out on a deck when surrounded by weathered wood anyway. When you patch up the deck with composite, at least, you know you won't have to make the same repair in a couple of years.

When deciding on decking, get the big picture. When you shop for composite decking, try to look at full-sized decks make from the variety you're thinking of buying. If a friend or neighbor has built a deck in a style of composite you particularly like, ask for the name of the product and who the supplier was. You also may find full-size examples of composite decking at builder showrooms and large home shows. If possible, examine a deck that has been exposed to the outdoors for a year or more, so you will have a good sense of how well the material weathers in your climate.

Driveways: Change One Word, Free Your Weekends

If you own a big wide stretch of asphalt to park your car on, maybe every three years you say, "I think I'll seal my driveway next weekend." It's a hideous, messy task that can easily stretch into a backbreaking two-full-day chore, depending on the size of the drive. You have to clean the asphalt meticulously, haul enormous buckets of sealer around, dump the gooey stuff onto the driveway, and spread it carefully with squeegee-like tools that are ruined after one use. All the while, you're breathing nasty fumes and splattering your shoes and clothing with indelible black splotches. Slamming your hand in a car door would be more fun.

Well, *How to Cheat at Home Repair* may save you a whole lot of misery on this score. While people who make and sell driveway sealer will tell you the stuff provides essential protection to the asphalt, skeptics say that such products are largely cosmetic—the biggest benefit is that they give your driveway a like-new look. Sealing the little cracks that appear in your asphalt is unarguably important, because water seeping through can cause erosion that undermines the asphalt. Also, ice will expand little cracks into big ones and eventually into potholes. But patching a few little cracks can be managed as a simple ten-minute project using crack-filler products you can pick up at your home improvement store. That leaves plenty of time for golf the same weekend.

If you love the look of a freshly sealed driveway, by all means follow your heart. You're in charge, after all. But I'm just suggesting a small change in phraseology: Every three years say to yourself, "I think I'll *paint* my driveway next weekend." We're talking about the same project, but this puts the emphasis on its cosmetic nature. When you think of it in this light, I'll bet you'll find a much more fun way to spend the weekend. And I'll bet this every-three-years chore stretches to every seven years. That's a lot of free weekends. You owe me, buddy.

Oil spill: When driveways dial 9-1-1. Sometimes one handyperson project begets another. That's what used to happen whenever Tom Scherphorn's son changed his automobile's oil in the driveway— there was often a little pool of spilled motor oil that was a project unto itself. As with much of the world, the solution lies in who you know. The Scherphorns are acquainted with a firefighter or two, so it's not hard to track down a source of the absorbent chemical that firemen use to clean up fuel and oil at accident scenes. Just sprinkle it on, let it sit for an hour, sweep it up, and throw it away. You may already have an alternative absorbent product right in your house: cat litter. Or you can drop by a janitorial supply store and buy a can

Deicer: Ready to Change Course, Old Salt?

If you're a traditionalist still using real salt to melt ice on your sidewalk or driveway, it's time to switch. Real salt—the stuff that reads SODIUM CHLORIDE on the package—will harm your lawn and other plants, will harm the soil, and will harm the environment elsewhere when it seeps into waterways. It will also hurt your pets' paws when they walk through it and damage your shoes when *you* walk through it. On all scores, the gentle alternative is the deicer called calcium chloride, which is widely available by the bag in regions that get wintry weather. Calcium chloride costs a tad more than real salt, but the investment in damage prevention is well worth it.

of the granules that custodians shake onto liquid messes (Super-Sorb is one brand). Park the can right in your garage so it's handy.

If there's oily residue left after you've swept up the absorbent chemical—or if your spill was small in the first place—the cleanup solution is as close as your kitchen. Squirt some grease-cutting dishwashing liquid (Dawn works particularly well) onto the spill and scrub it with a stiff-bristled brush or broom. Then use a wet mop to get the detergent up.

The Unwanted "Window" in Your Siding

When you patch damaged vinyl siding, you can make the job as complicated as you want to. A purist will have you buying special one-time-use tools for extracting old siding, driving special nails to a specific depth, and driving yourself nuts with more nit-picking details. The easier approach will save you money, time, and aggravation—and in the end will repair your siding just as invisibly. (Guess which version you're about to find in a book called *How to Cheat at Home Repair*?)

No matter how you repair your damaged siding, the biggest challenge lies in finding a new piece in the correct color to serve as

Strike While the Siding Is Warm

Repairs to your vinyl siding are best done as a warm-weather project. If you try to do it in the winter, the siding you're working with will be brittle and more likely to crack when you don't want it to. In T-shirt weather, the siding will be more supple and cooperative.

your patch. If you saved some unused siding from the original installation—well, aren't you the visionary—you're home free. Otherwise, if you know the original source of your siding (say, a contractor or a home store), check to see if they have that style and color in stock, or if they can put you in touch with the manufacturer. If all else fails, buy a piece of siding that's as close in color as you can find. The repair won't be totally invisible, but there's a way to cheat around that, too: Remove a stretch of siding from an inconspicuous part of your house and use that for your repair job. Then install the slightly-off-color piece in the inconspicuous spot.

Let's say you're repairing your siding because an exuberant young athlete in your household smacked a football against your house, leaving a four-inch (10-cm)-wide hole in the siding. When your blood pressure returns to normal, start your repair by familiarizing yourself with the basic structure of your siding. Almost all vinyl siding is designed to run horizontally on a wall, and each panel interlocks with the siding just above it and just below it. Typical vinyl siding has a top with rectangular holes in it (called the nailing strip, because nails driven through the holes hold the siding to the house). Just below the nailing strip is a ridge that grabs onto the panel of siding just above it. Along the bottom of the siding is a folded-in edge that locks onto the panel of siding just below it.

Now let's gather a few items and start on the repair: Aside from a new piece of siding, you're going to need a device for cutting the siding (a utility knife or tin snips), a straightedge (a T-square if you have one, for getting the straightest lines), some adhesive (get

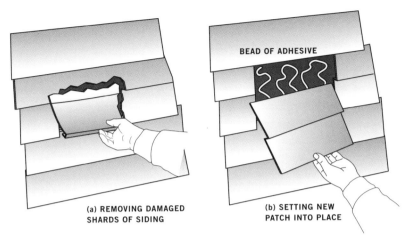

BEAD OF ADHESIVE

(a) REMOVING DAMAGED SHARDS OF SIDING

(b) SETTING NEW PATCH INTO PLACE

Remove damaged vinyl siding (a), lay a bead of adhesive in the gap, latch your new vinyl siding patch to the strip of good siding just below the hole, and press it into place against the adhesive (b).

polyurethane caulk at your home store, or some other siding adhesive), and a pencil.

1. Cut the damaged part of the siding off your wall. Use your straight-edge and pencil to mark vertical lines a couple of inches (7–10cm) to the left and right of the shattered vinyl, and then add a horizontal line just above the hole. Use your tin snips or utility knife to cut the damaged siding along the pencil lines. When you cut, be careful not to damage the panels of siding above or below the one you're working on. The vinyl that you remove will include the damaged spot down to the bottom of the panel. The old vinyl above the damaged spot should remain intact.

2. Decide how wide you want your siding patch to be. Your patch should be at least two inches (5cm) wider on each side of the hole you have created. So if the gap is now six inches (15cm), the patch should be at least a total of ten inches (25.5cm) wide. Also use your artistic judgment: It's possible that an even wider patch would look more

HOME EXTERIORS

Winterize the Outdoor Spigot

If you get cold winters, your gardening duties plummet to just about nothing by late fall. That's a good time to take care of a one-minute task that will save you a lot of heartache when subfreezing temperatures arrive. Go inside, find the valve that governs your outdoor water spigot, and turn it off. Then go back outside and open the spigot to let any water remaining in the pipe dribble out. Don't reattach the garden hose. Having taken this little precaution, you know that the water inside the pipe will not freeze, expand, and burst inside your house—spawning a whole series of repairs from plumbing fixes to flood damage remediation.

like an intentional segment of siding that a narrower one. So you might opt for a patch that's twelve or eighteen inches (30.5cm or 45.5cm) wide. On your replacement siding, use your straightedge and pencil to mark vertical lines where you need to cut the patch. Make your cuts as straight as possible.

3. Make a test fit. Let the bottom of your patch interlock with the top of the siding panel that runs just below the damaged siding. Hinge the patch up against the wall. There's no need to lock your patch onto the siding panel above it, so we're going to trim away the nailing strip at the top as well as the ridge that would have done the locking-on. You want the top edge of your patch to tuck neatly against the siding panel above it, so mark that height on your patch. Take the patch off the wall, use your straightedge and pencil to mark the trim line across the top of the patch, and make the cut.

4. Above the hole you cut in the damaged siding, apply a horizontal line of your adhesive to the original, undamaged part of the siding. Make sure the line of adhesive is a few inches (7–10cm) narrower than the patch.

5. Once again, lock the bottom of your patch to the panel of siding below, and press the patch into place over the hole in the damaged siding. Find a sturdy object, such as a hefty board, to lean against the patch while the adhesive dries (check drying time on the package).

SO WE SEE that cheat-at-home repair traditions work as well outside the house as they do inside—choosing materials that slice eons of labor off our to-do lists, fixing the easy problems, passing off the tricky problems to experts, and letting go of myths and misconceptions that complicate our lives needlessly. Ah, isn't it great communing with nature!

OOPS!

Backyard Barbecue

Wyndmoor, Pennsylvania, resident Tom Scherphorn once lived in a set of row houses with tiny backyards. A neighbor decided to kill weeds on his little postage-stamp-sized piece of real estate by sprinkling them with gasoline. The fumes from the gasoline wafted down a back stairwell and into his basement, where they encountered the pilot light of the water heater or furnace. The result: a literal backyard barbecue, which was quickly controlled by an alert neighbor with a fire extinguisher. Embarrassingly, a fire department training session was taking place nearby. Twenty eager fire vehicles showed up for the festivities.

Next time, how about just yanking those weeds out of the ground?

Pest Control: Send Those Unwanted "Guests" Packing

NATURE CAN BE SO DARNED ENVIOUS. EVER SINCE HUMANS FIGURED OUT HOW TO MAKE FIRE, COOK FOOD, AND BUILD HOUSES, THE ANIMALS AROUND US—FURRY ONES, FEATHERED ONES, SLITHERING ONES, AND CREEPY-CRAWLY ONES—HAVE BEEN SNEAKING IN TO SHARE OUR WARMTH, FOOD, WATER, AND SHELTER. FORTUNATELY, THERE ARE MYRIAD SIMPLE THINGS WE CAN DO TO REMOVE THESE TEMPTATIONS AND EVEN MAKE OUR HOMES DOWN-RIGHT UNAPPEALING TO SUCH PESTS. SURE, IN EXTREME CASES YOU MAY WANT TO CALL IN PROFESSIONAL PEST-CONTROL PEOPLE. BUT USE THIS CHAPTER AS A CHECKLIST OF QUICK-AND-EASY MEASURES YOU CAN TAKE TO FORE-STALL THE DAY YOU HAVE TO MAKE THAT CALL.

CHAPTER
11

General Pest-Proofing

One way to limit household pests is to fix some of the exterior conditions that make your home seem so inviting to bugs, mice, and other critters in the first place. Here are some changes that experts recommend making to the exterior of your house. For his input, a grateful tip of the hard hat goes out to Reggie Marston, a home inspector in Springfield, Virginia, and the "house detective" on Home & Garden Television.

Outside the House

If pests feel welcome all around your house, right up to the foundation, siding, and roof, then those curious little devils are always going to be looking for a way into your house as well. Here's how to make the exterior of your home less inviting to a wide range of pests.

◇ **Cut away any trees, shrubs, vines, or other vegetation that are overhanging, next to, or on your house. "This growth is just a highway for the pests to crawl up, get onto the roof and find an opening into the attic," says Marston. "Before you know it, there's a family of pests in the attic, and they're not even paying rent."**

◇ **Don't put mulch next to your house. Ants love to nest in it, says Henry Hendrix of Scottsdale, Arizona, brand manager for Combat Insecticides.**

◇ **Use garbage cans that seal tightly, and make sure no trash, food, debris, or rotting wood stays for long anywhere in the yard.**

◇ **If you have a stack of firewood, pile it up off the ground (on a discarded pallet or a store-bought metal stand) and away from the house. Keep in your house only enough wood for the next fire.**

◇ **Survey the exterior of your home for gaps—even tiny ones—that insects or rodents could use for entry. Pay close attention to spots** where wires or pipes enter the house. Use, caulk, expanding foam, steel wool, or wire mesh to fill any gap that looks even slightly suspicious. (Mice, for instance, only need a quarter-inch [6-mm] space to slip through, while rats can enter your house through a gap that's barely more than a half-inch [13mm] wide.) If there are spots where your siding is so close to the ground that you can't easily see the spot where house and foundation meet, use a mirror to get a good look.

◇ Remove any debris piles near your home, including branches, stones, and bricks. Rodents and other undesirables will set up housekeeping there.

◇ Make sure all your windows and screens are in good shape.

◇ Before you bring items into your home, check them for pests. This goes for firewood, boxes, paper, houseplants, and even furniture.

◇ Make sure your chimney has a wire mesh barrier called a chimney cap. (See chapter 10.)

◇ Check that your downspouts and gutters are clear so they will move water away from your house. Otherwise, your gutters will dump precipitation against the foundation of your house, where it will seep inside and provide pests with a ready source of water.

Inside the House

Lifestyle habits inside the house also can play a big role in whether pests feel welcome in your home.

◇ Clean up any crumbs, spills, grease spots, pet food, baby-flung mashed carrots, and other food sources quickly—in the kitchen and anywhere else people eat. Dispose of used bottles, cans, and other food packaging immediately.

◇ In your pantry, keep boxed or bagged food sealed in plastic bags or plastic containers that seal firmly. Don't let vulnerable foods stand in one place for long, where pests can nibble away at them without your noticing.

◇ If your pets don't eat all the food in their bowls, remove the food—don't let it sit around all day, says Hendrix, the Combat brand manager. Store pet food in rigid, airtight plastic containers.

◇ Don't let paper clutter accumulate, says Henry Hendrix of Scottsdale, Arizona, brand manager for Combat Insecticides. Cockroaches and other pests will make a home—and sometimes even a meal—of piled up newspapers, magazines, and cardboard boxes.

◇ If you store birdseed or grass seed in the garage (or out in the shed, for that matter) keep it in metal or plastic bins that have tight-fitting lids. Otherwise, these spaces will become very popular with the neighborhood rodents.

◇ Before you pack away clothes that are out of season, wash or dry-clean them.

◇ Mop, sweep, and vacuum floors weekly. Clean the hard-to-get-to areas at least once a year—including the pantry, cabinets, and under the stove and refrigerator.

◇ Use a duster or broom to knock down any spiderwebs you find inside. If you do this weekly, spiders will have a tough time building new webs and laying eggs.

◇ Vinegar repels ants. So mix a 50/50 solution of white distilled vinegar and water in a bowl, dip in a sponge, and wipe down your kitchen counters.

◇ If you have bugs in your house and you're trying to drive them out, remember that spraying an insecticide will only kill the pests that you see. It will also repel any other bugs that come along; they will just go elsewhere in your house. On the other hand, the bait traps you can buy commercially trick the bugs into carrying poisoned food back to their nests—which means a lot more of the bugs get wiped out.

◇ To discourage rodents, see that your drain covers are in place in the garage and basement. Also, if there's a letter slot in your front door, make sure it has a spring-loaded cover. If you live in an apartment, tape over any gap under your kitchen and bathroom sinks where pipes emerge from the walls.

◇ Pests in your house won't survive without a source of water. So get any leaky plumbing fixed, says Hendrix. Also, insulate pipes and appliances that develop condensation on the outside. If the tray underneath a houseplant fills up when you water the plant, empty the tray.

◇ In the attic, check that the screening over the gable vents on the side walls is intact. Marston, the home inspector, says that in older homes he almost always finds vent screens that are either torn or rusted out.

◇ Bugs hate a well-ventilated attic. So add that to the reasons to improve the airflow in yours. Review the advice in chapter 8.

Inside and out, seal up the eaves. Framing carpenters who build roofs frequently leave gaps between the roof sheathing (the plywood base of the roof) and the facia (the side board that gutters attach to), Marston says. This neglect leaves thousands of entryways for pests to slither through. He recommends using screening, metal flashing, or wood to cover these gaps. First, seal all these gaps in the eaves of your home that you have access to from the attic, since that won't require ladder work. (Remember to leave the soffit vents open.) Sketch out a map, or make a mental note, of any gaps that you couldn't reach in the attic. Attack those spots from the outside—use a ladder or, if the gaps are particularly high, add the job to your handyperson's to-do list. In some cases, you might need to slightly lift overhanging roof shingles to get access to the place where the roof sheathing and facia meet.

Pest-Specific Advice

Now that you have made the exterior and interior of your home unwelcoming to bugs, mice, and other invaders, let's look at several measures you can take to ward off specific pests. Not all critters behave the same, after all, so techniques for repelling them vary, too.

Watch for bats on their way to "work." If bats are roosting in your attic, your first step in evicting them is to find out how they're getting in and out. In warm weather, spend a week walking the perimeter of your house at sunset. Watch closely for any vents, cracks, or crevices where bats emerge on their evening hunt for food. (Bats can slide through surprisingly small gaps.) Make note of any spot that bats are using as a door, but leave the hole alone for the moment. In the fall or early winter you can put up barriers, after the bats' babies have learned to fly. Otherwise, you'll trap them inside your house.

When the time comes, here's how to make those "bat doors" a one-way exit.

1. Buy some screening or hardware cloth (wire mesh) at your hardware or home improvement store.

2. During the daytime, duct-tape a rectangle of the screening to the exterior of your house over each bat exit. Tape the screening across the top and down the sides, but not at the bottom. If you leave the screening slightly loose, the bats will be able to get out of your house but not reenter.

3. Watch the bat exits for several more evenings. When you're sure they're gone for good, fill up all the gaps with caulk or expanding foam. Be thorough. You can be sure that the bats will come back to check on their old haunt occasionally.

Give bats alternative lodging. If you don't like the idea of bats roosting in your attic, encourage them to set up housekeeping elsewhere: Give the little guys a house of their own. Remember, bats do your neighborhood a lot of good by gobbling up insects, so giving them a place to live—other than your house—is a good strategy. Browse the Internet to find vendors of houses that are specially designed to accommodate bats. If you're thinking of evicting bats from your attic, set up your bat house a few months in advance so they'll already have an eye on the new location. Mount your bat house at least fifteen feet (4.5m) off the ground and in a spot that gets direct sun for at least six hours a day. You can put the bat house on the

Your Backup Spray

Let's say there's a flying insect rampaging in your home—perhaps a wasp or mosquito. You don't have a flyswatter, and you're reluctant to use bug spray inside. Well, squirting the little devil with hairspray is a reasonable plan B. The sticky stuff will send the intruder into a tailspin.

side of a human structure (your house, your barn, your shed, for instance), on a separate pole, or in a tree.

Move quickly to trap mice. Once mice set up housekeeping inside your home, they will breed fast enough to make a rabbit blush. So at the first sign of mice, act aggressively. Closely inspect the outside of your house for gaps and cracks where mice might enter. Either fill any cracks completely with a durable exterior caulk, or stuff them with steel wool, which mice can't gnaw through. Buy a lot of mousetraps for any room where you suspect the critters are active. *A rule of thumb:* In the entire house, you should have twice as many traps as you think you have mice.

Mice are most comfortable walking next to walls, so set your traps around the perimeter of the room. Put two or three traps near each other, and spread out your groupings in an irregular pattern. When trying to figure out where to place your traps, dust likely areas with talcum powder and look for teensy footprints the next day. Peanut butter and uncooked bacon make great mouse bait. Whichever you use, make sure the mouse will have to tamper with the trap's trigger to get the food. Set out traps for the entire house all at the same time, spend three days catching the little critters, and then remove your traps. Wait a week before setting them up again. Wear rubber gloves when you handle mousetraps so the little fellas don't detect your scent and get suspicious.

Turn off the "welcome light." To reduce the number of moths and

PEST CONTROL: SEND THOSE UNWANTED "GUESTS" PACKING

mosquitoes that sneak into your house, make some changes on the outside of your house—namely, your outdoor lighting. Flying insects, as you know, are attracted to light. If they're swarming around the entrances to your home in the evening, that increases the likelihood that they'll swoop into your house the moment someone opens a door. Switch from white bulbs to yellow bulbs, which don't attract bugs quite so readily. Also, don't use your outdoor lighting any more than you have to. Have an electrician install motion-sensing switches so your lights are on only when people are in the vicinity.

Put a moat around pet bowls. If you discover that ants are feasting on your pet's food, create a simple moat that will keep them at bay. Find a waterproof container that's shallower—but slightly wider—than Fido's food bowl. A food-storage container or a pan will do. Set the food bowl in the middle of the container and add an inch or so (2–4cm) of water to the container. Now add two drops of dish-washing liquid to the water, thus eliminating surface tension that might allow ants to cross the moat. You also can buy ant-repelling moats at pet stores and over the Internet. They come in various sizes—smaller ones for pet bowls and larger ones for use in the pantry, at a picnic, or while you're camping.

Apply boric acid lightly. You can use boric acid to discourage cockroaches, but only if you apply it correctly. The easiest form to use comes in squeeze bottles (available at hardware stores and supermarkets) that will spray the fine powder where you aim the nozzle. Boric acid is not a "more is better" kind of deterrent. Apply only a very light coating—cockroaches will avoid a thick coating. Spray the boric acid under and behind your major appliances—the refrigerator, stove, dishwasher, washing machine—as well as under sinks and spots where pipes pass through walls and floors. Keep boric acid away from food, children, and pets.

Make glass doors visible to deer. There are some human contrivances that deer just don't understand. The automobile is probably the first thing that comes to mind, if you've ever seen the sad consequences

continued on page 222.

Minty Bags Make Rodents Turn Up Their Noses

Have you ever awakened in the morning to find the garbage bags from your trashcan chewed open and dragged around the yard? The hair on the back of your neck stands up as you imagine the rat, possum, raccoon, or other pest that was responsible. As you know, your valiant *How to Cheat* books staff is ever on the alert for cutting-edge products that will eliminate routine hassles from your life. Now you can put an end to these garbage raids simply by using a new kind of garbage bag.

Repel-X garbage bags are manufactured with eucalyptus, wintergreen, and mint oils molded into the plastic. The resulting minty odor reduces your pest problem in two ways: It masks the odor of your garbage, so prowling critters, such as rats, possums, and raccoons, will be less likely to approach your garbage in the first place. The odor also annoys such critters. "Rodents have very sensitive sinuses, and that's how they can smell garbage for miles around," says Repel-X inventor Joe Dussich. The concept behind repelling rodents with pungent herbs has actually been around a long time, he says. Gardeners have long planted mint around vegetable plots to keep hungry intruders away.

These are not kitchen-size garbage bags. They come in thirty-nine-, forty-five-, and fifty-five-gallon (147.5l-, 170l-, and 208l-) sizes. You're meant to place your regular kitchen bag inside your Repel-X bag and then plop it outside—you won't even need to use your trashcans to protect your garbage from interlopers any more, Dussich explains. "And not only that—your garbage smells good!"

Repel-X bags first hit the market in 2007, but originally were only distributed as an industrial product—to apartment building managers, parks departments, and restaurants, for instance. They're popular in New York City, where there are reportedly eight or nine rats for every human. At this writing, Dussich's company, the JAD Corporation of America, was planning to release Repel-X bags as a consumer product in 2008 in supermarkets, home improvement stores, and other mass merchandisers. The company was expecting to distribute internationally by the end of 2008 as well. They are available to homeowners at the website NoMoreRodents.com. The bags are billed as natural and nontoxic.

PEST CONTROL: SEND THOSE UNWANTED "GUESTS" PACKING

when deer wander obliviously into traffic. But deer also are clueless about window glass. A floor-to-ceiling sliding glass door is made to be seen through, after all. Deer do just that without registering the fact that there's a large breakable object between them and the interior of your house. So if deer visit your neighborhood, put some thought into any large windows at the back of your house. When deer get the idea that there's something edible inside your home, they've been known to crash right through window glass to get a meal. Just imagine how much damage a bleeding, panicking deer can do to the interior of your house. Take out a little deer-proofing insurance for your house—it's easy and inexpensive. First, understand that emerging from your back door and feeding deer will give the critters the idea that you have food in the house, so stop that. Also, take measures to make your large windows appear more like a barrier. During twilight, lower blinds across such windows, or use stickers or suction-mounted decorations to create the appearance of an impassable obstruction.

Keeping Your
Home Safe

ONE OF THE PRIMARY IDEAS BEHIND "CHEATING" AT HOME
MANAGEMENT IS CHOOSING YOUR OWN PRIORITIES—NOT
BEING DISTRACTED BY THE PRIORITIES LAID OUT FOR YOU
BY MOVIES, MAGAZINES, ADVERTISING, YOUR NEIGHBORS,
OR AUNT MATILDA. IN TERMS OF HOME REPAIR, I PROPOSE
THAT YOUR NUMBER ONE PRIORITY OUGHT TO BE THE
SAFETY OF YOUR FAMILY. FOR INSTANCE, IF YOU HAVE TO
CHOOSE BETWEEN REPAINTING YOUR DEN AND MAKING A
FIX THAT WILL SAVE A CHILD'S LIFE OR KEEP YOUR HOUSE
FROM BURNING DOWN, I WOULD SUGGEST THAT THOSE
WALLS IN THE DEN LOOK PRETTY GOOD AS THEY ARE. GO
AHEAD AND MAKE YOUR HOME SAFER.

CHAPTER 12

Now, every home was built a little differently and every home has a different history of how it's been used, modified, and repaired. So making broad statements about where you will most likely find dangers in your home is tricky. For guidance, I consulted Reggie Marston, who has quite a stack of credentials in the home safety field. He has spent more than thirty-six years in the home construction field, personally inspected more than 5,500 homes in the last twelve years, and appears regularly on HGTV's *House Detective* show. He put together the following top-ten list of safety fixes for the typical home. Safety issues abound, but these are the tragedy-waiting-to-happen conditions that he finds most often during home inspections. Which means you will probably find at least a few that apply to your home. You can easily handle some of these fixes yourself, and others belong on your to-do list for a handyperson or some other repair professional.

I know that talking about safety puts a lot of people to sleep. And that safety-oriented repairs are not very showy. So if you would rather skip these items, go ahead and paint your den instead—you're the boss. Point out the new paint job to the fire-and-ambulance crew when they arrive. I'm sure they'll be impressed.

1. Inadequate Handrails and Guardrails

Falls account for about a third of fatal home injuries. Having easy-to-grab handrails and guardrails in the right places will go a long way toward preventing falls in your home. Anywhere there's at least a thirty-inch (76-cm) drop between walking surfaces (on decks and landings, for instance) you need a guardrail. The guardrail should be at least three feet (91cm) above the floor.

Wherever you have four or more steps, mount a handrail top to bottom. The top and bottom of the rail should be installed to prevent someone from snagging clothing and falling. This means the rail meets a wall or turns down to meet a support post. The handrail should follow the angle of the steps at a height of thirty-four to

Balky Garage Door Has Something in Its Eye

Does your automatic garage door refuse to close? In a way, that's good news because it probably means that one of the door's safety devices is doing its job. Modern garage doors have electric eyes mounted on either side of the door. A beam passes between them, and if the beam gets broken, the garage door won't go down. This prevents a person or object from getting smacked. Ninety percent of the time, a balky automatic garage door is simple to fix, says "Handyman Scott" Kropnick. Someone probably stored a possession in the way of one of the electric eyes. If not, look for other obstructions—even a cobweb can break the beam. If there are no obstructions, one of the electric eyes might be out of alignment. They can typically be re-aimed by turning a wing nut on the mounting bracket.

thirty-eight inches (86–96.5cm). Make sure the vertical supports (pickets or balusters) under a handrail or guardrail are secure and are no more than four inches (10cm) apart.

2. Deteriorating Garage Door Mechanism

When a garage door with an automatic opener is in perfect operating condition, it should stop and reverse itself before it can damage something in its path. But when such a mechanism is in poor repair, it can send an enormous about of force crashing into your car, a pet, or a person.

Automatic garage doors need yearly service. The alignment of the tracks must be checked, connections secured, springs adjusted, and wheels and hinges lubricated. Make sure your garage door springs are fitted with sturdy safety cables (many aren't). Essentially these cables run through the inside of each spring and are secured on either side of it. If the spring snaps, the cables catch and prevent

KEEPING YOUR HOME SAFE

the garage door from going into a dangerous free fall. Kits for installing such safety cables are available in hardware stores and home improvement stores.

Be sure to test the clutch adjustment on a garage door opener. On the overhead box you will find screws that adjust the "up force" and the "down force" of the door—basically, how hard the door pushes in either direction. If a door moves too forcefully, it could harm someone. Take a broomstick or another long object. Prop one end against the ground outside the door and stand inside holding the other. Let the door close on the broomstick and see whether the door reverses itself without pushing your arm down forcefully.

3. Inadequate or Missing Smoke and Carbon Monoxide Detectors

Whether your home has independent, battery-operated smoke detectors or the newer hardwired and interconnected variety, test these devices twice a year and give them fresh batteries. Replace any smoke detector that's ten years old or more. Have a smoke detector on every level of the house. There should be one outside of bedroom areas and one inside each bedroom as well.

If you have an appliance that burns fossil fuel in the home (these days, that would mostly be natural gas or oil), install a carbon monoxide detector on each level of your house. The same applies if you have an attached garage with a door between the house and the garage.

4. Blocked Escape Routes from Bedrooms

Make sure there are at least two ways to escape from every bedroom in the event of fire. One escape route could be the regular bedroom door, and the second could be a window—provided it's large enough for a person to pass though. You also want bedroom windows to be large enough for a firefighter to enter while wearing an air-tank backpack. Make sure that bedroom doors and windows open and shut easily. Door locks that require keys won't do, and neither will windows that have been painted shut. Also, do not place large, hard-to-move furniture in front of a bedroom window. If there is only one way in and out of your basement, don't use it as a sleeping area.

5. Improper Electrical Work

How many times have you read about house fires that were attributed to faulty wiring? Right—too many times to count. As discussed in chapter 4, the odds of an amateur doing a safe job of home electrical wiring are just about zero. And the odds of slipshod wiring causing a fire or electrocuting someone are frighteningly high. There are so many other home repair projects crying for your attention—projects that fall within the skill range of us everyday folks—that there's no need to venture into the realm of home wiring. If there's any suspect wiring in your home—perhaps your own attempt, or work done by the previous homeowner twenty years ago—have a professional electrician redo it. A little pride isn't worth dying for.

6. Breached Fire Separation Walls

If you have a garage built in or attached to your house, there should be a protective shield of fire-resistant walls and doors between the areas where humans live and the areas where cars and lawn-mowers live. The idea is that if a fire breaks out in your garage, the fire separation walls and doors will give the fire trucks time to arrive before the blaze spreads to the main part of the house. In many homes, however, this safety feature is unwittingly weakened. For instance, homeowners may punch a hole through the wall of the garage into a living space for some reason, they may install a pet door through a fire separation door, or they may install pull-down stairs through the ceiling of the garage to gain easier access to the attic space above. Talk to your handyperson about patching up any such breaches with materials that meet the fire code.

7. Flue System Flaws

Any appliances that rely on combustion of fuel—gas furnaces and gas water heaters, for instance—have a flue system designed to carry combustion gases up through your house and release them above the roof. (Those gases include deadly carbon monoxide.) You probably already know that such appliances should be inspected and serviced at least yearly (get the flue inspected, too). Combustion appliances also need enough free space around them so they get adequate oxygen for burning.

However, did you know that allowing combustible materials too close to some kinds of flues in your home could be a serious fire hazard? You may have to do some research to find out how much clearance is required around you type of flue. Among the flues that consist of a bare metal pipe, some require that no combustible materials remain within one inch (2.5cm), and others require a clearance of six inches (15cm) or more. This clearance applies to the entire path of the flue through your house, and it applies to stored possessions near the flue as well as the construction materials that the pipe passes. The problem is that the gases inside the flue are quite hot and the flue itself heats up as well. So any of your home's wood framing that is too close to the flue will get desiccated over the years and could burst into flames. Find out what clearance is required for your kind of flue, and track its path from basement to roof, looking out for combustible materials that aren't keeping a respectful distance. Such mistakes are often the result of reroofing jobs and attic finishing projects.

8. Large Vegetation Close to the House

There are numerous reasons why having sizable vegetation close to the house is a bad idea. Big trees pose the most obvious threat. In a storm, overhanging limbs can crash down and punch a hole in your roof—and possibly injure a person inside. Or worse, the entire tree could topple, crushing your home and some of its occupants. Large shrubs near the house can pose a different kind of threat, providing a hiding place for an attacker or burglar. And, as discussed in chapter 11, vegetation near the house can provide shelter to vermin, which will spend their leisure hours looking for gaps in your walls so they can get inside.

9. Stoves and Large Furniture without Antitip Brackets

Install antitip brackets on any large furniture or appliance that a child might attempt to climb. A falling bookcase, wardrobe, entertainment center, or even big-screen television could kill a child.

One of the less obvious places for an antitip bracket: the freestanding stove in your kitchen. A child could step on the open oven door, and that leverage could pull the stove over—and dump scalding food or water from the stovetop onto the victim. Such an accident could happen to you, too, if you were to place a heavy roast on the open door. Antitip brackets for stoves typically fasten to the floor at the rear of the stove, and the back leg of the stove slides into the bracket. You can buy antitip brackets at home stores. However, if you have a gas stove, you will need an appliance professional to install one for you.

10. Water Temperature Set Too High

Overly hot water is a danger to small children and elderly people. They may dip into scalding water and fail to get out quickly enough to prevent serious scalding. So if you have small kids or elderly people in the house, make sure your hot water is no more than 125 degrees Fahrenheit (52°C). Here's how to test that: Take a cake or meat thermometer to the tub where children or elderly folks are most likely to bathe. Turn on the hot tap long enough to be sure you're getting newly heated water, then insert the thermometer to check the temperature. If it's over 125 degrees Fahrenheit (52°C), turn the water heater down. Most water heaters have a temperature control dial on the side.

SO HOW DOES your home stack up against this list of common safety hazards? I'll bet you have added at least an item or two to your to-do list, and I hope they get top priority. Correct these items to protect your family, yourself, your possessions, and any guests who occasionally share your living spaces. You may not receive a medal for making such fixes, but they'll go a long way toward keeping your name out of the newspaper—the kind of story with a headline that begins "Tragedy Strikes . . ."

Getting Help: Finding and Working with the Best Repair People

WHEN SOMETHING NEEDS FIXING IN YOUR HOME, THERE'S A SIGNIFICANT CALCULATION YOU HAVE TO MAKE THAT'S CRUCIAL TO SUCCESSFUL CHEATING AT HOME REPAIR: DECIDING WHETHER YOU CAN EASILY HANDLE THE REPAIR YOURSELF, OR IF YOU SHOULD CALL IN A PROFESSIONAL. *HOW TO CHEAT AT HOME REPAIR* IS DEVOTED TO SIMPLE HOME REPAIRS THAT WE ORDINARY FOLKS, WITH NO SPECIAL TRAINING, CAN ACCOMPLISH WITH COMMONLY AVAILABLE TOOLS. THE FLIP SIDE OF THAT COIN IS HAVING THE WISDOM TO CALL IN A PROFESSIONAL WHEN YOU REALIZE THAT YOU WILL HAVE TROUBLE DIAGNOSING THE PROBLEM, ACQUIRING THE TOOLS AND MATERIALS NEEDED FOR THE REPAIR, MAKING THE REPAIR CORRECTLY, OR DOING THE REPAIR SAFELY.

CHAPTER 13

But hiring a professional repairperson is not as simple as picking up the telephone. You want to be sure that the person who walks in your door with a toolbox is trained and competent, charges reasonably, is insured, and has a good reputation. Yes, this involves a little research, but that effort is minuscule compared to the consequences of turning an incompetent, uninsured worker loose on your house. When you do find good repair professionals, you want to maintain a good relationship with them so they'll be happy to return when you need them next. So let's take a look at getting, and keeping, the right kind of help. A grateful work glove salute goes out to repair professionals Tom McCormick, David Lupberger, Raymond VinZant, Dave Shapiro, and Scott Kropnick for their input.

Finding a Repairperson

When you need work done at your house, picking a repairperson or a repair company at random out of the phone book, or making a snap judgment based on a nice display ad, is a recipe for disaster—what electrician Tom McCormick calls "phone book roulette." If that's all the effort you put into hiring help, you can expect continuing episodes of shoddy work, exorbitant prices, and unreliable workers. You will only know true sanity as a homeowner when you have established a good relationship with trustworthy repair professionals in at least three categories: a general handyperson, an electrician, and a plumber. You might also want to add to that list heating/air-conditioning and appliance repair professionals. Here's how to get to that blissful state:

Start by asking people you know and trust. Begin your search for the perfect repairperson by asking neighbors, friends, and colleagues about great workers they use repeatedly. Also check with local home inspectors, real estate agents, architects, and lumber yards—they typically know which home repair professionals have the best reputation.

Get references. When you first talk to a prospective repairperson, ask for several names of recent customers, along with their contact information. A reliable professional will gladly provide this information. Call all his references and ask about their experience with your candidate. Was the work done well, on time, at a reasonable price? Would they hire him again?

Look for a license and insurance. A licensed contractor is more likely to do work well and up to code. Make sure your repair professional is insured in the event of damage to your home—say, if a newly installed pipe bursts in the middle of the night, flooding your living room.

Check for past complaints. Contact the local office of the Better Business Bureau, or your local government's consumer protection office, to find out if your candidate has any history of consumer complaints lodged against her.

Find out how workers are screened. If you are considering using the services of a large company—which may send any number of different repair people to your house—call the company and ask what standards they use for hiring. Do they conduct background checks of prospective employees, and do they test for drug use, for instance? On the Internet, check the repair company's website and look for any language about hiring and work standards. Then conduct a search on the company's name to see if any complaints surface.

Resolve the permit issue upfront. Ask whether a permit is required for the work you want done. If you have any doubts after talking to your repairperson, call the local building department. If your repairperson asks *you* to get the permit, find a different repairperson instead. You're probably talking to an unlicensed repairperson, and you—not the worker—will end up liable if the work does not meet code.

Get details of the job in writing. Before you hire a worker for a large project, get a written proposal—don't rely on a verbal agreement. Include the location of the repair, the type of materials to be used, brand names and specifications of significant items, and any other specifics about the work. Make sure the proposal includes removal of old materials and fixtures. Also specify when the work will start, whether the work will be continuous or interrupted, the color of materials, and the locations of new fixtures.

The Care—and, Yes, Feeding—
of Your Favorite Repair People

Let's say you finally find that rare breed of repair professional—someone with superb credentials, who does great work, who charges a reasonable rate, and who you are personally comfortable having around the house. Congratulations! Now make sure you build a good relationship with this repairperson. When someone likes working for you, he is more likely to give you priority over other customers, is more likely to respond when you have an emergency, and is more likely to treat you fairly. Here are some pointers developed after conversations with repair people about the kinds of customers they love and the kinds of customers they despise.

Don't theorize—stick to the facts. When describing a repair that needs to be made, stick to observable facts. Don't try to diagnose the problem or use terminology that you don't fully understand. That will only confuse matters on the off chance that the repairperson assumes you know what you're talking about. Don't try to tell the repairperson how to do the work. But do provide all the pertinent details about what conditions you can see and what is not working as expected. For a plumbing problem, for instance, tell the plumber when and where you found a leak, the make and model of fixtures involved, and describe any noises you might have heard.

Clear the way. Before your repairperson arrives at the house, move any storage boxes and other personal items away from the areas where the work will be done.

Treat workers like guests. If you treat repair people like "hired help," they're going to hate working in your house. You don't have to be a management genius to know the perils of disgruntled workers. Instead, treat repair people like any other guest in your home. Point

Schedule Twice-a-Year Repair Visits

It's a given that you're going to have a handyperson out to your house at least two times a year, and probably three or four times. So whip out your appointment calendar and call your handyperson right now to schedule two appointments, spaced six months apart. Spend the intervening time making a list of projects for each visit. You will rest assured that several nonemergency projects around the house are going to be taken care of (all in one service call, too), and your repairperson will be glad to have future work on the calendar. A day or two before one of these repair dates arrives, call your handyperson and review the tasks you have on your list so he'll be sure to bring all needed materials.

out where the bathrooms are should they need one, and at the very least offer drinking water if not soft drinks, coffee, or tea. If you have more than one worker in the house for a big project, treat everyone to a pizza or a box of doughnuts. Workers who feel good about you will be more likely to do extra work without charge or otherwise give you a break on the final bill.

Let them do good work. Don't ask your repairperson to skimp on materials or ignore regulations in order to lower the cost of the job. No one likes to do shoddy work, and a good repairperson has to stand by the quality of the work done.

Keep in contact during the job. Be available during the work to answer the inevitable questions about your preferences. Either remain in the house or be reachable by telephone.

Work through mistakes calmly. If your repairperson makes a mistake, don't get angry or have a heated discussion. Remember that all workers are human and capable of the occasional mistake. Discuss the possible solutions calmly and rationally. If you made a careful hire, you already have put a lot of effort into finding a repairperson you trust. Trying to find a new worker to take over the job will cost you much more in terms of time, money, and energy than settling the matter with the repairperson you already have. Besides, any new worker will be a stranger who is still capable of making mistakes.

WELL, IT FEELS pretty good now, doesn't it? Through these thirteen chapters you have armed yourself with the *How to Cheat at Home Repair* mind-set, you've learned scores of the sneakiest, corner-cutting fixes imaginable, you've learned how to select low-maintenance materials for your home, you've learned the misconceptions that can sap hours out of your home life, and you've learned how to select and display your tools in the most strategic ways. What's more, when a home repair is beyond your abilities (or you just don't have time for it), you have the number of top-notch repair professionals on your speed dial. Welcome to the cheatin' life!

INDEX

Type S fuses, 65, 66

U

Underwriters Laboratories, 62, 63
"Ultra-low-maintenance" decking, 204, 205
Upholstery, thread holes in, repairing, 35, 36
Utility knives, use in home repair, 16

V

Vacuum cleaners
    changing trajectory of, 34, 35
    removing dust from wicker furniture with, 40
    wet, removing basement leaks with, 176
Vegetation, closeness to home, 229
Veneer, loose, 32
Vinyl flooring, 124
Voltage testers, 59

W

Wallboard, basement, 177
Wallpaper, use of in home, 123
Walls
    holes in, repairing, 111
    mounting objects to, 122
    patching material for, 112
Washing machines
    differences in models, 167
    leaks in, 164
    maintaining, 164, 165
    supply line hoses, replacing, 101
Waste lines, inspecting main, 103
Water heaters
    flushing, 99, 100
    "on demand," 103
    valves for, periodically checking, 99

Water marks on furniture, and towels, 32
Water rings, rubbing away, 27, 28
Water softeners, 102, 103
Water temperature, setting of, 229, 230
Water valves
    periodically shutting them off, 99
    shutoff, finding, 100, 101
Wax fillers, and furniture refinishing, 26
Weeds, killing, 211
Wet vacs, removing basement leaks with, 176
White vinegar
    removing stains with, 129
    repelling ants with, 216
    using on drinking glasses, 188, 189
    use on clogged showerheads, 86
Wicker furniture
    painting, 41
    preserving, 39, 40, 41, 42
"Wiggly," 59
Windows
    cracks in, repairing, 145, 146
    latches for, 143, 144
    screens in, repairing, 146, 147
    shades for, lazy, repairing, 147
    stuck, freeing, 142, 143
    weep holes, clearing out, 144
Wine stains, removing from carpet, 132
Wood decking, composite, 203, 204, 205

Z

Zip ties, use in home repair, 20

ABOUT THE AUTHOR

JEFF BREDENBERG, author of the *How to Cheat*™ book series, spent the first two decades of his publishing career working for newspapers, writing and editing in Chicago, Denver, St. Louis, and four other cities. He has written, edited, or contributed to more than twenty-five books on the subjects of home management and health. He is a frequent contributor to home-oriented magazines as well. He has also published three science fiction novels—*The Dream Compass, The Dream Vessel,* and *The Man in the Moon Must Die*—plus several short stories in magazines and anthologies.

Bredenberg lives in the suburbs of Philadelphia with his wife and two sons.

Learn more about Bredenberg at www.jeffbredenberg.com and www.howtocheatbooks.com.